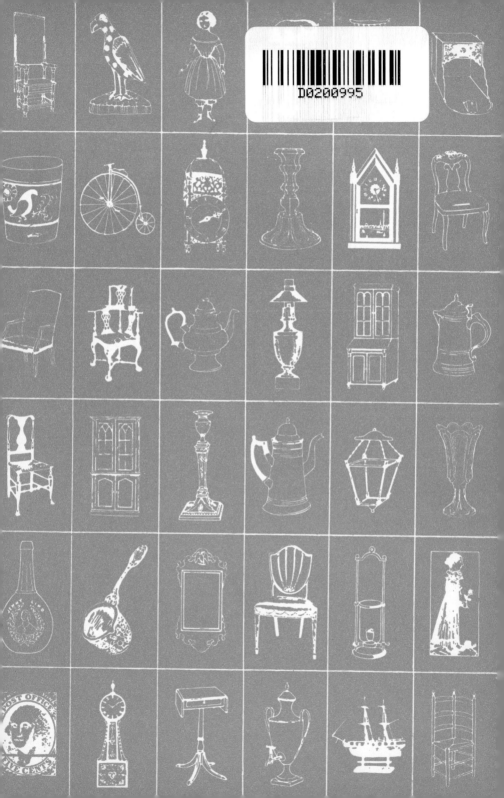

THE PRIMER OF
American Antiques

THE PRIMER OF
American Antiques

BY CARL W DREPPERD

ILLUSTRATED

Doubleday & Company, Inc.

GARDEN CITY, NEW YORK

1952

COPYRIGHT, 1944
BY CARL W. DREPPERD
ALL RIGHTS RESERVED, INCLUDING RADIO, TELEVISION, AND MOTION PICTURE

PRINTED IN THE UNITED STATES
AT
THE COUNTRY LIFE PRESS, GARDEN CITY, N. Y.

Acknowledgments

THE preparation of this book, in both text and illustrations, engaged the interest and the wholehearted co-operation of many people. Many of the illustrations have been generously loaned. And a host of patient researchers, who have prepared monographs and books dealing with American antiques, have contributed in no small measure to the text.

Acknowledgment is, therefore, made to B. Altman & Company for the use of illustrations; to Mr. Thomas H. Ormsbee, editor of *The American Collector;* to Lockwood Barr; to Evangeline H. Bergstrom; to Esther Stevens Brazer; to the Bruce Publishing Company for use of some measured drawings of early American furniture; to Colonial Williamsburg; to the Condé-Nast Publications, Inc., for use of innumerable pictures of American antiques; to Crown Publishers for illustrations used in McKearin's *American Glass;* to the Bureau of Foreign and Domestic Commerce of the United States for illustrations used in *Furniture—Its Selection and Use;* to Doubleday, Doran and Co., Inc., and the Garden City Publishing Company for the use of innumerable illustrations from a dozen or more of their books; to *Furniture World* for photographs from which line drawings were made; to Ralph T. Hale & Company, publishers, of Boston, for illustrations used in *Encyclopedia of Antiques;* to Harper and Brothers for permission to use illustrations from *The China Hunters Club,* one of America's first books on antique china, pottery, and porcelain; to William Helburn, Inc., publishers, for illustrations used in *Collection of Scale Drawings of Colonial Furniture;* to Houghton Mifflin Company of Boston, for permission to make drawings of photographs used in *Colonial Furniture of New England;* to the Museum of the Huguenots at New Paltz, New York, for pictorial material; to Ellouise Baker Larsen for illustrations used in *American Historical Views of Stafford-*

ACKNOWLEDGMENTS

shire China; to Ruth Webb Lee, author and publisher of *Sandwich Glass* and *Pressed Glass*, for use of many line illustrations; to The Macmillan Company of New York for use of line drawings appearing in books by Thomas H. Ormsbee; to Robert H. McCauley, Esq., of Hagerstown, Maryland, for permission to make line drawings from his book on Liverpool pottery; to George S. McKearin for many illustrations of glassware; to the Metropolitan Museum of Art, the Philadelphia Museum, the magazine *Antiques*, for permission to make line drawings of photographs supplied by them; to the Wallace Nutting Estate for the right to use line drawings and make line reproductions of photographs supplied by them; to the Parke-Bernet Galleries of New York for permission to make line drawings of innumerable objects in their various catalogues; to the Pennsylvania Society of the Colonial Dames of America for illustrative material; to the Pitman Publishing Corporation for the right to use drawings from their book *Furniture Styles;* to the *Reader's Digest* for the right to use line drawings; to Charles Scribner's Sons for permission to make line drawings of illustrations used in Mr. Luke Vincent Lockwood's *Colonial Furniture in America;* to Scott Publications, Inc., for use of illustrations from the *1944 Specialized U. S. Stamp Catalogue;* to Valley Forge Park of Valley Forge, Pennsylvania, for permission to reproduce the fireback in Washington's headquarters; to the Walpole Society for many line illustrations used in the *Glossary of American Antiques;* to Lawrence C. Wroth of the John Carter Brown Library, Providence, Rhode Island, for data and illustrations; to the Yale University Museum for photographic material; to the Grand Rapids Publishing Company for permission to make drawings of pictures in *An Exemplar of Antique Furniture Design.*

In addition, splendid assistance has been given personally by Stephen Ensko; Harry Shaw Newman; Irving W. and Charles W. Lyon; Arthur Sussel; Benjamin Ginsburg; Alice Winchester, editor of the magazine *Antiques;* Thomas H. Ormsbee, editor of the *American Collector;* Joe Kindig, Jr.; John L. Ruth; Dr. and Mrs. Arthur Greenwood; Mr. and Mrs. Bertram K. Little; Helena Penrose; Louis Hertz; Frank O. Spinney; Herbert H. Hosmer, Jr.; Richardson Wright, editor of *House & Garden;* and Beatrice G. Crane.

Finally to the artists who drew some three hundred pictures for me, and to the wood engravers who, all unknown, over a century ago made many pictures now used again in this book.

Preface

Even primers need prefaces. When the primer deals with so multifold a subject as American antiques, a preface is mandatory. First, it must be assumed that the reader of this primer is desirous either (1) of having a thin layer of knowledge about a great many different kinds of American antiques, or (2) of pursuing the acquisition of specialized knowledge in respect to some or many of the items mentioned. Both kinds of readers should start with facts about the social and political complexion of the American colonies and of the first half century of our life as a new nation. Otherwise there will be some wonderment as to why certain styles and types of furniture persisted over many years in some districts, and why almost none of them is found in other districts.

New England was settled primarily by yeomanry and artisan classes from England. That is to say by farmers, craftsmen, and tradesmen. These people were not stupid boors, but sternly religious dissenters at desperate odds with the Court and the established religion of England. They knew, and even enjoyed, good solid Elizabethan furniture in their English homes. They knew good food. They worked for a living, but were not bond servants, serfs, or tenant farmers. They owned land. They had trades, owned artisans' shops, or were small merchants. Their ministers were learned scholars, albeit stiff-necked and prone to dissension. Such peoples are not, and never were, "the first by whom the new is tried." Generations of them clung to the same habits, and forms, and things. They came here to settle and stay. They came to consolidate and multiply, and wax well to do in their own way. There was no thought of exploitation in their minds. No idea of quick profits from Indian trade; no hunting for gold or silver. Theirs was the escape device of the persecuted. They left England under a cloud of persecution. before

vii

Charles I had fallen to the armies of their fellows who stayed at home and, under Cromwell, fought it out with the Church and Crown, and won.

Virginia, on the other hand, was settled and controlled by English chivalry; by gentlemen and others seeking to rehabilitate family fortunes and, later, to find an asylum from the rising tide of Puritan domination under the Commonwealth of Cromwell. In spite of his fortitude, the Virginia gentleman planter was keen for improvement in the pattern he was schooled in: in keeping abreast of the new, the smart, the fashionable. That type of mind will readily throw out the old, give it to bondsmen, servants, and slaves, and enjoy the newest conceits. Consequently, we can picture, for example, Byrd's "Westover" as in a continuous state of change in so far as its furnishings, its pictures, mirrors, floors, fire tools, et cetera, were concerned, while the Fairbanks house at Dedham, Massachusetts, remained just as it was for a century, inside and out, and in that respect had a thousand other New England houses for company.

The Dutch in New Amsterdam were there to make money, to exploit the resources of the Hudson Valley, and to trade the raw materials and furs of America for the goods, and the gold, of Europe.

The Swedes, who were first to settle in what was later Pennsylvania, were simple yeomen of the same basic type which settled New England. The Swedes impressed indelibly upon the shores of the Delaware and Schuylkill the blockhouse and the simple furniture styles which, a century later, were copied by German and other immigrants.

The Dutch also were in the Delaware, Schuylkill, and Hoarkill valleys. The latter two names are themselves of Dutch origin. The very term "Pennsylvania Dutch" is said to derive from the New York Dutch, so designating their brethren in Penn's Land.

Philadelphia, a Swedish village in 1682 when Penn arrived, by 1710 had become a rich metropolis. The Quakers who expanded it lived well, and surrounded themselves with good things. Welsh ironmasters were soon taking good iron out of the Pennsylvania hills. The rising tide of immigration, from Switzerland, Moravia, France, Holland, and other European lands, made Philadelphia the busiest port in the colonies. With that immigration came a flood of English, Scotch, French, Dutch, and Swedish cabinetmakers, silversmiths, artists, and other luxury craftsmen. Every new town in Pennsylvania became a little Philadelphia, with Lancaster almost a twin to the City of Brotherly Love. The Swiss-Amish and Swiss-Mennonite farmers, the German Schwenkfelders, the polyglot group of Ephrata, and the

Moravians at Bethlehem and Lititz, adapted existing simple forms of furniture which today are wrongly designated as Pennsylvania German or Pennsylvania Dutch. They are, actually, a combination of English, Flemish, Swiss, Welsh, Dutch, and Swedish styles, blended into a pattern that suited the users and which, in many forms, persisted until the middle of the nineteenth century.

Therefore, in this primer you are asked to take, not only with a grain of salt, but also with your tongue in your cheek, much of the current pro-German promotion that has been, and is even today, being circulated about Pennsylvania pioneer furniture. Study history on your own. And don't think everything with a tulip, bird, or heart on it is "Pennsylvania." It isn't. It can be anything from early seventeenth-century Swedish or Swiss to English, Italian, Dutch, French, or Spanish. For that's where America got the tulip, and the tulip was in Pennsylvania in profusion before the hordes of immigrants from the *Vaterland* arrived.

Similarly, there is much pleasure and no little profit to be had in a study of the blending of arts, crafts, and forms evident in the pioneer furnishings and furniture of new states as they were settled and admitted to the Union. The English influence, through Virginia, on Kentucky and Tennessee; the New England influence on upper New York; the Connecticut and New York influence on Pennsylvania; the blending of New England, Pennsylvania, and Maryland forms in Ohio; provide rare fun as studies which reveal variables, and retrace the trails of peoples at work forging this nation into a super world power.

In order that your pleasures may be manifold and your search made easy, many books of reference are mentioned in this primer. Have no hesitancy in reading any of the recommended books with an open mind. In fact, to enjoy some of them you'll need a wide-open mind. Whatever this primer lacks in data, information, and pictures, these other books will give you. Some of them devote pages to matters herein dismissed with a line or two of type. Nowhere, up to this time, has there been an effort made to produce an American antique primer such as this—a primer that, it is hoped, will be a signpost pointing to the crying need for a vastly enlarged work: an encyclopedia of American antiques. To whoever takes on that job, our heartiest good wishes and heartfelt condolences!

CARL W. DREPPERD

Contents

CONTENTS

Foreword

BY CHARLES MESSER STOW

CARL W. DREPPERD IS A CONSULTANT to industry, but he is also an antiquarian. Whether he was led into professional research by antiques, or whether professional research lured him into the field of antiques, I do not know. The two callings, however, are somewhat akin; their followers have to be both inquisitive and acquisitive.

Mr. Drepperd has applied the scientific methods of his business to the unscientific status of his avocation—his interest in American antiques. The results have been beneficial both to him and to that part of the public blessed with the collecting instinct.

This book, I am sure, would not have been undertaken unless Mr. Drepperd had been convinced there was a need for it. Coming from Lancaster County, Pennsylvania, naturally he is not much given to embarking on unprofitable or unworthy ventures. I have no doubt that when he first talked with his publishers he was able to lay before them a graph showing by its rising curve the number of copies that should be printed for the first edition, the number that should be sold in successive editions, and, very likely, the sales to be expected ten years hence. That is the way the research analyst works.

Lest someone should scoff at a scientific approach to a problem such as collecting antiques, or, for that matter, question whether or not a problem demanding scientific approach even exists, let me certify that it does. Let me certify, also, that given the population of a community, Mr. Drepperd can tell, with astounding accuracy, the number of craftsmen of various sorts at work in that community at almost any period during its history.

Research workers have the healthy habit of checking and rechecking their findings. Therefore, Mr. Drepperd asked me to read the galley proofs of this book and requested me to measure his own optimisms and his own considered opinions against the background of my judgment.

Now, I am not a scientific prosecutor of research, and I cannot draw a graph to illustrate either tangible or intangible things. Terms like "ratio," "factor," "triangulation," are meaningless to me, though in the scientific approach they are apparently essential. In the last quarter of a century, however, I have watched the fluctuations of the public's interest in antiques, the changes in collecting moods, and the subtle variations in taste. This experience I was glad to put at Mr. Drepperd's disposal.

At the outset, I can say without fear of contradiction that the country-wide interest in antiques never has approached anywhere near eclipse, even in the dark years of the depression. Some collectors, of course, have had to sell their collections because of economic pressure; some collectors have died and their collections have gone into museums or have been dispersed. But for every collector who has stopped collecting or who has died, two others at least have begun.

Naturally there are many grades of collecting. Mr. Drepperd's book contains seventy-two chapter headings, meaning that he discusses seventy-two different categories of antique objects that might be collected. There are many more. Certain fashions run through the field of collecting, waxing and waning. At one time pattern glass was hunted assiduously by thousands of persons who liked that type of collection. Just now even greater numbers are searching attics and storerooms for buttons, and the button craze flourishes even as pattern glass did once. There was a great demand a few years ago for shelf clocks of the early type made by the Willards and others, before the quantity production men of Connecticut began to turn out their machine-made products. Now, dealers tell me, there is little demand for this type, but banjo and tall clocks are sought. Nobody, not even a scientific research worker, can tell why these things are so, any more than anyone can explain the fashions in women's hats.

Many new collectors are starting just at this time, and for a good reason. It has been discovered that antiques are a concrete form of history. In fact, the New York State Historical Association at its annual meeting of 1944 gave official recognition to this form of history by allocating one entire session of its three-day meeting to discussion of antiques. The association's quarterly publication, *New York History*, contains a section devoted to antiques.

In the last few years conceptions of the nature and purpose of history have been changing, both with teachers and with the public.

The tendency toward specialization in education very likely is responsible for this change. We now have social, economic, political, military, religious, and a score or more other kinds of history. Antiques are recognized as a legitimate branch of historical study and are classed as cultural history.

As far back as the early 1930s the late R. T. H. Halsey gave a course at St. John's College, Annapolis, on early American artistry as exemplified in the objects called antiques. At Yale University the Garvan collections of American silver, furniture, glass, prints, and paintings are used in the same kind of courses given by John Marshall Phillips. These lectures were so popular among students that the number of the classes had to be doubled. History was regarded once simply as a record of events, chiefly military and political; now a tendency is to consider it a record of the human beings engaged in those events, and of those who observed and reacted to the events.

Statistics of historical societies in the United States and Canada show that in the last eight years the number of active organizations has increased 56 per cent. This proves, of course, that more and more persons are becoming interested in the country's past. Interest aroused betokens a desire to share in the work connected with it. Most of the historical societies have had nuclei of collections in the form of documents and relics, usually connected with military affairs. These collections are being expanded to include objects used in the daily life of the past, thus becoming historical museums in a truer sense.

Professor Theodore M. Greene of Princeton has called history both a science and an art: ". . . a science in so far as it searches for and discovers regularities and patterns in the flux of the historical process, and as it succeeds in expressing these recurrences with descriptive, scientific precision; an art in proportion as its task is the imaginative reconstruction of historical individuals, episodes, movements, and periods with due regard to their human significance."

Since history has become humanized, so to speak, collectors of antiques have automatically become historians, and their contribution is re-creating the daily life of those persons who have made history. Knowing the home surroundings of a historical character is a help in determining his thought processes. Understanding these, reasons for his course of action are easier to comprehend.

Mr. Drepperd, using his slide rule, has come to the conclusion that a great many people are becoming interested in antiques and are wanting instruction. I have backed up this conclusion, using my own clumsy methods of observation. Hence, this book appears, designed for those who desire elementary teaching in culture history, that is, in antiques. It does not go deeply into matters affecting connoisseurs or touch on questions that occupy advanced collectors. It is what its name implies, a primer of antiques.

1

Seventeenth-Century Tables, Chairs, Settles, Forms, and Stools

DRAWING TABLE

This, the furniture of what Wallace Nutting has called the Pilgrim century, is apt to be wrongly attributed, geographically, when calling it Pilgrim. It is, rather, the furniture of the settlers of New England, Virginia, Maryland, and New York, together with the furniture of the Swedes and Dutch in what was later Pennsylvania, and the furniture of Penn's colonists after 1680. It is a matter of record that Penn, in writing instructions to his agents in America, told them to have prepared certain articles of furniture, indicating that joiners were already here in his colony, and also that he was bringing much furniture with him. Whatever he did bring with him was either Tudor or Carolean in style, but when he arrived he found the Dutch styles which, later, were popular in England as William and Mary furniture.

GATE LEG TABLE

Virginia seventeenth-century furniture was elaborate, massive, and ornate, in either the high style of Queen Elizabeth's reign, or in Carolean style. Little of it was saved, but it is mentioned in many surviving documents, such as inventories, wills, and estate records. The Swedes' styles reflect the Dalecarlian and other Swedish provincial furniture of the early seventeenth century. These are somewhat of a pattern with Elizabethan, but simpler in form

BUTTERFLY TABLE

I

HIGH-LOW STRETCHER TABLE

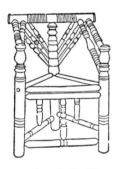

TURNED CHAIR

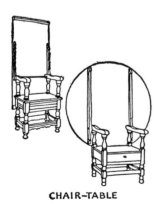

CHAIR–TABLE

and style. When decorated, this furniture was painted, or embellished with studding of nails or bosses. The Dutch, of course, had the *kaas*, or great cupboard, typical of The Netherlands, and furniture based on Chinese styles brought to the homeland by the Dutch East India traders. They also had certain Spanish designs, implanted upon their art consciousness by the Spanish conquest of the Low Countries. Maryland furniture reflected the higher styles of England, very much as did Virginia. New England had its simple Tudor and its own variants, as produced in the New England colonies.

Notable among the seventeenth-century items of furniture, fashioned of oak, maple, hickory, and walnut, are the drawing table— a form of extension table with fairly heavy bulb-turned legs (in the finest examples the bulbs are slightly carved), heavy stretchers bracing the legs near the ground, and a tripart top composed of a fixed top which covered the main framework of the table in one great planklike piece, and two sliding halves which, nested under the main top, could be drawn out to extend the table to almost twice its length. These slides, or draws, from which the table derives its name, were very ingeniously contrived. They operated a sort of angular wedge and falling tackle of heavy wood construction which, upon their being drawn out full length, lifted them on an exact level with the fixed top. They had to be rather forcibly depressed to be shoved back under the main top when returning the table to normal dimensions. Drawing tables of American make are excessively rare. Certain ones that have been in this country for three centuries were obviously imported.

The gate-leg table is another form of extension table which rested a fixed top on a frame of turned legs and stretchers, and had two large drop leaves which were supported on

2

movable legs in the form of single or double gates swinging out on both sides of the table.

The butterfly table is apparently a distinctly American development, but sometimes also credited to Spanish influence (from heaven alone knows where), which was a dainty extension table. Its chief characteristics are an oblong, narrow, fixed top, supported on a frame of four turned legs, canted or slanting outward, joined near the base with stretchers, and having two wings, pivoted on top rails and stretchers, which swung out to support two drop leaves. Both the gate-leg and butterfly tables had what is known as a tongue-and-groove joint on the edges of leaves and top at their juncture. This is just what the name implies. The fixed table top had a rounded channel hewn along its edge; the falling leaf had a rounded projection which fitted in that groove when the leaf was up. When hanging, such leaves part from the top and show a wide air space. When the "table joint," formed of a large half-round projection on the top and a similar concavity on the lower side of the leaf, is used, no gap appears; the joint is close whether the table is open or closed. The tongue-and-groove joint is a mark of seniority on both gate-leg and butterfly tables.

The "high and low stretchered" turned table is now a very rare type, characterized by ball, button, or sausage turnings, the stretchers of which are placed high between the wider-spaced legs and low between the narrow-spaced legs, with an extra joining stretcher between the two low, short stretchers; and tables of similar nature but with one heavy turned ball on each leg.

Turned 3-legged chairs as illustrated. These were a relic of medieval England and were once collected by Horace Walpole, the great English connoisseur.

The chair table, illustrated, which was a

CROMWELLIAN CHAIR

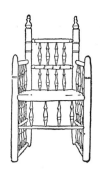

BREWSTER CHAIR

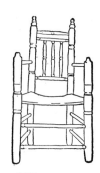

CARVER CHAIR

DAY BED

WAINSCOT CHAIR

UPHOLSTERED CHAIR

piece of dual-purpose furniture; a table when the back was tilted down over the arms of the chair, and a high-backed chair when it was tilted upright, and the turned Turkey-work chair, sometimes called "Cromwellian" —an early upholstered chair with a turned frame. Brewster and Carver chairs; both turned, rush- or bass-bottomed, and named for the Pilgrim Fathers who once owned chairs of the type.

The wainscot chair, made in the tradition of cabinetwork, and now exceedingly rare.

The stuffed chair with turned legs and shaped arms and with upholstered back and seat. The settle; literally a high-backed and scroll-ended "sofa" of all-wood construction, admirably planned to keep off draughts, and moderately comfortable with a cushion on the seat and some cushions on the back. These were made in plain and wainscot styles. The day bed, *canapé*, or sofa, of Carolean style and of Flemish origin, more frequent in Virginia and Maryland than in New England. A similar purpose sofa of William and Mary style used in New York and Pennsylvania; and a turned frame, rush-bottomed style, of New England and Pennsylvania.

It is evident, however, that most styles of day bed, in lesser degree than the local favorites, were used in all colonies. Stools, which were the first chairs, and which for the first decade or two of colonization were about the only seats generally available. Forms, or benches. Stretcher, refectory, and other "long" tables. Carolean caned chairs of rich turning and carving, made and sold in America, not only in the seventeenth century, but well into the eighteenth. These items, together with chests, court, press, and on-frame cupboards, and wooden utensils, made up the household furniture of the seventeenth century. Mirrors and clocks were scarce. But herewith are illustrated at least one example of each of the major items, a mirror and a clock of the period. The following books are recommended for further study of this furniture and the period:

Colonial Furniture of New England, by Irving W. Lyon, M.D.
Furniture of Our Forefathers, by Esther M. Singleton.
Furniture of the Pilgrim Century, by Wallace Nutting.
Colonial Furniture in America, by Luke Vincent Lockwood.
Homes of Our Ancestors, by Halsey and Tower.
Early American Furniture Makers, by Thomas H. Ormsbee.
Furniture Treasury, by Wallace Nutting.
Pine Furniture of Early New England, by Russell H. Kettell.
Tudor to Stuart, by Blake & Reveirs-Hopkins.

JOINED STOOL

TRESTLE TABLE

17th. CENTURY CLOCK

17th. CENTURY MIRROR

SETTLE

CAROLEAN CHAIR

2

Seventeenth-Century Press
and Court Cupboards

PRESS CUPBOARD

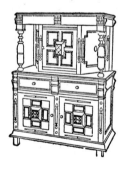

THESE TWO kinds of American furniture of the first colonial century reflect (with the exception of Swedish types) the England of Henry VIII and Queen Elizabeth. They are altogether Tudor in style and are an evolution from furniture of the early Middle Ages. Thus New England and Virginia press and court cupboards are an American link with England after the Norman Conquest; with Merrie England at her best. Now, so rare that almost every known example is recorded, press cupboards and court cupboards may well be considered a closed opportunity. But less than twenty years ago a very fine one was found in a hen house in Virginia. It was immediately pronounced "New England" and eventually sold at an amazing price. However, it may well have been a Virginia press cupboard. As noted in the Foreword, Virginia settlers had Tudor furniture, and her artisans made it for a while. But in that dominion there was more eagerness for new styles, and hence the Tudor furniture of Virginia was discarded before 1700. Carved, turned, and fashioned of oak, maple, and pine, employing every art of the carver, joiner, turner, and wainscoter, court and press cupboards have paneled doors and ends, turned posts, applied turned decoration, carving on flat surfaces and on bulb turnings, and some were even further embellished with paint:

6

black, white, and red. They date from 1630 to
1690 in America. It is doubtful whether they
were made after 1650 in England.

The terms "press" and "court" derive from
early English usage. In 1400, and even earlier,
anything called a "presse" or an "almerie" was
an enclosed, or closable piece of furniture—a
cupboard. Finally almerie, press, and cupboard
became synonymous terms. The very fine cupboard became a "court" or stately piece. But
the court or stately piece remained a more
open piece, in order to display plate of gold
and silver, fine trenchers, and other garniture.
Finally, the press cupboard was given also the
name livery cupboard. Its use was to hold
linen, sometimes clothing (livery), and sometimes food. We are safe in accepting the definition of court cupboard as the open type,
either both above and below the "board" or
partly enclosed above the board. Also, we can
accept "press cupboard" as meaning a cupboard fully enclosed both above and below the
center "board" or closed below and partly enclosed above. Both types are illustrated in typical examples of American make, dating about
1680. So also is the Swedish cupboard-on-frame
introduced about 1650 into what is now Pennsylvania by its Scandinavian colonists. The
press cupboard has carved tulip decoration
on the lower door panels; applied ornaments
on upper door and drawer panels and the
stiles; turned bulbous posts; and carving on
the cornice. The court cupboard is open at
bottom, with a deep shelf, has heavy bulbous
turning, turned decoration, an elaborately
paneled door, and two huge drawers. The
Swedish cupboard is fully enclosed above and
entirely open below. It is not carved or decorated.

The books mentioned in Section 1 are recommended also for further study of press and court cupboards.

COURT CUPBOARD

PRESS CUPBOARD

SWEDISH CUPBOARD

3

Seventeenth-Century Chests

SWEDISH CHEST

HUGUENOT CHEST

STILE AND RAIL CHEST

These items of household necessity offer the first evidence of things to come—evidence of American craftsmen melding styles without regard to Old World craft traditions. In New England, joiners made chests after the Tudor style but had something of their own to say in every one. In New Amsterdam, chests of Dutch design were the order of the day. Certain of these reflect Eastern (Chinese) designs —the same source which provided much inspiration for later William and Mary and Queen Anne styles. And also, it should be noted, the same source which Master Chippendale later tapped for some of his most charming designs!

To what was later to become Pennsylvania, the Swedes carried the Scandinavian tradition in chests of architectural pattern, decorated in brilliant colors. The chests of Virginia, of course, echoed the Tudor and Carolean styles of England. At Saint Augustine, and at Santa Fe, Spanish chests were implanted on North American soil. The Huguenots, fleeing to America before 1700 and settling in New York, New England, Virginia, and Pennsylvania, recreated their traditional chests and even elaborated upon them. And, since the chest was item number one of household goods, it is not to be wondered at that the chest joiners extended their freedom and melding of styles into other items of furniture.

8

A "joined" or "joyned" chest is a chest framed together with mortise and tenon, and often paneled. Old inventories mention joined chests, wainscot chests, paneled chests, cutwork chests, inlaid chests, and engraven chests, as well as plain chests and board chests, leathern chests, and carved chests. They are known in the simple chest form, and with one, two, and three drawers. When the four-drawer chest was made, it was no longer a chest, but a case of drawers. Oak seems to have been the favored chest wood, although maple, pine, and walnut examples exist. The finest examples are the New England chests with tulip decoration carved on the panels. Disbrowe, Hadley, and other named chests are modern terms deriving from the names of original makers or the places where the chests were first found, or found in some numbers. One signed Disbrowe chest is known, made by Nicholas Disbrowe of Hartford, about 1686. The examples of real early American chests here illustrated include the signed Disbrowe; a two-drawer chest with tulip carving (about 1680); a simple chest with molded stiles and rails and carved panels; a Swedish chest of the type made or used in New Sweden (later Pennsylvania) about 1660; a Dutch chest of about 1660; and a Huguenot-influence chest from New England (about 1690–1710).

DISBROWE CHEST

TWO-DRAWER TULIP

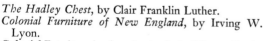

DUTCH TYPE CHEST ON STAND

The Hadley Chest, by Clair Franklin Luther.
Colonial Furniture of New England, by Irving W. Lyon.
Colonial Furniture in America, by Luke Vincent Lockwood.
Furniture Treasury, by Wallace Nutting.

4

William and Mary Furniture

THIS engaging furniture style, virile in design and almost masculine in gender, arrived in America, via the Dutch colonist, before William of Orange and Queen Mary were invited to the throne of Britain to replace the wholly unpopular despot, King James II. Its characteristics include the double hood, the square flat top, the trumpet-turned leg, and the flat, shaped stretcher. Showy burl woods were used to make the finest pieces, some inlay is known, also carving on stretchers and feet. Some William and Mary furniture is japanned and some is painted in imitation of burl. The curled, shaped foot, of Carolean design, is to be found on the English transition pieces (furniture made under both the old- and the new-style influence). This shaped foot and other curlings of Carolean design derive from Flemish styles. With the William and Mary style came the forms now called lowboy and highboy, but then known as two-piece chests of drawers, chests of drawers on frames, and dressing tables. In America, William and Mary furniture was made in beds, tables, sofas, day beds, chests, dressers, high chests, arm and side chairs, stools, mirrors, clocks, wardrobes, cabinets, and desks. Some of the earliest slope-front desks on frames, of William and Mary style, had an extra pair of trumpet-turned, hinged, or gated legs, which swung out to support the falling desk leaf. A multiplicity of legs (from six to eight) is found on the cabinet pieces, sofas, and day beds.

The brasses on William and Mary furniture consist mainly of an escutcheon with a hollow-cast drop handle, often generally of pear shape. They are either plain, or sparsely or elaborately decorated. This furniture was used in New England, New York, Pennsylvania, and Virginia. Maryland, loyal to James in spirit, if not disloyal in fact to the Protestant Orangeman, William, apparently did not take to the style. However, the Royal Governors appointed by William (and it is a matter of record that his reign marked a housecleaning in England's colonial policy) appear to have favored the style which his coming to England made popular. American William and Mary furniture is now quite rare, and any piece of it is correspondingly valuable.

The various pieces here illustrated and identified were either made in America, or were imported from England or The Netherlands between the years 1680 and 1725. Early English Queen Anne furniture held to this general form, or style, for several years. Some Queen Anne highboys are exact replicas of William and Mary, with the exception that the trumpet-turned legs are replaced with cabriole legs. The William and Mary style, however, lasted longer in America than in England.

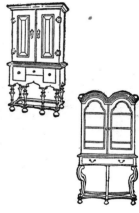

American cabinetmakers used walnut, curly and burly maple, ash and walnut, and even cherry, or a variety of wild cherry, in the construction. When veneered with burled walnut, ash, or maple, the cabinet sections were made of pine, or deal.

Colonial Furniture in America, by Luke Vincent Lockwood.
Colonial Furniture of New England, by Irving W. Lyon.
American Antique Furniture, by Edgar G. Miller, Jr.
Practical Book of Period Furniture, by Eberlein and McClure.

5

Queen Anne Furniture

T<small>HE</small> characteristic feature of Queen Anne furniture, named for the daughter of James II who succeeded William of Orange and Mary to the throne of England in 1702, is the cabriole, curved, or cyma-curvate leg, ending in a shaped foot. The Dutch developed this style from the Chinese with whom Dutch traders were in constant touch through the Dutch East India Company. William and his queen, Mary, themselves Dutch, were responsible for the introduction of the style into England. But before the style was in England, it was in America—in New York, and in Pennsylvania, where the Dutch had crowded the Swedes before Penn arrived, and where they stayed in large numbers in continuous touch with The Netherlands.

Therefore, American Queen Anne, or Dutch-style cabriole-legged furniture, is older in America than it is in England. Also, the style persisted here for almost a century, especially among small-town, village, and country cabinetmakers. Six fine Queen Anne chairs in one of America's greatest collections were made in 1753, by Michael Lind, a Swedish cabinetmaker of Lancaster, Pennsylvania, as a wedding gift for a good friend. The Queen Anne style is represented in candlestands, tilt-top tables, drop-leaf tables, arm, side, and corner chairs, sofas, lowboys, highboys, chests-on-frames, chests, cases of drawers, stools,

desks, desks-on-frames, mirrors, clocks, silverware, pewter, china, and glass. Certain examples of these are among the marginal illustrations. The dates range from 1700 to 1780.

When Chippendale and earlier Georgian designers began to develop a new style, they
clung to the basic Queen Anne forms until
they hit upon the square leg, flat carved, or
molded, and the fretted and spandreled forms,
now known as Chinese Chippendale. Many
different feet were used as terminals of the
cabriole leg of the Dutch or Queen Anne style.
These are the pad foot, drake foot, snake foot,
duck foot, et cetera. Queen Anne furniture
in America was made in pine, maple, curly
maple, walnut, mahogany, cherry, pearwood,
and poplar, used either exclusively or in combination. The brasses, drawer pulls, escutcheons, et cetera, also reflect the Chinese taste
and are sometimes called "willow pattern."

American Antique Furniture, by Edgar G. Miller, Jr.
Practical Book of Period Furniture, by Eberlein & Mc-
　Clure.
Period Furniture Hand Book, by G. G. and F. Gould.
The Period of Queen Anne, by Blake and Reveirs-
　Hopkins.

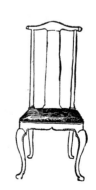

6

Chippendale Furniture
in America, 1725–90

A̶NY ATTEMPT to analyze, expose, and elucidate on the furniture styles of Thomas Chippendale in "primer" form is ordained to failure.
The subject is too big, even, for one book.
Thomas Chippendale, shrewd and resourceful
user of borrowed motifs in designs for furniture of all kinds, published *The Gentleman
and Cabinet-Maker's Director* in 1754. The
novice, and even the educated student of furniture styles, will often call a piece of Georgian
furniture, made before Chippendale's book
appeared, Chippendale. And no wonder. Chippendale borrowed from the Georgian styles,
which were in almost direct imitation of Queen
Anne in line and form, just as he borrowed
from the French cabinetmakers of his day,
and from the Dutch, the Spanish, and the
Italians. Also he borrowed from the Chinese.

Consequently, the title line of this section
should read "What Is Called Chippendale-
Style Furniture in America, 1725–90." Just
how much of it is copied from Chippendale's
book of designs, in its various editions, is a
matter for deep study and not quick reading.
But what is important to expose in this primer
is the fact that American cabinetmakers, albeit
in some cases English-trained, developed, improved, and improvised on Georgian, Chippendale, and other contemporary designs, and
created a style of their own which, in turn,
resulted in the making of much furniture that

14

is lovelier, more exquisite, and finer than that made under the Chippendale-design influence in England.

Goddard of Rhode Island, and Savery, Randolph, and Gostelowe of Philadelphia created furniture that is better than the peer of England's best Chippendale.

Similarly, several hundred other town and country cabinetmakers in America were making both modified and elaborated Queen Anne-style furniture that ranks with much English Georgian furniture. When these cabinetmakers saw what their city brethren were producing in the Chippendale manner, they, too, began making it. Just as with other furniture styles which preceded it in America, more Americans per thousand of population appear to have had a piece or two, or a set, of Chippendale-style furniture, than was owned and enjoyed per capita in England. There, it was for the royal, the lords, peers, ladies, and gentry. Over here, if you had the money to buy it, it was yours. And the price was right. Importation of English-made furniture of this period undoubtedly was carried on. It is most likely the imports entered ports south of Philadelphia where native cabinetmakers of great talent were scarce. It takes custom to keep a fine cabinetmaker alive.

A Boston, Newport, Hartford, New Haven, New York, Philadelphia, Charleston, Lancaster, Albany, or Baltimore cabinetmaker had as much custom as he could handle because there were plenty of people for customers. Virginia, the Carolinas, and Georgia were not big-town colonies; they were colonies of great plantations—mostly self-contained and self-supporting except for their classic and luxury needs. Philadelphia and New York made Chippendale furniture was, undoubtedly, also shipped south to other colonies. The illustrations here assembled cover the major items

made in Chippendale style in America. Some of them are "country Chippendale," which means they were made by cabinetmakers in villages and small towns. The styles are simpler, the decoration rudimentary. But they, too, are valuable today. Mahogany is the most favored wood of this period, but walnut was often used, also maple, curly maple, cherry, fruit wood, pine, and poplar.

Thomas Chippendale, by Oliver Bracket.
Chippendale and His School, by Blake and Reveirs-Hopkins.
Blue Book of Philadelphia Furniture, by W. M. Hornor, Jr.
American Antique Furniture, by Edgar G. Miller, Jr.
The Gentleman and Cabinet-Maker's Director, by Thomas Chippendale, with a Supplement by Walter Randell Story.

7

Block-Front Furniture

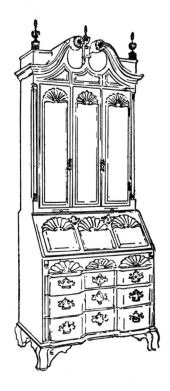

CONNOISSEURS on both sides of the Atlantic may differ in opinion regarding nearly all American antiques, but when it comes to block-front furniture they reach an oasis of unanimity. They agree it is the handsomest of American productions and that, apparently, it is original with us. Of course there are dissenters who claim the style isn't original with us and that it derives from The Netherlands and Spain. If this be so, and it is still a moot point, then we shall probably find that the Dutch and the Spaniards got their inspiration from the Chinese. However, until the case for the dissenters is proved—and up to now there is no proof worth talking about—we can rest content with the feeling that the very finest furniture produced in America during the second half of the eighteenth century is our very own furniture—New England block front.

America's great block-front design now appears to be definitely established as the brain child of two Newport, Rhode Island, cabinetmakers: John Goddard (1723–85), who was born and who died in Newport; and John Townsend who, born at Newport in 1733, worked there until at least 1769. Some authorities claim he then removed to Connecticut. Others claim he stayed in Newport.

The block-front design, or style, these two master cabinetmakers perfected was achieved by so carving and working the façade of a piece of furniture that it presents a series of

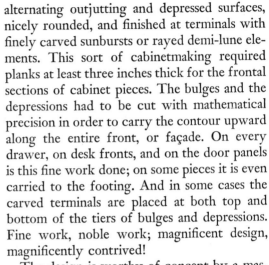

alternating outjutting and depressed surfaces, nicely rounded, and finished at terminals with finely carved sunbursts or rayed demi-lune elements. This sort of cabinetmaking required planks at least three inches thick for the frontal sections of cabinet pieces. The bulges and the depressions had to be cut with mathematical precision in order to carry the contour upward along the entire front, or façade. On every drawer, on desk fronts, and on the door panels is this fine work done; on some pieces it is even carried to the footing. And in some cases the carved terminals are placed at both top and bottom of the tiers of bulges and depressions. Fine work, noble work; magnificent design, magnificently contrived!

The design is worthy of concept by a master architect. Its execution called for master craftsmanship. After Goddard and Townsend had set the style, other New England cabinetmakers took it up. They, too, produced superlatively good work, and for this very simple reason: only a superlatively good cabinetmaker would try to make a block-front piece of furniture! Hence only good ones tried and they, in the main, succeeded. That is why every piece of block-front furniture thus far found has been considered worthy of the designation "fine." Even the attempts at block-front work, with very shallow depressions and low-relief bulges, made "upstate" in Massachusetts and New Hampshire, are now considered better than just good furniture of the eighteenth century.

Block front has been called "Chippendale" in style, but so to designate this American masterpiece of styling is to decry it. It is, rather, based upon what Chippendale himself began to work with: Queen Anne styles as reflected in early Georgian furniture. He went his way, with feathers, frills, rococo, and what have you. Goddard and Townsend went their way

18

and developed a style that Master Chippendale
might well have wished was his own. For a
number of years a few people thought Chippendale had made some block-front pieces.
There were, and are, a few pieces in England.
But they have more recently been adjudged
as imported—from America. When? Either by
returning Royal Governors who carried them
home with them; by returning officers who
served here with King George's forces in the
Revolution; or shipped to England during the
quiet exodus of American antiques between
1870 and 1900. It seems the cult of antique
collecting became quite a vogue in England
after 1870. Newly rich nobodies were bidding
for the newly poor "somebodies'" furniture.
There wasn't enough of it. So a group of
English dealers began buying up Chippendale,
Tudor, Queen Anne, and William and Mary
furniture over here. Also they purchased a
good deal of Bristol delft and Staffordshire
tulipware that had been here for at least two
hundred years. One such dealer, issuing a
monthly catalogue in England during the
1880s, pictured a great deal of furniture from
America—even some blown-mold bottles from
Pittsburgh and Ohio glass factories.

The fact that block-front furniture is now
almost unobtainable except by virtue of accidental new discovery of a piece or two, or the
dispersal of a great collection, the student of
American antiques need not neglect study, or
be denied appreciation, of this great furniture
style. Made only in cabinet pieces: kneehole
desks, dressing tables, highboys, slope-fall
desks, bookcases, et cetera, the style is so distinctive that with only the term "block front"
in your mind you'd recognize a piece on sight.
The magnificence of the designs is difficult to
reproduce in the small drawings we must use
in this primer, but you who are intrigued by
what is said here can go on and on, reveling

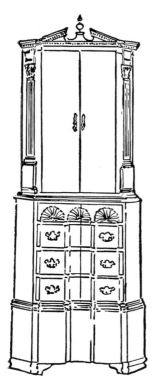

in block-front design, by studying the volumes listed below. It is *the* great American design of the great age of cabinetmaking, and a noble design of which we can be justly proud. It appears to have been made from 1748 to 1780.

The desk shown at bottom of page 17 comes from The Netherlands and is, perhaps, the kind of example on which proponents of the foreign origin of the style rest their case. The large corner piece, shown on this page, is now in an important American collection. The top is a restoration. The base is considered to be original. All other illustrations of block-front furniture are of pieces in museums or in notable private collections.

American Antique Furniture, by Edgar G. Miller, Jr.
Furniture Treasury, by Wallace Nutting.
The magazine *Antiques* (May 1922; February 1923; April 1929).
Early American Furniture Makers, by Thomas Hamilton Ormsbee.

8

Adam Furniture

THE ONE BIG GAP in the scene that is the American reflection of classic English and Dutch furniture styles during the eighteenth century is found in the almost non-existence of Adam furniture, or furniture in the Adam style. With us, Hepplewhite marks our break with Chippendale. In England, it is Adam that marks the break. But that break came in England at about the time we were making our own "break" with Old Lady Britain, and were setting up housekeeping on our own. This is not to say that some Adam styles did not trickle into America. They did, but chiefly as mantels, mirrors, chairs, and pier tables only. Adam established the reception for the classic style in England. The brothers Adam were primarily architects and never were cabinetmakers. When they designed a house they designed the furniture for it.

It is the reflection of Adam, in Hepplewhite, that we enjoy in place of the Adam style. Adam's classic styles derive from Grecian and Roman forms. These, especially the Greek, were further revived by the Dutchman Robert Hope who, retiring to England, issued a book of designs that greatly influenced our Federal styles. Mention of Hope will be found in the Federal-style section of this primer.

Robert Adam and His Brothers, by John Swarbrick.

21

9

Hepplewhite Furniture

GEORGE HEPPLEWHITE's *Cabinet-Maker and Upholsterer's Guide* was first published in London, 1788. His designs seem to have captured the immediate fancy of American cabinetmakers and the American public. This is quite natural. After any war, and particularly after a war that has been won, the people as a whole are sufficiently elated to be lifted out of wartime conservatism and have an ardent desire for something new. Americans found one answer to this desire in furniture of the Hepplewhite style and, within twelve years, seem to have ordered more of it than they ordered of Chippendale style in any twenty years of Chippendale's furniture popularity. Hepplewhite's designs mark a full and complete departure from Chippendale. The tapered square leg, the flat or serpentine front, the bow front, delicate inlay, and classic, airy, and light form are its characteristics. Beds, tables, dining-room furniture, sideboards, tea tables, card tables, butlers' sideboards, hunting boards, corner cabinets, chests, clocks—mention what you will, even twin beds and chamber closets—you'll find it made in the Hepplewhite style in America. The wood most favored was mahogany, with inlays of white holly, box wood, and colored woods. The brasses are classic, in keeping with the designs.

Almost every cabinetmaker in America made furniture in the Hepplewhite style. In the back country they used walnut, pine, cher-

ry, maple, fruit wood, and poplar. Some of
the back-country Hepplewhite has little or
no inlay—but the styling is there. The illustrations here given are exemplary of the great
dozen years of feverish Hepplewhite furniture making in America. Hepplewhite furniture has been found from Saint Augustine, Florida, to Boothbay Harbor, Maine, and from
the coast line thus bracketed, as far west as
the Mississippi. As the people moved into new
territories and states, they took some household goods with them, and often, between
1790 and 1810, it was Hepplewhite furniture
they carried with them, at least in part.

American Antique Furniture, by Edgar G. Miller, Jr.
American Furniture & Decoration, by Edward S. Hal-
loway.

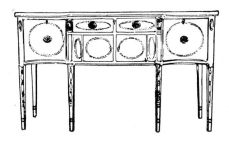

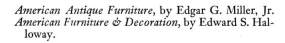

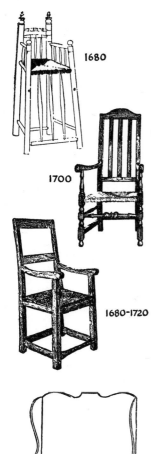

1680

1700

1680-1720

1830—1840

1680-1700

10

Pioneer and Cottage Furniture

To CALL this furniture "folk" is to do it and
the people who made and used it a gross injustice. There is a vast difference between what
the Germans call *Herrenvolk* and what the
American pioneer called "Folks." The former
designation is for robots in thinking and in
action. The latter is a compliment. When you
are folks to people who understand, you are
a real person: hospitable, congenial, social, and
all else that spells friend. It may well be maintained that in Pennsylvania the Germanic immigrants continued in the folk tradition. Certainly it is true of those who banded themselves into religious communities. At Ephrata,
at Snow Hill, and along the Perkiomen Creek,
religious sectarians held forth and flourished
for a while. But to say the things they made
are German is not quite true. Their forms and
styles were drawn from memory, and from
those used in the surrounding country. There
is Swiss, Swedish, Dutch, and German influence in most of them. So, too, with the
houses and furniture created by or for the
immigrants out of the Palatinate who were
removed to London by Queen Anne, shipped
to New York, finally to New York State
(Livingston Manor, et cetera), and who then
migrated to Pennsylvania. On their mean-
derings and treks they fell heir to many
ideas not German. The Zellers who built the
Zeller Garrison House in Lancaster (now
Lebanon) County were not German but
French, from Deux-Ponts. They built in a

manner that is redolent of France, and their real name was Sellier, or Cellier.

The Shakers and other sects of religious-communal type made many things within what might be called a folk pattern. But the pattern is a simplification of existing forms and styles used contiguous to the settlements.

Early American pioneer and cottage furniture is actually a slightly blurred copy of contemporaneous styles used by the gentry and the middle classes. Often the blurring is only simplification and practical adaptation to pioneer and cottage needs. A great deal of early New England furniture was pioneer furniture. A great deal of early Swedish and Dutch furniture is in the same category. The pioneer and the cottager (in many cases the cottager became a pioneer on a new frontier where, as a pioneer, he soon became a cottager again) required, made, and had made for him things that would last. Solid wood construction and good ironwork were mandatory. Rush seats and rope seats were preferred to upholstery. Chests that would stand plenty of punishment were a delight. Because most of these pioneers and cottagers were not peasantry, but proud spirits out to carve a new heritage for themselves, they demanded also some natural beauty in their furnishings. Of course this is not to say they demanded beauty as aestheticists demand it. They demanded it from instinct and perhaps subconsciously.

And so in pioneer and primitive American furniture we find day beds, chests, chairs, tables, clocks, settles, bedsteads, and other things. A lot of what is now collected as belonging in this category is actually out of it. Sink benches were just kitchen pieces: low cupboards with an open well in which the dishpan was kept. When this well was lined with "zinc," it became zinc-bench or sink-bench. Between 1800 and 1890 these were in

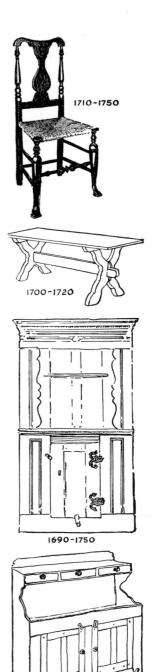

1710-1750

1700-1720

1690-1750

1800-1860

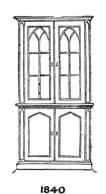

1760-1800

1840

1690-1750

cottages, cabins, town tenements, and in the kitchens of farmhouses. Shoemakers' benches are tradesmen's shop furniture. Most weavers' stools come, not out of houses, but out of weavers' shops. Taps (liquor bars) come out of taverns. Schoolmasters' desks are out of schools or offices. Wagon seats were seldom if ever used in a home. Collect such quaint things if you like them, but collect them for what they are. There is no pioneer halo over them. Some of the pioneer and cottage furniture here pictured is not uncommon. In fact, you'll find some of it illustrated in *Godey's Lady's Book* and called cottage furniture. There was an American vogue for country-style cottages and villas in the 1840–50 period. This caused the transplanting of a modified form of Tudor cottage to America. Some of these had bathtubs installed in trapdoors under the dining-room floor! In this period the New England settle of 1660 was resurrected and used as a sofa in cottages and inns. These mid-nineteenth-century cottages were furnished with much goods that is today collected as primitive.

Pioneer and cottage woodenware, pewter, et cetera, are included in the sections dealing with those items. They were not, with the possible exception of some woodenware, pioneer or cottage made. They were just good stout wares selected for the purpose of use, with a touch of the beautiful or the gaudy.

It is a matter of record that almost all pioneer and cottage furniture was made by specialized workmen: carpenters, joiners, cabinetmakers, et cetera, who, locating in a pioneer settlement, at once went to work. They were needed. So were coopers, tinsmiths, and other artisans. Towns grew fast, and in many cases the makers of fine and even luxury furniture were not two years behind the makers of what we call pioneer and cottage furniture.

Pine, cherry and walnut, maple and hickory, buttonwood, poplar, and even cedar were used in this kind of furniture. It may be on the crude side, or verge upon what collectors call "country made," or it may be so engagingly forthright and honest that it just screams "pioneer." Call it the "vanguard and the baggage" furniture of America, if you like. You'll be close to the mark. It was made there first, wherever the "there" may have been, and it stayed longest before discovery by collectors. But please do not call this folk furniture or folk art unless you want to be as silly, well, as the people who do call it that and worship it as such. We have no real folk art in the European sense. European folk art is a sort of crystallized peasant tradition in textiles, pottery, metal wares, furniture, habits, and customs. In America, what is called folk art, folk architecture, et cetera, is really an attempt at duplicating classic or current styles from memory of the form. Thus the workman tried to reproduce without benefit of clear pattern or models, but to the best of his craft ability.

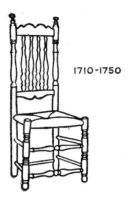

1710-1750

1750-1770

1680-1740

Pine Furniture of Early New England, by Russell H. Kettell.
Furniture of the Pilgrim Century, by Wallace Nutting.
Early American Craftsmen, by Walter A. Dyer.
Shaker Furniture, by E. D. and F. Andrews.
The Story of American Furniture, by Thomas Hamilton Ormsbee.
Early American Furniture Makers, by Thomas Hamilton Ormsbee.

1770-1840

1690-1750

11

Introduction to American Federal Furniture

There is, as yet, no book about American Federal furniture. In fact, this primer calls it Federal in the hope that the name will be adapted and generally used. But there is plenty said about this furniture in some twenty-five books dealing with American antiques in general. Federal furniture, representing the American melding of Hepplewhite, Adam, Hope, Sheraton, and French Directoire, is the furniture of America feeling its oats, growing at a great rate, and expanding all over the map. Everyone who knows his American history knows that between 1800 and 1848 we expanded at a rate that made the rest of the world gasp. At one fell swoop we took over the Louisiana territory. We gulped Florida for dessert. Texas joined us and added to our world-power status.

Furniture was desperately needed during this expansion period. The cabinetmakers responded with furniture that not only satisfied creature comforts and needs, but which reflected our national desire to gloat over our coming of age and being a great world influence for democracy.

So long is the scale of Federal furniture, from gamut to ela, from low to high, that each intervening note in the scale is a platform upon which to stop and get your breath. Federal furniture—and Federal-style—exists in every imaginable kind of item. It is found reflected in pump handles, soap dishes, clocks, watches, silver, mirrors, wallpaper, carpets, floor cloths, painted floors, linen, fancywork, tinware, pewter, britannia ware, brass, stoves, pottery, stoneware—everything. In preparing the following sections, no less than fifty examples of each object illustrated were studied before a final choice was made. These candidates covered a geographic area reaching from Saint Louis and New Orleans to Charleston, South Carolina, and Newburyport, Massachusetts.

The unquestionable badge of Federal furniture has been thought to be an eagle; cast, carved, engraved, painted, stenciled, or inlaid. This, of course, is an error. The eagle is evidence, but not the password. In this Federal group of styles we find furniture by Duncan Phyfe, New York cabinetmaker, and some hundreds of others who, unnamed, and unhonored, made furniture in substantially the same style, albeit some made it with a much heavier and less facile hand. Also, we find the clocks of Simon and Aaron Willard, mirrors made by hundreds of looking-glass makers, and even the lowly spool-turned furniture which seems to have entered the scene, tentatively, at least, about 1815.

The list of reference books recommended for further study of this period alone may look forbidding. However, there is something of general interest, and much of particular interest, for you in each one. So vast is this field that illustrations in the following sections cover only the major kinds of furniture, and the most important phases of Federal design. Every kind of cabinet wood was used in Federal furniture. There is solid furniture, inlaid and painted furniture, stained and grained furniture, stenciled furniture, and furniture cast in iron. Our Federal period began with our discovery of Adam, the Jeffersonian love of classic forms, our adaptations and melding of Sheraton and French-Directoire styles, our interest in the Greek revival, and our touch with the French of New Orleans and the Spanish of Florida. It ended with the downfall of the Adam influence, the disappearance of the Greek style, the complete submergence of Sheraton, and the apparent eclipse of taste that marked the period of our war with Mexico. The next step was our entry into the Victorian maelstrom—the furniture of which is now considered as falling within the category of antique.

Approach this Federal period and enjoy its study as a new experience. From Adams to Jackson, at least, it lasted in full strength and glorious power. Into the Van Buren administration it ventured. Then came the beginning of the end. By 1840 it was done; done in by the heavy, stolid, but showy post-Empire furniture of which the less said the better.

American Furniture and Decoration, by Edward S. Holloway.
Furniture Masterpieces of Duncan Phyfe, by Charles Over Cornelius.
Southern Antiques, by Paul H. Burroughs.
Sheraton Period, by Blake and Reveirs-Hopkins.
American Antique Furniture, by Edgar G. Miller, Jr.
French and English Furniture, by Esther Singleton.

12

Federal Furniture
of Sheraton Influence

THOMAS SHERATON's *Cabinet-Maker and Up-holsterer's Drawing Book* first appeared in 1791. Almost at once the designs of this new-comer in the furniture field shook the swiftly grown tree of Hepplewhite popularity and sounded the final requiem for Master Thomas Chippendale's. Few worshipers at the shrine of Sheraton's styles realize they derive from an eccentric—an original who was successively a Baptist minister, teacher, inventor, and furni-ture designer. Ruthlessly he dubbed Chippen-dale and Hepplewhite designs as "antiquated," and proffered his own, borrowed from Adam, Shearer, and other English designers. These, it must be admitted, were also the mainsprings that Hepplewhite had tapped.

Sheraton, in his *Cabinet-Maker and Uphol-sterer's Drawing Book*, offered fresh, new con-cepts. The characteristics of this phase of his work are: adherence to angularity and re-strained curvature of form; straight lines for the blocking out and execution of a design; reliance mainly on reeding, inlaid ovals, bosses, cartouches, and vase forms for the achieve-ment of beauty and decoration. After the be-ginning of Napoleon's reign as Emperor of France, Sheraton fell under the spell of French Empire and fell flat as a master designer. In America, rather than in England, his basically sound designs persisted, melded here not with the Empire style, which caused his decline in

England, but with Directoire, which made both styles unique with us, and deserving of the separate distinction of "Federal." That is why so many things we have been calling Sheraton over here are not recognized as such by English connoisseurs and experts. Not that it matters one whit what English connoisseurs and experts think. In fact, to ask their opinion of our furniture is almost fatuous. It's almost like asking another man what he thinks of your own wife. A question verging, one might say, on poor, if not bad, taste.

The original, or first-period Sheraton, as exemplified in his first books, persisted in our Federal mating of styles until the Van Buren administration. Toward the end it was competing with heavy Empire, but not embracing that monstrous effort at originality. The Federal style of Sheraton dominant, blended with some Directoire, or Directoire dominant, but blended with some Sheraton, went out of fashion when Mr. Van Buren did the same thing.

There was a new deal in taste. Those who indulged in it to the full had a full house—all jokers. By the time of the Mexican War our public taste was awful in respect of new furniture and impeccable in respect of what we were keeping to pass on to posterity as antiques. The pictures here displayed are of pure Sheraton styles in sofas, chairs, beds, sideboards, et cetera, and of the same styles blended with Directoire. There are several books dealing with Sheraton styles in America. *American Antique Furniture*, by Edgar G. Miller, Jr., is one this primer recommends. But by all means strive to see either an original or a reprint of Sheraton's *The Cabinet-Maker and Upholsterer's Drawing Book*. Most libraries have one or the other. You need not bother with his *Cabinet-Maker's Dictionary*, published in 1803. Avoid contact with his Empire styles.

Elsewhere in this primer you can read about America's own *Cabinet-Maker's Assistant*, published at Baltimore, in 1840, and the styles it laid before the eyes of our ancestors. There you will find "Empire" at its unbelievable worst.

It should be noted here also that Sheraton was a designer of dual-purpose and experimental furniture. Perhaps our own Thomas Jefferson got his furniture-gadget ideas from Sheraton. Among Sheraton's fancies were ottomans or sofas with seat-heaters (!), folding beds, couch tables, bookcase-washstands, stepladder tables, and game-board sewing stands. It is doubtful whether furniture of Sheraton style, copied from his own design books, was made in any cities of America other than Boston, Salem, New York, Philadelphia, and Baltimore. Sheraton's designs were not all popular in England. His chair designs seem to have met with little favor at home. In America, melded with Directoire, his chair designs became a part of our Federal style.

Sheraton Period, by J. Blake and A. Reveirs-Hopkins.

13

Federal Furniture
of Directoire Influence

THE FRENCH DIRECTOIRE or Directory style was developed during the last decade of the eighteenth century, and continued through the first decade of the nineteenth century. That it influenced American cabinetmakers' styles for a longer period in America than in France is, perhaps, due in no small part to the fact that Napoleon was made Emperor of France in 1804, and a new style, Empire, was immediately put into process of development. French Directoire has been called the most simple, the most lovely, and the most elegant furniture style of its time. Its chief characteristics derive from the studied, resourceful use of the curved line. It is reflected at its best in chairs and sofas of both elegance and comfort, in graceful tables and stands, in beds and in mirrors. As with all classic styles, the Directoire could be followed in furniture for the masses as well as the classes. In France it was a new national style acceptable to all, and "all" did not include the nobility. That had been liquidated, or had emigrated. The Directoire began with the execution of the King and his consort, Marie Antoinette. The best of France's designers went to work for the people instead of the nobles. You can read about this era in political history, or in the romances of Dumas, Dickens, or Sabatini. But in viewing the Directoire style itself you can see furniture for the people at

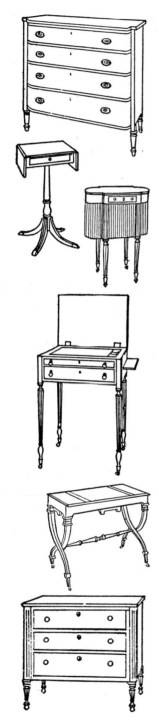

its ultimate best; far superior to the political system that gave it birth.

This Directoire style, combined with some aspects of Sheraton, influenced the work of the New Yorker, Duncan Phyfe, and scores of other cabinetmakers who were Phyfe's peers, even though they are obscure at this distance of time. American Directoire-influence Federal-period furniture still cries for a sympathetic biographer who will tell its story in both words and pictures. The style is so happy a blending of connotations having both masculine and feminine appeal that the book, when written, might well be the wise collaboration of a male and a female appreciator.

America's admiration and sympathy for the cause of the French people who, after all, were seeking in their own way exactly the liberty we in America had won, led us into ready acceptance of the Directoire style. But if it was sympathy and admiration for France that opened the door, it was the style itself which won America's heart. We clung to it so tenaciously that our own acceptance of its successor in France, the Empire style, was registered only after the Emperor who motivated it had become a prisoner of the English at Elba and Saint Helena. In view of the fact that we had a bit of trouble with England in 1812, and had our own capitol burned by them, we may well have accepted the late Emperor's styles just to spite Old Lady England. We spited no one but ourselves and our own taste. Had we clung to this Directoire style—and it deserved clinging to—we might well have used it in the development of an American style for the entire nineteenth century, and thus have avoided the Empire and Victorian horrors altogether.

The illustrations have been selected as those best demonstrating the curved line and the sheer beauty of Directoire styles under American influence—or the Federal styles under Directoire influence—whichever designation you like. They include representative pieces: beds, sofas, chairs, stands, tables, and desks. Traditional fine cabinet woods—mahogany, walnut, and maple, as well as poplar, cherry, and other fruit woods—were used in making our Federal Directoire-influence furniture. The painted fancy chairs of Directoire influence were of soft woods, with rush, caned, or upholstered seats.

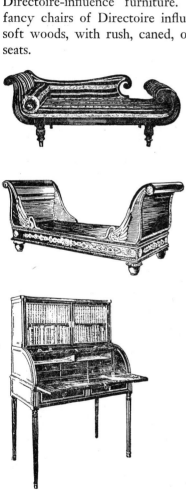

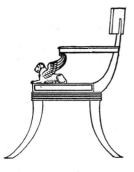

14

Federal Furniture of Greek-Revival Influence

To THE analytic student of political history, the Greek-revival influence on furniture which was pointed by the publication of Thomas Hope's *Household Furniture and Interior Decoration*, London, 1807, may well have paved the way for international sympathy for the cause of Greek independence two decades later. Perhaps *Marco Bozzaris* (remember the Turk was dreaming of the hour when Greece, her knee in suppliance bent?) recognized the Greek-revival influence as an early form of lend lease. At any rate, Hope and other enthusiasts made Doric, Ionic, Corinthian, Parthenon, and Acropolis household words. The classic got into our blood stream, already conditioned by the Directoire, the spread of art as a study for all people—and our belated discovery of the designs of the brothers Adam.

The Greek-revival styles of Hope, Adam, and others are found in our furniture as a blending. We can isolate them only in terms of their dominance in certain articles of furniture, and in the use of Greek decorative forms, particularly the "anthemion," or honeysuckle, the lyre, acanthus, and patera. Hope spoke for the line of beauty; the beautiful necessity; for structural beauty and beauty in structure. His also was a voice which presaged the coming of functional design. That he, or his philosophy, influenced Jefferson is obvious. But more

obvious still is the Greek-revival influence on American town, city, and farm architecture, of 1810–30. Our new states abounded in it. In Ohio, farmhouses, schoolhouses, barns, pigsties, corncribs, and outhouses were as Greek in style as the streets of Athens in 500 B.C. Department stores, bazaars, groggeries, hotels, banks, all were Greek in style. Happily, many of these little gems of the Greek revival still stand. And no longer are they razed with impunity. A farmer planning to demolish a Greek-revival barn or other structure is apt to have an indignant committee from the nearest Historical Society demanding that he let it stand. He usually does.

Since this primer cannot attempt to cover Greek-revival architecture either as a style or a motif of interior decoration, the only illustrations for this section are examples of Greek-influence furniture, regardless of their median source of advocacy: Adam, Hope, Shearer, Sheraton, or the Directoire.

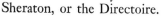

15

*Federal Furniture
by Phyfe and His Peers*

"Aᴍᴇʀɪᴄᴀɴ ᴄᴏʟʟᴇᴄᴛᴏʀs are a bit hipped on names," said an English collector several years ago. One suspects he was looking down his nose when he said it, but he spoke the truth. We are name hunters in more ways than one. Take Duncan Phyfe, for example. Born 1768, died 1854, working 1794–1845, he was a superlatively *good* cabinetmaker. We can put the period right there and still do Phyfe justice. But we didn't and we haven't. We have made Phyfe a demigod almost; a sort of American Chippendale or Hepplewhite. Which he was not, and did not aspire to be. Other good cabinetmakers were working at the same time Phyfe was turning out his furniture in New York. They were working in New York, Boston, Salem, Albany, Baltimore, Philadelphia, and elsewhere. Much of their work is as good as Phyfe's. But old Duncan is enthroned as the standard by which, or with whom, the work of all the others is judged. They're better than, as good as, not quite so good as, or 'way below, Phyfe!

One error has been in associating the work of Phyfe the cabinetmaker with the idea of Phyfe as the designer, rather than as Phyfe the *user* of good patterns and styles. Also we have used the feminine technique of refusing to look at his poor styles, and by this simple act of not looking have ignored their existence. Some of his protagonists have gone so far as to hope

Phyfe's poorer stuff will never be viewed, or
reviewed. Evidently this idol had at least one
foot of clay. The fact is that some of his later
things after, say, 1830, are as awful as any
other super-Empire stuff made by any other
cabinetmaker. But was this Phyfe's taste or his
customers'? He may have become the New
York fashion to such an extent that the rich
brewery trade came to him for furniture in
what *they* thought was high style. Cabinetmaking, not designing, was his business. It is
to be presumed he made what his customers
wanted. And got his cash. The furniture made
in Phyfe's best years—and the best years of
his contemporaries, wherever they worked—is
a happy blending of Sheraton, Hope, and the
Directoire. What resembles Empire is most
likely Hope influence, for Hope also influenced
the Empire style.

Most of the chairs by Phyfe and his peers
are after Hope and Sheraton with a frequent
sweep of curve that is pure Directoire. The
sofas, largely, are Directoire inspired, although
some are almost pure Sheraton in basic form.
You can readily tell them apart in our pictures.
The tables of this period are more Sheraton
than Hope or Directoire, but the admixture is
there in many of them. In every piece of the
Federal furniture of this era there is one price-
less ingredient: freedom to do as the cabinetmaker wished with good shapes and forms and
décor and be damned to traditions. That is the
Federal part of the designs.

So much has been written about Duncan
Phyfe and the so-called Phyfe style that this
primer need not concern itself with intimate
details of the lives and works of Master Phyfe
and his fellows. The same furniture was made
by less skilled cabinetmakers in many small
towns and villages all over New England, New
York, Pennsylvania, and eastern Ohio. The
work of their hands is honest, but on the stodgy

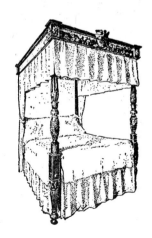

side. It verges on "Empire" even though the cabinetmakers who made it probably hadn't heard of Empire when they fashioned it. That points to the secret of Phyfe and his good fellow craftsmen. They were light-handed. They appreciated the styles they were blending. They had that combined nicety of feeling and dextrousness of touch that spell beauty: the creation of masterpieces even by nobodies. Baltimore, to knowing collectors, is a high spot of fine cabinetmaking in this particular era of the Federal period. The cultural position of Baltimore in the first several decades of the nineteenth century is seldom appreciated by people other than its natives. We should consider, though, that Baltimore was right next to Washington. It reacted to, and acted upon, Washington. For years Baltimore was the center to which Southern aristocracy looked for style guidance, beauty, and cultural advantages. Out of this fine city on the Chesapeake we have furniture of Federal-period styling that is second to none made elsewhere in the Union.

Pictured are the chairs, tables, and sofas of the Phyfe era in the Federal period. The list of books, certain of which are also recommended in other sections, is worthy of your study. And may some lady or gentleman from Maryland be inspired to write, research, and picture the furniture of Baltimore made in this very same era; as good as, if not better than, the best the era produced elsewhere.

This furniture is largely of mahogany, although cherry, fruit woods, walnut, and maple were used. Greek decorative forms are found inlaid and carved on it; the lyre is used in chair backs, sofa ends, and table pedestals. Curving bulges out of cubical forms. Inlaid panels, carved eagles, shields, and stars, cast and polished brass feet are almost trademarks. Reeding on flat surfaces, slender reeded

40

vase forms, and some leg carving mark its movement from first to last. There is also that engaging habit of extending the legs of chairs and tables upward to the seat or top, terminating in disks, dished or rosetted. For some years after the Phyfe vogue started every table and chair with the lyre motif was gleefully called Phyfe. The sofas of Sheraton and Directoire fashion, made no matter by whom, and where found, were imagined to be by Phyfe. When the size of his shop and store was examined, it became obvious that Phyfe couldn't have made all, or half, or even a quarter of the furniture attributed to him. He was revealed in much the same light as we have revealed him in this primer, and as having not one, not two, not three, or four peers, but a noble company of them, most of whom have yet to achieve publicity and fame. But the furniture he and they made is ours to collect and ours to hold—grand furniture to collect and grand furniture to own.

Furniture Masterpieces, by Duncan Phyfe, by Charles Over Cornelius.
Early American Furniture, by Charles Over Cornelius.
Duncan Phyfe and the English Regency, 1795–1830, by Nancy McClelland.

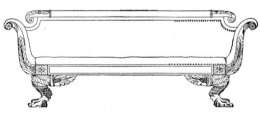

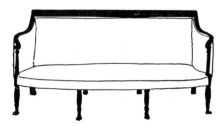

16

Post-Federal and Pre-Victorian American Furniture

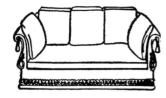

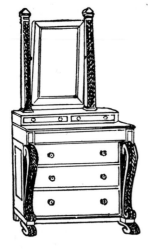

THAT excellent magazine *House and Garden* has, on occasion, printed expositions of good taste and poor taste in decoration and furniture styles. Which precedent, even in this primer, permits attention to a style that is the epitome of poor taste in furniture design. But since the taste was American, and because a great many Americans had it, they also had the kind of furniture this section must deal with here and now. In 1840 John Hall, architect and draftsman of Baltimore, published *The Cabinet-Maker's Assistant* embracing "The most modern style of cabinet furniture; exemplified in New Designs." These new designs mark the decline and fall of Adam, the Regency, Sheraton, and the Directoire. They mark also the persistence here of the Empire style evolved in France in 1803–10, to please the Emperor Napoleon.

This is the furniture which, shipped on riverboat furniture stores, was purchased at every landing stage on the Ohio, Mississippi, Missouri, Tennessee, and other rivers. It moved up the Connecticut and the Delaware. It penetrated the bayous around New Orleans. It was carried to every inlet on Chesapeake Bay. It crowded its betters in every home in the land. Heaven alone knows what kind of song it crooned, but it seems to have been accepted with general squeals of delight. When it lost popularity, it was to Victorian furniture—the era of walnut, rosewood, and horsehair, the nadir of fashion which marked the stuffy reign of young Victoria and the far stuffier old Victoria.

This is the furniture which, made in factories, was sold by warehouses and emporiums. This is the furniture almost any cabinetmaker *could* make. And this, too, is the furniture which the uninitiated think is "colonial." You've probably heard it called that from Pittsburgh to the Rio Grande; from Grand Rapids to Los Angeles. Most of it isn't yet one hundred years old, nor has its approach to the century mark mellowed a single line of it. Which is not to say it was all bad. Some of the bedposts are rather nicely designed. There is the faintest touch of Sheraton in some of the sewing stands, and there is a dim echo of Directoire in some of the sofas. A few of the stools look comfortable and are worthy of houseroom today, if kept in dark corners.

Yet, if you like any of this furniture, that is strictly your own business. But do not permit a liking for it to develop if your mind is still wide open about what to collect *if* you collect, and what to dispose of if you have a houseful of American antiques. Undoubtedly, it is the kind of furniture Abraham Lincoln had in his first home. It was the last word when Vandalia was the capital of Illinois and before the six-bell Conestoga teams were pulling out of Saint Louis for the land of gold. In spite of prejudices, this furniture is truly of the period of 1840–60, and it belongs in any Midwestern or Mississippi Valley house built in that era. The illustrations are taken directly from Hall's book of designs. This book has just recently been reprinted in facsimile in a limited edition. We recommend it as the one book for study of this style.

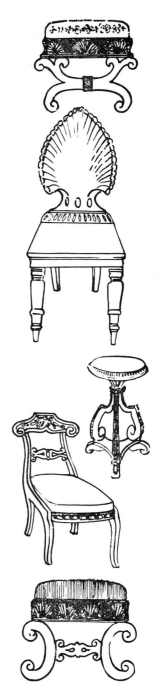

17

Victorian Furniture

If any furniture requires a study of its background, it is the thrice-hybridized ugly flower called Victorian. If we were speaking of horses, we could say the fashion was sired by frustration and damed by memory of better days and better deeds. Once upon a time, in every American town, there was a Mr. Complexowitz, a Mr. Shakkamodian, a Mr. Gesundheit, or some other Portygee or furriner who, in his little business, was aping the manners of his betters. He was laughed at. But he was diligent, and crafty, and smart at his calling, whether it was shoemaking, candymaking, or beer brewing. He waxed rich. And suddenly in that town it was no longer fashionable to laugh at him. It is something like that now in respect of the furniture collectors once laughed at as Victorian.

Twenty-five years ago only the very poor would buy it at sales of household goods, and even they turned up their noses at it. A lot of it went to the penny man, the junk dealer who'd bid a penny on every lot and take what the penny bids brought. Now sofas and chairs that went for ten cents and twenty cents a quarter century ago are bringing ten times as many dollars. This new evaluation has pulled Victorian furniture right up through mediocrity into high fashion. It will never be a style, but it is now the fashion, and spinach or not, it is dressed up and served with hollandaise, mushroom, and champagne sauces.

The Queen for whom it is named came to the throne of England as a waif and stray. She was the niece of William IV, who ascended the throne on the death of his brother George IV. Without direct issue, William died, leaving the throne vacant. Victoria, after much political squabbling and the lining up of power parties, was finally elected to succeed. There was a question of her getting the place even up to the day of her coronation; in fact, even to the hour of that ceremony. And her place was insecure for a few years after the throne had been handed to her on a platter and the Germanic Hanoverian line kept in succession. A German princeling, Albert, was selected as her consort. "*Gesundheit*" was again heard at Windsor. Beer, hock, and Liebfraumilch were the tipple, and no doubt apple fritters were served with the ham.

One should really read and study the history of England during this period in order to realize to what cultural depths it had fallen. The great estates and the peerage both sadly needed rejuvenation. The age of machinery had arrived and fresh, new men of the common people were rising to power. They had yet to learn the meaning of high-placed taste, but they knew how to make shillings grow into pounds quicker than you could say "beaver." The furniture of the period of Victoria's coronation, 1837, was on a parity with what we ourselves were coming to—heavy Empire, in which paternity of design could no longer be noted. It was Adam, Hope, and the Empire of France so coarsened as to verge upon grossness. To this hodgepodge the designers of England grafted decadent Chippendale and the furniture styles prevalent in France before the Directoire. What could be the result? Nothing but what it was: Victorian fashions.

Which is not to say it was all bad. Some of

it completely eliminated the heaviness of the late Empire and went back to first causes. The result was furniture that was almost a reproduction of the overdressed Chippendale of England and America of about 1765, or reproductions of the French styles of Louis XVI.

The cabriole leg, the flowing line of Directoire, the classicism of Adam and Hope, are all in Victorian-furniture fashions. Everything in one pot; not a meal, but a mess. Pedestal tables lost their lovely vase-turned members and shaped feet. The feet were fret-sawed and gouge-carved. The turnery was an effort to see how many shapes could be devised. Horsehair became the favorite upholstery fabric for the furniture, but tufting, satins, silks, and brocades were also used. Whatever classic forms the fashion adapted as a motif, it "improved" by foreign gilding and decoration. It reflected the reign, the temper of the people, and the state of mind of the population—not only of England, but of America.

With us, the state of mind resulted in a bloody civil war. England had a few wars too. For a while England was the secret ally of our Confederacy, for profit in the form of cotton to keep her Lancashire mills going. The more we look at the furniture, regardless of how we feel about it, the better it looks when viewed in relation to the age that produced it.

Victoria, with the aid of many good advisers, reigned a long time. Her son Edward began to grow irksome over Mamma's long life. He was afraid he would never get to the throne. Before he ascended the throne for a short reign the knell had been sounded for Victorian fashions. The gay nineties didn't mark its end in America—that was marked by the Centennial Exposition of 1876, at Philadelphia. There, American antiques were restored, as a heritage, to the American people. When we saw what we had discarded for late Empire and Victo-

rian, we got new ideas. Grand Rapids and other spots in America were marked for an increase in population. Furniture factories to turn out other than Victorian fashions were destined to be founded and to grow. Spool beds were to be made again. Early Empire chairs were to be revived, then some Directoire. The little ripple on the pool, or puddle, of Victorianism that was Eastlake was chucked out bodily. More attention was paid to William Morris. A vogue for China collecting started. Sideboards, aping the joinery-turnery press, and court cupboards of the seventeenth century were turned out in golden oak!

The death pains of the Victorian fashion were as horrible as the birth pains. Boston had a revival of Chinese influence. Turkish styles came in. Home after home had a Turkish nook, complete with dim red harem lamp and ottoman!

Victorian furniture was made in every common cabinet wood: walnut, mahogany, rosewood, fruit wood. It was carved with fruits, vegetables, flora, and fauna. Massive sideboards with clusters of carved wildfowl, vegetables, and fruits were made. Chairs with and without arms; gadget furniture; lampstands; tables; dining tables that extended to thirty feet—these were the talk of the town and the country. Everybody had this furniture. It was sold everywhere. At least ten million American homes were either full or half full of it. Only our disastrous fire rate kept it within bounds.

And now it has hit the jackpot. It is popular; it is again a vogue and a fashion. But that carries its own warning. Fashions come and go. Unless you can afford to invest a few thousand dollars in the fashion, and then liquidate your holdings at a tenth of the cost, don't follow fashions in antiques. Follow styles. Good styles. But if you have Victorian chairs, tables, bureaus, desks, sofas, and whatnots,

now is the time to dispose of them. Collectors born of the war industry are about. Department stores are selling Victorian furniture and selling it fast, along with country-made sink-benches and such things. Perhaps they find it hard to get the earlier American furniture. But you who collect still have some three thousand good antique shops to visit and the sales of several great auction galleries to follow. Many fine collections of American antiques are now coming to market; to auction. What is being sold there, and who is buying it, is a far better guide than following the fashion. Yes, it's a harder job to do. Being an individualist even in personal taste is always harder than to follow a style. If you really like Victorian furniture, collect it. If you are doing a house in true period style, say west of the Mississippi, Victorian furniture of 1840–70 is indicated—but leavened with furniture of an earlier age, of a pattern with what the early settlers carried with them and cherished. Memphis, Saint Louis, Natchez—in fact the entire Mississippi Valley scene—demand *some* Victorian furniture. But choose it with as much, or even more, care, as the critical buyer of 1840–60 would have exercised. Don't just buy Victorian. Buy the best Victorian. The best is not too bad, but mediocre Victorian was—and is—awful. The worst Victorian was, and remains, a lot of unholy horrors.

18

Dual-Purpose Furniture

If you have ever read Goldsmith's *Deserted Village*, you may remember the lines: "The chest contrived a double debt to pay—a bed by night, a chest of drawers by day" . . . Also, if you have followed the fortunes of that great lot of patent models sold by the Federal Government to Sir Henry Wellcome, who planned to set up a museum of them and died before he could do so, you'll know they are now being sold and that, at the first sale, a patented "bed-in-chest" model was sold. Its date is almost a century after Goldsmith's comment.

Dual-purpose furniture was perhaps at its peak in the eighteenth century. Secret drawers, which made a desk, a chest, or a cabinet a kind of "safe"; Franklin's chair, which became a set of library steps; beds which tucked into high wardrobes; small tables which extended to big ones—these were almost common. The table of the Pilgrims which also became a chair by tilting the top was reproduced in the following century, but in high style. The late Wallace Nutting was much interested in this type of American furniture shortly before his death. Some of his findings were published in the magazine *Antiques* for October 1940.

Collecting Antiques in America, by Thomas Hamilton Ormsbee.

19

Spool Furniture of 1815–65

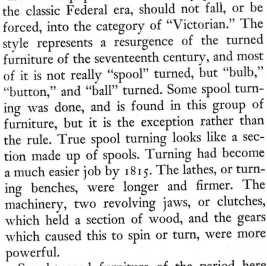

This once-popular furniture, a by-product of the classic Federal era, should not fall, or be forced, into the category of "Victorian." The style represents a resurgence of the turned furniture of the seventeenth century, and most of it is not really "spool" turned, but "bulb," "button," and "ball" turned. Some spool turning was done, and is found in this group of furniture, but it is the exception rather than the rule. True spool turning looks like a section made up of spools. Turning had become a much easier job by 1815. The lathes, or turning benches, were longer and firmer. The machinery, two revolving jaws, or clutches, which held a section of wood, and the gears which caused this to spin or turn, were more powerful.

Spool-turned furniture of the period here considered was popular in both mansion and cottage. To suit the taste and the purses of all people, it was made in walnut, maple, mahogany, cherry, poplar, and buttonwood. The fine woods were finished naturally; the soft woods were stained and varnished, or painted and decorated. Chairs, stools, music benches and chairs, settees, single and double beds, washstands, towel racks, night stands, chests of drawers, hatracks, music stands, umbrella stands, and other household furniture, including tables of various sizes, were made. By 1840 spool furniture was the product of factories which supplied furniture stores, warehouses, river boats, and store wagons with the finished product. Many local cabinetmakers made this kind of furniture. Turnery shops supplied cabinetmakers with ready turned lengths in all diameters, styles, and woods. Today spool furniture is collected largely for furnishing young girls' rooms, servants' rooms, and attic spare rooms. It is very engaging furniture, informal, yet satisfying. Illustrated are objects made in the spool style and the major varieties of spool turning, including the genuine "spool."

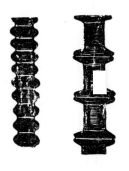

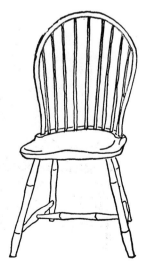

20

Philadelphia, Stick, or Windsor Chairs

BY THESE NAMES, and several others, purely colloquial and regional, such as "hickory," "chicken coop," and "bird cage," are designated the most delightful colonial and Federal-style furniture for the people devised and made in this country. Equally at home in a formal drawing room or a charcoal burner's cottage; in tavern or church; on a door stoop in a back street, or on the veranda at Mount Vernon, these chairs have been part of the American scene since 1725. Then they were called Philadelphia chairs because, somehow, they originated, evolved, or were "newly invented" in the City of Brotherly Love. Because there was an English stick chair called Windsor, heavier and more cumbersome, somewhat like, but vastly inferior to, the Philadelphia chair, the name Windsor was given the American chair. The research job concerning the Philadelphia chair's origin is still to be completed. It looks now as though a Welsh, Swedish, or Manx joiner had a lot to do with it.

The main characteristics of the chair are its all-wood, joined, and keyed construction, its shaped, conforming saddle seat which made wood as comfortable as upholstery, and a give in the resilient slender spindles which made the back comfortable. Once the construction pattern was set, a great variety of models was produced. These include the loop-back, the sack-back, and the comb-back. From each of these sprang a series of variants. These are illustrated, and in the illustrations are more clearly defined than by words.

The turned legs of Windsor chairs are divided into three general categories. The Philadelphia, or Pennsylvania, type terminating in a ball; the New England type terminating in a tapering section below the vase; and bamboo turning which was generally used in all later Windsor models. These chairs, from first to last, 1725–1875, were made in huge quantities. In that century and a half the form gradually changed to a heavier, more stolid, but far-easier chair to make. The light touch and the earnest desire to make good Windsors seem to have come to an end about 1840. After 1800 they were made by the same men who turned out the popular "fancy" chairs of that era. The makers almost always advertised themselves as "Windsor and Fancy Chairmakers."

Some of the most delightful Windsors are not perfect in their bending and spindle spacing. There are almost as many saddle-seat patterns as there were makers. In conforming, subjectively, to the saddle-type seat, individual makers went objective on many occasions. They made shallow saddles, deep saddles, narrow saddles, wide saddles, and they shaped some of their seats almost like hearts without points, the lobes to the front. Brace-backed Windsors are the scarcest and most desired variety. From two to four braces, springing from an extension of the saddle seat at the rear, rise upward, as extra spindles, to brace rails and combs of the back. The four-brace is almost unique. Also, sometimes, the chair-back spindles were not made continuous, but were "staggered." This vagary is also rare. On occasions a maker also added turning to his spindles. That variety is now quite scarce. No matter how much a matched set of Windsors

may look alike, they vary. Each is as individualistic as a snowflake. One doesn't need a microscope to see the difference. Look closely; examine the chairs. The differences are there.

Many but by no means all makers of Windsors marked their chairs. The marking was usually done with a branding iron on the bottom of the seat. According to best authorities, and from a scanning of inventories, account books, et cetera, Windsor chairs were never finished in natural wood, or mahoganized. They were painted; mostly green, but some were painted black, some yellow, some red, and some white. Sometimes decoration, in the form of rings and tracery, was added to spindles, arm rails, and turning. Chairs of Windsor type have been found with evidence of as many as a dozen repaintings. They were much-beloved chairs. Handy chairs. For many years they were harder to buy from owners than Queen Anne and Chippendale chairs. These chairs invite and engender sentimental associations in owners and collectors.

Illustrations include the major varieties of Windsor, Philadelphia, or "stick" chairs made between 1725 and 1825. The woods usually are poplar for the saddle seats, hickory for spindles (mostly spoke-shaved by hand), hickory for the bows, arm rails, and other bends, and hickory, maple, ash, et cetera, for the turned legs and stretchers. Stretchers are often spoke-shaved in the lowlier examples; turned in the finest ones. The carved knuckles on arm-rail terminals are a study in themselves. The more spindles in a back the rarer the chair. Nine-spindle backs are preferred; eleven-spindle backs are almost unknown. Seven-spindle backs are usual. Five-spindle are very late. Double- and even triple-comb backs are known. Also double- and triple-bow backs. Writing-arm Windsors are quite scarce, but an

54

eternal object of collectors' search. They are ideal writing chairs—and reading chairs. The large, shaped writing board is canted just right for reading and writing. It is probably the prototype of the "side-arm" lunchroom chair.

Windsor Chairs, by Wallace Nutting.
The Story of American Furniture, by Thomas Hamilton Ormsbee.
Early American Furniture Makers, by Thomas Hamilton Ormsbee.

21

Fancy Chairs for the People

As has been noted in the section titled Federal Furniture of Directoire Influence, the Directoire was a people's style, created by the best designers of France. In turn, Master Sheraton in his design books gave us the benefit of his once-clear vision in the same philosophy. Taking the best from both styles, America evolved a kind of fancy chair for home and cottage that was so delightful it went into mansions and aboard the "Pleasure Barges" which, to the Americans of the first quarter of the nineteenth century, were what night clubs were to prewar Americans. Ritzy, keen, smart, and just too, too something-or-other. Regarding these pleasure barges, let it be said they did much to popularize the fancy chair. *Cleopatra's Barge* chairs was almost another name for our fancy chairs because they were so plentiful on that barge of pleasure in Salem Harbor. But they were introduced to less pleasure-minded men and women on the ice-cream barges which plied our canals, navigable rivers, and creeks. They were in theater boxes and hotel lobbies. They were standard equipment on river steamers for deck and cabin. By 1825 almost every town had at least one "Fancy and Windsor Chairmaker." Cities had them by the dozen and score.

Lambert Hitchcock, of Connecticut, had the brilliant idea of setting up a mass-production unit for these chairs, along the lines then being

followed by the clockmakers of Connecticut.
"Why make one, or even six at a time?" he
reasoned. "Let's cut them out by the hundred,
paint and decorate them as clock tablets and
dials are painted, and rush seat 'em the same
way." He did just that. His factory gave name
to the town of Hitchcocksville. By 1826 he
was turning out fancy chairs at a great rate,
and mighty fine chairs they were. He stamped
them with his name. Today a genuine Hitchcock with that stamp on it is a highly desirable antique. Hitchcock was succeeded by the
firm of Hitchcock, Alford & Company. It remained in operation until 1843. By then the
American taste had undergone a violent change
(see section "Post-Federal and Pre-Victorian
American Furniture," page 42), and the
happy vogue of the fancy chair came to an
end. Apparently only in small towns and in
the custom cabinet shops of true masters, pur-
veying to the remaining gentry of taste, did
the fancy chair and the styles it sprang from
persist. Which is to say, in mansion and cottage
good furniture still was used, but in the great
middle-class home it had passed, or was passing, from the scene.

The illustrations of fancy chairs here shown
include examples made by "Fancy and Windsor Chairmakers" from Boston to Pittsburgh,
Cincinnati, and points West. Happily, the
fancy chair, too, traveled on river boats and
was sold by warehousemen. It was a staple;
perhaps our second staple article of furniture,
and with its twin staple, the Windsor, it bears
witness to our good public taste which decided
two such lovely things should be our first
favorites in furniture as merchandise.

Early American Furniture Makers, by Thomas Hamil-
ton Ormsbee.
American Antique Furniture, by Edgar G. Miller, Jr.
Antiques Magazine, August 1923.

22

Rocking Chairs

This item of furniture appears to be an all-American invention. It has been credited to Benjamin Franklin and to other great Americans. But chances are the inventor was a New England householder, and that he made the first rocker as a combined chair and cradle to hold his wife comfortably on the seat with the baby in a crib section. Such rocker benches are known and appear in styles that indicate the years 1760–65 as the date of development. When the rocking-chair idea was born, not only new chairs with rockers were made but thousands of existing chairs were equipped with rockers. Any chair within the type or kind of furniture we have termed pioneer and cottage was a candidate for rocker application. And a great many were elected. A fairly sure guide to the fact of conversion, especially in respect of the kind of rockers called "carpet-cutters," is that when the rockers are applied either to the inner or outer side of the legs, in a niche cut out of the leg section, they were converted from straight chair to rocking chair. We find Windsors, slat-backs, splat-backs, and even banister-backs so converted. But when the chair was newly made as a rocking chair, the legs were made heavier at the terminal points, or had no taper; they were slotted upward in the legs and the rockers were fitted in these slots. Then a pair of pins, or dowels, were driven through the legs where the rockers were affixed.

Later the rocker was broadened to at least four times the width of the narrow carpet-cutter type, and pulled down in height to a thickness of one to two inches. Often such rockers were made of bent hickory. The legs of the chairs, plain or tapered, were fitted into the· rockers. The carpet-cutter type was not bent, but shaped by cutting from boards one half to three quarters of an inch thick.

Once it was introduced, the rocker took America by storm. There were rockers of Windsor type, of slat-back, banister-back, and fancy-chair type; made with and without arms; broad or narrow in the seat; and high or low off the floor. Most of the Windsor rockers originally made as such have bamboo-turned rather than vase-turned legs. With the advent of the fancy chair—the painted and freehand or stencil-decorated chair with rockers—we see the development of that great American institution, the Boston rocker. Boston rockers were made in so many forms and in so many variants of each form that a collector, if he willed, could have a houseful of American rockers of this general type without duplicates. For all they are called "Boston," this type rocker was made everywhere in the land. To borrow a typical salesman's phrase—they were made from Canada to the Gulf and from Maine to California. Which is almost, but not quite, true. They were made, not only in every state in the Union, but also in Canada. And England. And France. And Holland, Sweden, and Germany. The civilized world grabbed the American rocking-chair idea just about the time they were getting ready to adopt another invention of ours—central heating by a warm-air furnace. Travelers have told me they have noted Boston-type rocking chairs in Sweden, Finland, Russia, and Turkey. They may, possibly, have been American-made rockers. Our chair-

makers who, by 1840, were a well-organized group, many of whom had developed into factories, were in the export business. They shipped Boston rockers to Europe and to South and Central America. They loaded them on river boats, canal boats, coastal trading steamers, and on Conestoga wagons. They had salesmen out with wagonloads of them, everywhere. They had drummers carrying samples. That is the quick-fact story of the American rocking chair. There is much more to be told than is told here, but these presents epitomize the saga. Our illustrations cover the various rocker types, both converted and original, and depict some of the variants of major Boston-rocker styles.

The Rocking Chair—An American Institution, by W. A. Dyer and Esther Fraser.

23

Buffet or Corner Chairs

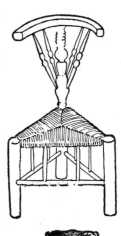

My friend, Bruce Millar, in *American Collector*, October 1941, epitomized the history of these chairs in one line—"Two Centuries of Comfort." Springing from a Flemish design of the sixteenth century, reaching England during the turnery craze and achieving almost madhouse proportions, the buffet or corner chair was vastly improved, and continued through the Carolean, William and Mary, Queen Anne, Georgian, and Chippendale periods, with many variants in the form of simpler turned examples and some purely pioneer types. It was revived again during the Victorian period, again in the Morris style, and finally crashed the gates of Grand Rapids and the pages of the Sears-Roebuck catalogue. In this one paragraph we have compressed not two, but three centuries of comfort history.

The buffet chair is comfortable. By the eighteenth century it had earned for itself the term "roundabout chair." It is a chair to loll in; to stretch in. Pull up a stool and make it a couch. Sit in it sidewise, to the right or left, or straight to the fore. Change your position as often as you please—you'll find comfort. In quoting Mr. Millar's title, we have at least broken the ice toward quoting further from his own interpretive study of this type of chair: "They are comfortable. They are economical of space. Their construction gives them strong constitutions. Their design makes

them ideal for several uses. They have cheerful, inviting personalities. And even a novice couldn't make an utterly bad one." What more could be said? One almost expects an old friend to have these attributes—but a piece of furniture?—almost never! It is the buffet, the corner, the roundabout chair that is the almost never. It *is* an old friend. People who hate antiques (and there are such people) seem to fall in love with these chairs at first sight, or first seat. The most satisfactory explanation thus far for the universal appeal of these chairs comes from a psychologist who has fallen for them himself. He says: "The development of this chair fills an age-old need, desire, and yearning of men. It is not only that it looks comfort—it is comfort." And so it is. Even overdressed and disguised in a multiplicity of turnery, it was comfort compared to other chairs between 1560 and 1600. Simplified as to turnery, it spelled comfort in America from 1640 to 1680. Then it took on added grace and added comfort in the William and Mary style. More still in the Queen Anne style. Also in Georgian and Chippendale; even in Chinese Chippendale. In hickory and pine it spelled comfort in cottage and cabin. That is its story and here are the pictures.

There is no book about corner-chairs, although almost every book on American furniture has something to say about buffet or corner chairs. If you have access to a file of the *American Collector* for 1941, read Mr. Millar's great little essay. Or try your luck at finding a stray copy of the October 1941 issue in the stock of some dealer in back-number magazines. Only some words of warning: don't do it unless you, too, are willing to fall under the spell of corner chairs. They're one antique that gets under the skin of even the out-and-out anti-antiquarian!

24

Mirrors

1750

THE MIRROR, or looking glass, was not always made of glass. For centuries it was made of highly polished metal and, it may be presumed, the making of metal mirrors contributed much to the development of the fine art of working in metals. When glass was first used for making mirrors, it was not in an effort to improve mirror-making, but to make mirrors more cheaply. Sheets of glass were heated and then coated with hot lead. The glassmakers of Venice and the little island of Murano seem to have been the first to make plate glass. Venetian mirrors were the mirrors imported by England until the Duke of Buckingham set up a plate-glass factory at Vauxhall. Then Vauxhall mirrors became England's boast.

1840

Mirrors in America are found to have been scarce items of inventory up to 1680, except, perhaps, in Virginia and Maryland. The Dutch of New Amsterdam had them, and some few New Englanders. It is with the William and Mary period that mirrors became more plentiful. But with us mirrors of that period and mirrors of the Queen Anne period were never what could be called common articles of home inventory. Mirrors were cherished. Tradesmen and tinkers of those days advertised they resilvered mirrors, repaired mirrors, and salvaged broken ones by cutting down and reframing them. A piece of mirror glass was cherished, even when broken.

Mirrors are found advertised with fair con-

1760

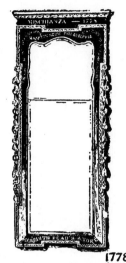

1778

1810

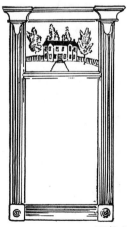

1830-1850

sistency after 1725. But still it was the glass and not the framing that you paid most for. Pictured here are the mirrors of the various periods, including imported and American-made mirrors, as sold by John Elliot of Philadelphia who, in 1756, offered "Pier, sconce, swinging, dressing, and pocket" mirrors and re-quicksilvered glass. Elliot seems to have been a mirror specialist from 1753 up to and through the Revolution. His son, John, Jr., carried on the mirror business. After 1800 innumerable mirror-makers appear on the American scene. The glass they silvered was in many cases American made. By 1820 mirrors were obtainable everywhere, and in a variety of sizes, shapes, and styles to please all tastes and purses.

Period styles in mirrors had a greater persistence than furniture in the same styles. We find resurrections of the styles of 1720 occurring in 1820. Gilt mirrors were made for a century, from 1740 to 1840. The glass in really old mirrors is quite thin, with the exception of the Italian or Vauxhall plate. The latter glasses are beveled, but the bevel is very faint, and seldom discernible to the eye. You must feel the edges to note the bevel. Crown glass was generally used. Hence some of the early mirrors show the faint curved lines that mark them as part of a huge circle of glass blown by the crown method. When mirrors were taxed in England, they were taxed according to size. Hence many early mirrors (especially the William and Mary and Queen Anne) are found made up of two pieces, the upper one sometimes engraved or cut.

The Queen Anne, Georgian, and Chippendale periods contributed most of our pre-Revolutionary mirrors. The Federal period yields us the greatest variety of truly American styles. To call certain of these Federal mirrors "Sheraton" is to decry their American design without adding one bit to Sheraton's stature. He had no mirrors in his drawing book. What the American looking-glass makers did was to produce a style of our own, and after 1812 the style literally screams America. The *Constitution*, that great warship of our Navy, is shown on the tablets of these mirrors winning all of her great duels. Our eagle perches atop these mirrors; scenes of American interest are painted upon them. And among them, thanks to the good and tasteful styling of the makers, one can find mirrors that are quite at home with the furniture of any period of colonial or Federal history, not even excepting the seventeenth century.

Made by expert craftsmen, and by village and small-town imitators, mirrors of the Federal period were available at prices ranging from one dollar upward. Most of the low-priced ones had amateurishly painted glass panels above the mirror. The frames were rather crudely made from molding cut by carpenters' planes. But even these have that charming something which gives stateliness to their more august relatives. The convex mirrors framed in round gilt frames, surmounted by eagles and other finials, whether made purely as decorative mirrors or as mirror-sconces, or sidewall candle brackets, lend an air of distinction to any room. You who collect antiques to furnish a room or a home can even find mirrors in the late Empire style which will not clash unduly with Hepplewhite and early Federal furniture. Explain it how you will—perhaps the gilding does it—but the late Empire mirrors, whether carved or made of split turned sections having applied ornamentation and rosetted corners, have more grace and charm than the furniture belonging to the same era. These are the mirrors which reflected the beringleted, hoopskirted, silk-clad maidens who bade farewell to the bril-

1770

1760

1770

liantly uniformed lads going off to the war with Mexico.

Most of the books recommended for study in the various furniture sections of this primer have something to say about mirrors. The mirror section of *American Antique Furniture*, by Edgar G. Miller, Jr., is a comprehensive study which deserves separate publication. But that can be said about the entire two-volume content of Mr. Miller's book. Dr. Irving W. Lyon, whose *Colonial Furniture of New England*, published in 1891, is our first great American book on antiques, disregards mirrors entirely. Other early writers, notably Esther Singleton and Luke Vincent Lockwood, Esq., give mirrors specific attention.

1760

1830

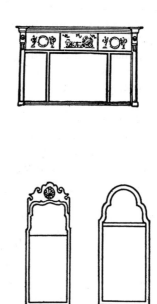

1720   1720   1710   1710

25

Cast-Iron Furniture

Fʀᴏᴍ Van Buren to Cleveland was the life
span of cast-iron furniture in the American
scene, yet within that span thousands of tons
of it were made and sold. It was the age of
architectural iron; the era that produced the
magnificent cast-iron balconies and railings
which today are the pride of New Orleans,
Charleston, and Savannah. It was the period
of cast-iron eagles, statues, deer, and roebucks.
It was the age that ran riot with its ornamental iron fences, its garden grottoes and
bowers. Benches, clothing racks, chairs, beds,
tables, and stools, cast in ornamental iron during this period—and especially between 1835
and 1856—reflect, of all things, the Directoire,
Sheraton, Adam, and the rococo!

Thanks to the fact, or due to the fact, that
after 1890 much of it was relegated to scrap
piles and sold as old iron, there is a scarcity
of this furniture today. Enough scarcity to
give it value and perhaps even virtue. Certainly, painted white, green, yellow, red, or
gray, to contrast with or match an interior,
it is more satisfyingly "modern" than most
so-called modern furniture. Not long ago a
shrewd antique scout, in asking me about this
furniture and who was likely to have some of
it, heard me say just one thing that set him
off on an excursion. That thing was: "Old-
time ice-cream parlors used to have this iron
furniture; at least the tables, with marble or
slate tops." Within a month he had found six

tables like the one illustrated, still doing duty in an ice-cream parlor that had first opened for business about 1878. The original proprietor's grandson said they had been bought, secondhand, from an ice-cream man who had retired about the time of the Centennial. The fireplace mantels here shown were offered painted in imitation of several popular marbles. The one with the rounded top was designed to receive a hot-air register. The square-faced one was for a real fireplace. Its date is 1845–50. A good many back-country founders entered the furniture field as a side line. They did not originate the patterns, but simply cast their own replicas from original castings. All the furniture was made in parts and fastened together with stove bolts. Thus it could readily be recast by any iron founder. It was usually cast from scrap iron. Hence the shipping cost did not deter its widespread use. It exists—or existed—in every state in the Union during the period of its making. And now, beyond question, it is antique—and worthy of preservation.

26

Children's Furniture and Toys

THE cosmic appeal of children may well, as philosophers say, be evidence of our recognizing in them the immortal projection and extension of ourselves. But regardless of, and without reference to, psychological reasons, we can contemplate a vast number of valuable antiques that are exclusively relics of past childhoods. Children's furniture may seem far too important a subject to dismiss with a paragraph, but without injustice to these engaging, exquisite, charming, and nostalgic relics of the past, what greater tribute can be paid than to say they are known in every style from Tudor to Victorian? Miniature highboys and lowboys, miniature chests, boxes, chairs, benches, stools, settles, beds; Tudor, William and Mary, and Queen Anne cradles; Windsor chairs and cradles. There are children's china, silverware, and pewter. There is children's everything. The values of children's furniture compare favorably with the values of adult furniture of its period. There may be fewer collectors of children's pieces, but what they lack in numbers they make up in enthusiasm. Therefore, any child's piece of furniture, or any miniature furniture of a period, made as playthings for children, is an American antique of value. It is exceedingly scarce to begin with, and perhaps never was common.

Children's toy collecting, somehow or other, seems to take the collector right out of this world. Hobbyhorses, dating as early as 1660

and down to 1876? There's a collector waiting for any one of them! Preferably the old and even crude ones. Dolls? There are opera stars, movie actresses, and great ladies of the stage who will walk ten miles for a true, authentic period doll. The earlier the period the better. They are known, and collected, over the same date range as hobbyhorses. There may well be 10,000 collectors of iron toys and as many collectors of lead, tin, and iron soldiers. Mechanical toys that "go," dating from 1825 to 1900, are collected as avidly as any antique in the entire category of Americana. Squeak toys, made in imitation of birds, beasts, and fowl, mounted on a little bellows, which when depressed emits a noise in imitation of the natural call of the animal, are quite important items of collecting interest. Galleries display them with great pride.

Miniature shops—shoemakers', butchers', grocers', hatters', fruiterers', milliners', saddlers', blacksmiths'—these are so choice as to rank ahead of a Noah's ark with its full complement of animals, all in pairs. A complete zoetrope, the actual great-granddaddy of the motion picture, with its first silly-symphony films in color, is something to prize. All that Edison did was to put an electric lamp in a magic lantern, run a zoetrope film made of celluloid through it, and he had the movie machine—from a child's toy! This toy is known in three forms and all of them are worth from $25 to $50 when complete. They sold, originally, at from $2.50 to $5.00.

Articulas are moving toys displaying people at work or play, the movement deriving from a heat turbine, or flywheel, which spins at a great rate in any updraft of warm air. They were homemade by the thousands and made in great numbers by toy manufacturers. The homemade ones, when cut from thin wood, hand-painted, and with a sheet-tin turbine wheel, are highly desirable.

Wood toys of all sorts made down to 1900 are collected. In 1900 the favorite toys for boys were wooden replicas of the United States naval vessels that had just vanquished the Spanish fleets in Cuban and Philippine waters. Some of these had wooden guns that fired wooden shells and exploded a cap. Other toys were disappearing coast-defense guns that rose up behind a fortress wall, fired a big rubber shell, and sank again. About 1840 there was a rare toy, probably of Chinese origin, in the form of a tumbling man. He was as limp as a rag, made of wood. You stood him on a series of steps, gave him a slight push, and then in a series of contorted gyrations he tumbled, without spilling, right to the bottom, head over heels, coming to rest right side up and smiling. There are collectors ready to part with a bond to get one of those.

Don't ask why. Toy collecting is a delightfully dangerous game. The danger is you'll go overboard and renew your youth—or keep it longer—which is even better. Our pictures of toys include the most desirable items, just as they were advertised to a waiting public in the years 1800 to 1880. Also there are a few of earlier vintage. We include no pictures of children's furniture because, with the exception of cradles and high chairs, when really of the period, such items duplicate the furniture illustrated in the various sections of this primer. We do, however, include other items which rightfully fall into the category of toys: Christmas garden pieces. The Christmas tree seems to have evolved from the ancient English "candle-trow," a tree-like fixture for many candles used at Yuletide and Twelfthnights. Christmas-tree gardens, originally crèches, or representations of the Nativity, soon became miniature villages, lighted with candles and tiny oil lamps. Mills that had a small stream pouring over the wheel, small

railroads that had running trains on the tracks, and small boats that paddled in small ponds— all these were used in Christmas-tree gardens. And all these are collected today. Toy collectors grin knowingly at Christmas when someone says, "Wouldn't it be grand to have this spirit all the year around?" They reply, "Collect toys, and your Christmases are eternal; they last all year around, every year."

27

Scientific Antiques

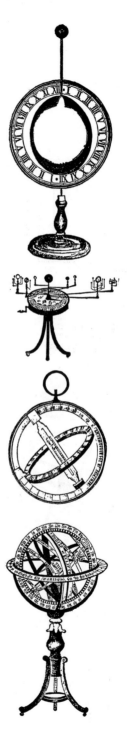

THEY have all kinds of names for partial or
ax-grinding histories which strive to prove
that the pot, the wheel, the blowtorch, or what
have you, is the theme or axis on which world
history revolves. History shouldn't be written
that way for, no matter what things, ideas,
objects, or devices we write about, they owe
existence to, were created, and used, by people. People make history of every kind save,
as the schoolgirl remarked, the "ogics"—the
zoologic, geologic, et cetera. Making scientific
antiques a major section in this primer is by
no means a writer's whim. All advances in
science, as they contributed to the comfort,
convenience, and education of man, were
made into, or incorporated in, some device
or other. Thermometers, barometers, orreries,
sundials, reading glasses, reflectors, bifocal
viewers (stereopticons), polariscopes, magic
lanterns, telescopes, scales, measuring sticks,
drawing instruments, terrestrial and celestial
globes—all of these were designed for household use, and in styles that made them a part
of the furnishing of a home.

True, the list was short in colonial days. But
by 1790 the list reads like a scientific instrument catalogue. Oddities in sundials include
a dial mounting a miniature cannon which,
loaded with powder, went off with a bang at
noon on sunshiny days because there was a
burning glass which focused the rays of the
sun on the touch hole at noon, sun time! Wall

73

dials. Window dials. Pocket dials (some of which date from 1650). Barometers in Sheraton style; thermometers in Sheraton and Empire styles. Globes of the earth, matched with globes of the heavens, that are literally things of beauty. Orreries that reproduce the motions of all the planets and moons in our solar system—in Sheraton style! As yet the collecting of such items is limited. But my good friend, Dr. Streeter, of Yale, leaves no stone unturned in enriching the collection he is building for that great institution. Wise collectors realize that no Early American interior is quite complete without the appurtenances of the Early American home when its period was "today" in the lives of the original owners. So they are buying scientific antiques when they can find them.

These antiques never were common or purchased by all and sundry. An orrery, in 1825, cost as much as a sofa by Duncan Phyfe. A pair of globes—celestial and terrestrial—cost about as much, or more. In 1848 Benjamin Pike, of New York, an instrument dealer of note, issued a two-volume catalogue of his wares. "No volume such as this exists," said Mr. Pike, "so I have decided to make one." He did. Amazingly, the cabinet styles he reveals in his copiously illustrated book are of at least two decades, if not four decades, earlier than its dating. Properly to illustrate this section of the primer we have drawn our illustrations from Pike's noble little volumes. All of these objects are antiques of value and collecting interest today. So, too, are certain objects not illustrated, but made in cheaper form. For example, there was a cheap folding globe, printed in colors on cloth, gored and mounted on a form of umbrella ribs. It didn't open as an umbrella but bulged right into globe shape when you raised the catch and pushed up on the rod!

74

28

Early American Silver

Do NOT HESITATE to enter this field, either as a collector or student for, as either, you have years of satisfaction and delight ahead. You may add a leaf, a twig, a branch, or a limb to the tree that is today's written history of American antique silver. This because, in spite of all we now know about it, we do not have data on more than two thirds of the silversmiths who worked here between the years 1650 and 1850. "Early American" is just as elastic a term in respect of the domestic silver production of our colonies and states as it is in respect of our native furniture and other antiques. Early New England silver is, roughly, of the years 1650–1775. So is early New Amsterdam and New York silver. Early Pennsylvania silver is 1690–1775, but perhaps far earlier if made by Swedish and Dutch craftsmen. But early Baltimore silver is later; later than Annapolis. Early Richmond and Virginia silver is later, and so, too, is early Carolina silver. Early Lancaster (Pennsylvania) silver is 1740–1800. Early Pittsburgh is 1790–1850. Early Saint Louis silver is 1820–60. Early silver, in fact, is "early" at best, in relation to the age of the town, city, or locale in which it was made. And there was a lot of it made. In New England, where production was high, and almost fine, silver was not purchased primarily for aesthetic or luxury reasons, but for the eminently practical one of laying down money in something useful that could be re-

converted into money if required. In New Amsterdam, the Dutch appreciated silver for its luxury, its beauty, and its value. In Philadelphia, silver was a badge of gentility. There America's finest late eighteenth-century silver was produced. In Virginia, and perhaps to a great extent also in Maryland and Carolina, silver was the accepted appurtenance of the home of a lady and gentleman. It was traditional. It was a must, both for personal satisfaction in one's estate and for display of that estate.

The American silversmith with the greatest build-up is Paul Revere. His midnight ride and the numerous legends and histories about him have given him popular position. But he was far from being our best, or even our second-best silversmith. And not all silver stamped REVERE is his work. Paul Revere was a good businessman. He hired other silversmiths to make wares for him which he stamped with his mark. At least ten silversmiths of Philadelphia topped him in craft mastery, and most of the other Quaker City silversmiths were his peers. Charles Hall of Lancaster made silver every whit as fine as Revere. So did other Boston, Annapolis, and New York smiths. In fact, so did the smiths of almost every early American city. Which does not alter the fact that Revere silver will continue to bring top prices. You can't dethrone a public idol.

The silver made in America in the seventeenth century is now worth an amazing price per ounce. That of the first half of the eighteenth century is almost as rare and valuable. Silver of the last half of the eighteenth century is still within the price range of many collectors, while that of the first half of the nineteenth century, not so avidly collected at this time, offers the new collector, or the old collector seeking a new pursuit, a rare opportunity to gather now what is bound to be collected very eagerly within a few short years. Early American silver styles, as recorded in our illustrations, followed the traditional and popular furniture and ceramic styles. The advent of tea and coffee drinking revolutionized and expanded the work of both potter and silversmith. Prior to tea and coffee, silver was used mostly for salt cellars, condiment shakers, beakers, tankards, inkstands, candlesticks, plates, cups, platters, spoons, ladles, knives, forks, and bowls. Tea and coffee added tea- and coffee-pots, creamers, jugs, tongs, strainers, sugar basins, slop basins, tea and coffee spoons, and a great variety of tea and coffee trays. Also, these beverages (including chocolate) became popular with the people. Those who could afford to drink them soon found a desire for silverware in which to serve them.

One factor of great collecting significance in the American scene, mentioned before in this primer, applies also to our silver. It is this: Seventeenth-century styles in silver persisted into the eighteenth century in New England. William and Mary and Queen Anne silver styles persisted there, in New York, and even in Philadelphia well into the Georgian era. In the back country some Queen Anne and early Georgian style silver was made by the smiths whose fellows along the seacoast were making silver mostly to match the style of Chippendale. Viewed as a whole, without reference to the points of production, our Federal silver reflects the Georgian, Chippendale, Adam, Hepplewhite, Sheraton, Directoire, and Greek-revival patterns, yet it was made mostly between 1790 and 1835.

Some 2,500 American silversmiths are now listed, with their known marks, in various books on this subject. Silversmiths' marks are themselves a most engaging study. Punched

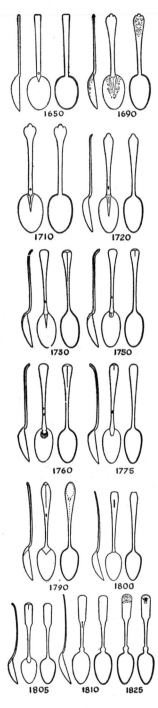

somewhere on backs of spoons or, rarely, in bowl or front of handle, on bottoms of hollow ware, and at various points on mugs, beakers, porringers, et cetera, the mark is the one identifying and consolidating link we have with the maker of the silver. Considering this, and the known listings of marks, opportunity for the new collector and student stands revealed. When you find silver of an unlisted mark in your locale, seek diligently in your local histories and your local newspapers' files of old issues to find mention of or advertisements of silversmiths. Study courthouse records and city tax rolls. Strive to identify the name or initials of the mark with the names or initials of silversmiths and jewelers you discover. Remember, that's how most of today's data were gathered, and take heart. There are at least two hundred cities whose silversmithing data are yet to be searched for. It should be mentioned here that hallmarks, as such, are not on American silver. The English custom of hallmarking the work of all silversmiths with stamps applied by the Goldsmiths and Silversmiths Company, or the Worshipful Company of Silversmiths, was a legal device to insure fineness of silver. A different stamp or hallmark was used every year. In America there was no comparable governing body, and hallmark stamps were rarely used. Notable in this rare category are the star quality mark of Cesar Ghiselin (1713), Philip Syng's leaf marks (1703), and the Baltimore assay marks, used from 1814 to 1830. Many silversmiths between 1790 and 1810 used marks to designate the standard of silver used. These occur as seventy-one different emblems in addition to the words PREMIUM, STANDARD, DOLLARS, DOLLAR, PURE COIN, AND COIN.

Connoisseurs of American silver regard the silver of the seventeenth century with awe, the silver of 1701 to 1750 with great respect and

78

high appreciation, the silverware of 1751 to 1775 with what might almost be termed mild contempt (the period during which the Chippendale style reigned supreme in furniture and when silver after the Chippendale influence was made with overdressed décor and in outlandish designs), and the silverware of 1776 to 1800 as the Adam-Hepplewhite-Sheraton classical period—mostly good, and mostly desirable. They seldom seek silver made after 1800, but a great deal of that silver was—and is—fine. Because it has not as yet been elected to high place it is still procurable.

Our illustrations display the various types of silver utensils made in America in various period styles. Incidental illustrations give examples of silversmiths' marks. For further and detailed information the reader is referred to the books mentioned below.

American Silversmiths and Their Marks, by Stephen G. C. Ensko.
Early American Silver Marks, by James Graham, Jr.
Early American Silver, by C. Louise Avery.
Historic Silver of the Colonies and Its Makers, by Francis Hill Bigelow.
Philadelphia Silversmiths and Allied Artificers, 1682–1850, by Maurice Brix.
Maryland Silversmiths, 1750–1830, by J. Hall Pleasants and Howard Sill.
American Silversmiths, by Ernest Currier.
The Silversmiths of the State of New York, by George B. Cutten.
Silversmiths of Delaware, 1700–1850, by Jessie Harrington.
South Carolina Silversmiths, 1690–1860, by Milby Burton.
Numerous pamphlets, catalogues of exhibits, and monographs on silver have been published by the Philadelphia Museum, the Metropolitan Museum of New York, the Museum of Fine Arts, Boston, the Pennsylvania Museum, Philadelphia, the National Art Museum, Washington, Yale University, and the Rhode Island School of Design. Books dealing with nonmetropolitan district silversmiths have been published (Example: *Utica Silversmiths,* by George B. and Minnie Warren Cutten), or are now in preparation. When in print and still procurable, museum bulletins on silver are modestly priced.

29

Sheffield Plate

Aɴʏ antique Sheffield plate in America was imported from England. It is not an American product of antique status although, in a modern sense, it has been made here for a good many years. Sheffield plate is silver with a copper core. Two thin sheets of silver were fused on a thicker sheet of copper, or a sheet of silver was wrapped around a copper bar and fused on it. This was the basic invention. The plated sheets could be worked into flat and hollow wares, and the total effect of solid silver given by drawing out the silver over the copper at edges, rolling it, or finishing it off with an applied ornamental border of wire or other silverwork. Silvered wire was produced by rolling the silver plate covered bar of copper until it was small enough to draw in a wire machine. It came forth as wire in any desired gauge, looking exactly like solid silver. With these two basics, a vast amount of near-solid silver was made. And because of the great opportunity for fraud, the making was under very strict control. "Plate" still meant solid silver in England, hence the designation of "Sheffield" and a new set of standards and markings. Sheffield plate of the early type was about half silver, or better. It would not admit of deep engraving, so either solid plates of silver were let in for an engraving surface, or solid-silver plates were fused on the finished ware. Much of the silver-coated drawn wire was used in Sheffield fruit baskets, trays, and allied pieces. Age and wear have caused the silver on this plate to wear thin. Often the copper core shows as a rosy blush through the microscopic layer of remaining silver. Where the silver is entirely worn away, the copper is bared.

Much Sheffield is embellished with crests, ciphers, and coats of arms of the lesser nobility and gentry of England. They used great quantities of it as utility ware. Much original Sheffield plate was imported by American jewelers and silver merchants after 1790. The English tax on silver of course encouraged its use there. Everything from a waistcoat button to a punch bowl was made of Sheffield plate. A good deal of the old plate is now being imported by antique dealers, and so popular is this ware that the imports are purchased at better than modern solid-silver prices.

Illustrated here are the types and kinds of Sheffield imported by America during the years 1790–1840. About that time our own budding silver industry was in process of formation, and the method of plating by galvano-electricity was coming into use. Instead, finally, of coming to making the equivalent of Sheffield plate in America—which we did not do before because the process demanded factory operation and widespread sale —we came to electroplated ware, and were soon making a bid for the world markets with that ware—cheaper by far than Sheffield

History of Old Sheffield Plate, by Frederick Bradbury. *Old Silver & Old Sheffield Plate,* by Howard Pitcher Okie.

30

American Pewter Ware

ALL our eating tools have evolved from utensils once used in the kitchen: the spit, the skewer, the knife, the ladle, the stirring stick, the tongs, the pot, and the bowl. A miniature bowl on a rod was the first spoon. The first fork was a two-tined skewer. The knife is a small cleaver. Cups and beakers are small pots. Plates are flattened bowls. Social classes were very clearly defined in the homelands of all American settlers. Kings had utensils of gold, the nobles and gentry had silver, the artisans had brass and pewter, the yokels and serfs had their hands—and used them in eating, to convey food from pot to mouth, until they made wooden spoons or could afford pewter and brass. By the time America was settled by organized groups, eating utensils were in fairly common use, although many families and individuals were content, or had to contrive, with but a few of them.

For at least five centuries pewter was the middle-class family's silver. At first composed of an alloy of copper and tin, and later with bismuth, antimony, and other low-melting-point metals added to the alloy, pewter was found to lend itself to casting in permanent brass and iron molds and easy to work on the anvil and planishing bench. Pewter workers originally may well have been out-of-trade armorers—men who saw their trade go to pot with the advent of gunpowder and guns. Certainly there is far finer craftsmanship in very early European pewter than that which ob-

tained in 1700 in America. The answer, of
course, is that the better craftsmen were in
silver, and the pewterer was not only below
him, but under the brazier. In fact, the pewterer finally fell to an estate below that of tinsmith. Which isn't a very auspicious prelude
to an enthusiastic note on American pewter.

Enthusiasm is possible because there was so
much pewter made, and so many pewterers
making it, that fine craftsmanship cropped out
every here and there. Also, the pewterers aped
the silversmiths (or maybe the silversmiths
aped the pewterers) in marking most of the
output with punches and stamps. Sometimes
they added an "*x*" to indicate superior quality
—which meant, or should have meant, that
there was more than the usual amount of tin
in the metal. Tin gives pewter quality. For
centuries a semi-precious metal, almost comparable to silver, and of a density and ductility
comparable to copper, tin was the master pewterers' best secret ingredient.

Early American pewter of the seventeenth
century is practically non-existent. That which
lasted a century or more was probably melted
down about 1810 when itinerant spoon mold-
ers toured the land with a melting pot and
a kit of molds. For a fee they'd take old pewter, melt it down, and rerun it into spoons
in their molds. Perhaps a great deal of flatware
and hollow ware, as well as damaged spoons,
were thus forever destroyed. Spoons and flatware were the chief production of the pewterer. These were both a casting operation,
although the flatware (trenchers, plates, shallow dishes, et cetera) was planished, or "skum"
on a lathe, or spinning chuck. High polish,
which of course did not last long because of
the quick-oxidizing character of lead, was thus
imparted to flatware. Spoons were polished
with sand and wood ashes and with many
privately concocted polishes.

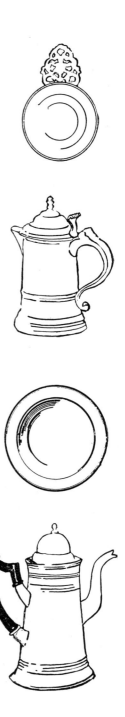

The pewterer also made hollow ware: tankards, beakers, mugs, bowls, candlesticks, oil lamps, and what in America are called porringers, but what in England were, and are, called bleeding bowls. Bleeding was the favorite remedy (and a sound one) of the early doctors, who were also called Leeches, after the bloodsucking aquatic worm they often used in bloodletting. Excess blood was caught in the "bleeding bowl." In America we seem to have used these as "porringers"—a pouring vessel—and also as eating bowls. These dishes, ranging from shallow to deep, and fitted with cast and flatware handles (shaped and pierced), in many and varied designs, are the most generally revered of pewter, although large trays, large plates, basins, and bowls are highly prized. But any bit of old pewter, if marked, is worthy of attention. Three notable books reflect the popularity of pewter as a collector's item. These are listed below. Our illustrations show the various pewter utensils and wares as made in the styles popular from around 1700 to 1850. Also, a few typical pewterers' marks are reproduced to show this important factor in pewter identification. You can compare most known marks with the records of the makers and thus date any identifiable piece with fair accuracy. To you who find a new mark, and also the record of the pewterer at work, there is some honor in store. The chances are fair that a goodly number of such cases will come to light. No expert has ever written the last word on anything but which was proved, and often by an amateur, not to be definitive because "everything" was not there.

American Pewter, by J. B. Kerfoot.
American Pewterers and Their Marks (Metropolitan Museum, New York City).
Pewter in America, by L. I. Laughlin.

31

Painted Tin, Japanned
Ware, and Tole

Pᴀɪɴᴛᴇᴅ ᴛɪɴᴡᴀʀᴇ exists in three kinds. There is the common painted and stenciled tinware designed for quick sale to all and sundry. There is the uncommon, elaborately painted, decorated, and gilded ware for the sophisticates. And there is the commercial product for shops and stores. In the first category were nutmeg graters, spice and tea canisters, boxes, cans, spill holders, basins, foot baths, and even bathtubs. In the second category there were trays, vases, *cachepots* and bough pots, garniture, and even items of furniture. In the third category there are huge bins, tea and coffee boxes, hutches, and goods containers. In both the first and second categories there are coal scuttles, umbrella stands, screens, tea- and coffee-pots.

When it is very cheap, it is "painted tin." When it is middle class, it is "japanned ware," and when it is very high-hat it is "tole." Consequently, when a dealer or a collector buys a bit of painted tin, the urge is to call it japanned ware. When it is japanned ware that requires a lift, it is called tole. You can tell the difference very easily. Japanning is the application of a tough dark brown (almost black) lacquer to tinware. This coating is very tenacious and forms a splendid wearing surface. When a few curlicues are painted upon this covering coat, in a few colors—yellow, green, red, blue, et cetera—it is painted tin.

When it is more elaborately hand decorated, with flowers, birds, emblems, and symbols; when the japanning coat is further covered with Chinese vermilion, brilliant yellow, or pale green, and the décor applied to that; or when the décor is dusted bronzing, stencil work, et cetera, it is japanned ware. And when the painting is exceedingly well done with pastoral scenes, bowers, historic scenes, and such, or when the embellishment is fruits and flowers of a quality approaching the formal painting of such subjects on canvas, then it is tole.

This art, in all categories of quality and style, derives from China. The Dutch East India Company brought it to northern Europe. The traders of Italy also seem to have carried it home and implanted the idea along the Mediterranean. We find it at its height of popularity first as tole, a conceit of the rich in the mid-eighteenth century. Soon it was taken up by the tinsmiths, who had the basic materials and who made many of the objects as items of everyday trade. This they painted, or had painted, and sold as japanned ware.

There was a tremendous lot of this ware made in America between 1790 and 1870. Newspapers appearing within this period carry more and more advertisements of tinsmiths making japanned ware. Retailers without manufacturing facilities sold it, or gave it away as a premium with a packet of tea or a pound of coffee. Spices, gunpowder, and other "keepdry" products were packed in it. Stencil cutters made the designs and applicators for its quick decoration. Production lines of girls, working at long benches, turned it out in the twinkling of an eye.

That is its compressed story. You may never find a chair in the painted tinware called tole. Or a bathtub. But you can find anything from an ice-water cooler to a coffeepot; anything from a nutmeg box to a lovely old serving

86

tray. Our illustrations depict some of the commonly made items, a few of the sophisticated, and one or two commercial items in this ware. If you have any of it, it is good to know it has value way and beyond scrap tin (which it isn't—it's just sheet iron and sometimes not even tin-plated) and that the more elaborately it is painted or decorated, the more valuable it is. Sometimes this ware is marked, usually with a small stencil application on the bottom or side. That marking makes it the last word in tinware—the aristocracy of the tinsmith's and japanner's art!

Early American Decoration, by Esther Stevens Brazer. *Antiques Magazine*, August 1922.

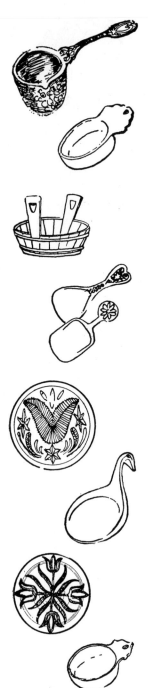

32

Woodenware

Hᴇʀᴇ is one forgotten, though important, item of Americana interest. No champion has come forth to do it justice, although one enthusiastic book has been written by a collector about her own collection. But the true appreciation of woodenware must spring from a multiple appreciation of why it was made, how it was made, and where and when it was made. "Treenware" is its early English name, designating ware made from trees. The native Indians of America, however, were making and using it before any explorer stepped on these shores. Wherever the pioneer landed and moved, woodenware was his first approach to new utensils. But beyond that, common sense indicated the use of woodenware in certain culinary tasks and in certain chores of food preparation and preservation. The dairy almost demanded non-breakable ware that was readily cleaned and scalded. Mixing and chopping utensils had to be non-breakable. So also casks, measures, and vats for pickling, corning, or salting. The preparation of bread was far more satisfactorily achieved in wooden trays, troughs, and bins. Baking boards, cake and butter molds are preferably made of wood.

In early America wood was readily at hand. Even the burls (gnarled, knotty protuberances on walnut, maple, et cetera), scarce in England, were found here in comparative abundance. Coopers, turners, and other woodworkers were here. And every settler had some tools of his own. Woodenware making began when the first colonists arrived, and it did not end for two and a half centuries. In fact, woodenware is still made. Again, the wooden spoon, stirring rod, temse (sieve), ladle, and paddle were traditional utensils, dating from so far back in history that to set a date is only to have it upset.

Spices and salt demanded tight wooden boxes. Flour required a wooden hutch. What wonder, then, that woodenware is found to have been popular and to have had universal use since 1620? That is why we have so much of it left today. Had all of it been saved, the antique market would be glutted with it. But only enthusiastic novices collect "everything" in woodenware. The discriminating collector goes after the masterpieces. The fine porringers (almost like the pewter ones in shape, but with shorter, flat handholds, rarely pierced save for a hanging-up hole), the fine burl bowls in all sizes, the decorative spoons, the carved wares, trammels (notched pairs of sticks to adjust a light or other object to varying levels when suspended from a hook), and butter, cake, and marzipan molds.

In the category of cake molds, molds from three inches square to almost two feet square have been found. Some are so intricately carved as to defy the imagination. But these, alas, are continental European and not American. Marks or names on such molds rarely indicate the maker. Almost invariably the name is that of the professional sugar baker who used them. Butter molds are known in well over two hundred different designs, and apparently of a date range that runs from 1780 to 1880. The late ones, no matter how much worn, are to be classed as factory-made. Early butter molds, or butter stamps—to give them a name that denotes their use—are quite desir-

able as a collector's item. Some misguided people have used them as curtain holdbacks, just to be quaint.

Certain molds which appear at first glance to be butter molds are, in reality, linen printing blocks. Most of these are homemade. Two of our pictures are taken directly from black-and-white impressions of original printing blocks of this type. Neither of these has a handle—the distinguishing mark of the butter stamp. Other of our illustrations show porringers, burl bowls, fine wooden spoons, trammels, boxes, a temse, dough trough, keeler, and scoop. There is also a tar bucket from a Conestoga wagon of about 1760, with a leather-thong handle. If you have ever heard the phrase "Setting the Thames on fire" and wondered how that body of water could be ignited, let this excursion into American woodenware set you right. It shouldn't read *Thames*, but *Temse*. Anyone who sieved diligently and vigorously was said to be "trying to set the temse (the sieve) on fire." Many woodenware objects are listed in the Glossary of Antique Terms in the final section of this book. Most of the woodenwares common to the American scene are therein noted and described as to shape, size, and use.

Everyday Life in the Massachusetts Bay Colony, by George Francis Dow.
Domestic Utensils of Wood, 16th to 19th Century, by Owen Evan-Thomas.

33

Early Blown Glass

THE PRODUCTION of "early" blown glass in
America covers a period of more than two
hundred years because there actually was,
or is supposed to have been, a glass factory
at Jamestown, Virginia, operating about the
year 1609. It is believed that the purpose of
this first venture was to make glass beads at
a cost of a few cents to trade for furs
and skins worth anywhere from ten to fifty
pounds! That kind of profit is enough to
encourage the building of a glass factory anywhere. But the real blown-glass history in
America begins with the factories of Lodewijk
Bamper, New York, about 1752; the Wistar
Glassworks at Allowaystown, New Jersey,
1739; and the Glassworks of Henry W. Stiegel
in Lancaster County, Pennsylvania, 1765. Of
these, Stiegel has received the best, and the
most, publicity. Stiegel glass was "collected" by
shrewd antique hunters of Lancaster as early
as 1900, when it could be picked up for a song.
Frederick William Hunter wrote a book about
it in 1914, and thereafter every piece of blown
glass, free-blown or mold-blown, was assumed
to be genuine Stiegel, especially if it was blue,
purple, violet, or amethyst in color, or clear.
Mr. Hunter also delved deeply into the earth
at the old Stiegel glass furnace. He dug up
fragments. Some of these were enameled glass.
Shortly thereafter a great deal of Swiss enam-

eled glass that had entered this country between 1790 and 1850 became Stiegel!

There are very few authenticated or documented examples of Stiegel glass. Some Stiegel wares were patterned after the designs of Bristol, England, and these, popular in the Colonies, paved the way for the acceptance of Stiegel's replicas. Also, Stiegel had some Venetian and Swedish glass blowers. They made glass in traditional Venetian and Swedish forms. He had some Swiss workers. They made glass in the patterns today known as *Alte Schweiss*—Old Swiss. Something of the French style was injected by Alsatian and Lorraine-born workers. In fact, one of the prize pieces in one of the most famous collections of Stiegel is a piece of French glass brought to this country about 1919. You simply cannot tell it from Stiegel, largely because we cannot tell exactly what Stiegel glass is, or what it should be. We can identify with far more accuracy the glasswares made by Wistar and other South Jersey factories. Their styles and patterns seem to have been organized and standardized. Amelung glass, made at the New Bremen Glassworks in Maryland, is very much like Stiegel. That is to say, it is very much like what we think Stiegel is. The early glass of Zanesville, Ohio, was sold as Stiegel for a good many years before it was properly identified and credited to its pioneer Ohio factory.

All this because of the emotional idea that Stiegel was *the* glassworks of early America, and that its output was colossal. It wasn't. It was in full operation only a few years. It was never free from financial troubles, and it may well be that glass was made there after Stiegel lost it. He built the glassworks to boom a town he had laid out. The town was a dream town, a sort of glory spot where he would act as lord of the manor; he, a German immigrant, would act out the part of a German baron! He ended in jail, for debt. The town struggled along. The name of the town is Manheim.

The glass factories of New England and New York State also made much blown glass between 1800 and 1840 that was once called Stiegel glass. Now it is recognized, at least as *not* Stiegel, even though there may still be some trouble in identifying the glass with a particular factory. Generally speaking, the beautifully blown and tooled (that is, shaped in the glass while plastic, not engraved or molded) glass in amethyst, blue, purple, and violet, probably made by Stiegel, is worth its weight in 24-carat gold. In this category of glass are found vases, sugar bowls, creamers, salt cellars, covered bowls, and basins. Engraved clear glass is also quite valuable, whether the Stiegel "type" or made by Amelung, or Sandwich.

Mold-blown or blown-mold glass is glass that was first subjected, as a gathering on the blower's pipe, to expansion in a two- or three-piece iron mold. This impressed a pattern on the bubble of glass which, upon removal from the mold, was then expanded and shaped into the desired form: a pitcher, bowl, creamer, inkpot, et cetera. Whatever pattern was impressed by the mold on the original bubble expanded and remained on the glass as it was blown. Such glass was made in the various colors above noted and in clear, transparent glass. Jelly dishes, service plates, compotes, vases, and other shapes were made, in addition to creamers and sugar bowls.

The New England and New York glass factories seem to have made a great deal of blown-mold glass. One factory, Pitkin, specialized in swirled or twisted decorated glass. This was achieved by blowing into a mold of upright reedings which, when expanded and twisted while the glass was plastic, delivered a charm-

ing variant of the usual patterns in mold-blown glass.

A tremendous production of plain blown glass came out of these New England and New York factories. Compotes, stands, vases, apothecaries' vials and wares, lamps, pitchers, milk bowls—everything in good glassware was made. This was sold, of course, as a straight commercial production. It could be purchased in thousands of general, glass and china, and grocery stores. Much blown glass once believed to be late eighteenth and early nineteenth century now stands revealed as having been blown as late as 1850.

Bakewell of Pittsburgh, from 1808, made many fine blown flint glasswares. This firm started the great Midwestern glass industry, and its production is deserving of much more attention by collectors.

The following list of glasshouses operating in America during our first two hundred years gives some idea of how many concerns were making glass. Some lasted a long time. Others folded up almost before they started production. The pictures of early blown glass display the scale from rich and rare to commonplace, but made within the two centuries, more or less, that in America marked the blowing of glass that can with propriety be called early.

Jamestown, Virginia, 1632.
Salem, Massachusetts, 1641.
Johan Smedes, New Amsterdam, 1650.
Evart Duijcking, New Amsterdam, 1650.
Shackamaxon, Philadelphia, Pennsylvania, 1683.
Caspar Wistar, Salem County, New Jersey, 1739.
Stiegel, Manheim, Lancaster County, Pennsylvania, 1765.
Philadelphia Glassworks, 1773.
Lodewijk Bamper, New York Glasshouse Company, 1752.
Amelung, New Bremen, Maryland, 1784.
Gallatin, New Geneva, western Pennsylvania, 1797.
Pitkin, Manchester, Connecticut, 1783.
Albany, New York, Glassworks, 1785.
O'Hara and Craig, Pittsburgh, Pennsylvania, 1797.

Temple, New Hampshire, 1780.

Bakewell, Pittsburgh, Pennsylvania, 1808.

New England Glass Company, Cambridge, Massachusetts, 1818.

Boston and Sandwich Glass Company, 1825.

Mount Washington Glass Company (New England), 1837.

Jersey Glass Company, Jersey City, New Jersey, 1824.

Clementon Glass House, Clementon, New Jersey, 1781.

No student of American glass can afford to be without the monumental yet modestly priced book *American Glass,* by George S. and Helen McKearin listed below. It is the kind of book which should exist about every category of American antiques. It has 3,000 pictures, ably compressed histories of all the known glass factories and their workmen, and a wealth of data which no student or collector can do without.

American Glass, by George S. and Helen McKearin.

34

Glass Bottles and Flasks

Nothing made in the entire gamut of American antiques so nearly approaches in numbers the size of our national debt in dollars as American bottles and flasks. To say that millions of them were made is to decry the production. Bottles were the first product of organized glasshouses. Bottles were made by 95 per cent of all our glass companies. And they were made in sizes from ten-gallon carboys to half-ounce vials. Bottles for wine, rum, cider, perry, and medicine; bottles for whisky, turpentine, Geneva (gin), and cordials. Bottles for nostrums, ink, cleaning fluid, camphene, kerosene, rattlesnake oil, and bear's grease. Bottles! Their uses were manifold, their design, pattern, and quality are legion. They came in all colors from black to clear white, plain and decorated, mold-blown, hand-blown, swirled, pontil marked, plain, and fancy. Within this subject American history is found written in glass, and the glass-blowing and fashioning techniques of England, Ireland, Sweden, Switzerland, France, Italy, Spain, and The Netherlands are found blended.

Hardly an American home but has at least one early blown bottle. Some barns still have rows of them standing on rafters. Some cellars have closets full of them. When Appert, the Frenchman, discovered the secrets of fruit preservation, bottles were made to hold preserved fruits, pickles, and condiments. Therefore, in this primer we can only prepare you for the gasps of amazement that will come from you when you finally bite into the history of American bottles and flasks. All we can do is to mention the high spots, here and now, as a foretaste of what is in store for you.

Standard bottle making in eighteenth-century America produced innumerable wine and other beverage bottles that are today collected by perhaps 10,000 enthusiasts. These date from about 1735 to 1800. The types shown here constitute those in most general use. The rarest are those with labels, or blobs of glass on the side, below the neck, impressed with a seal bearing initials, the name of the contents, or a date. The dated ones, of course, are rich prizes.

Next in order, and far more important in terms of values and of interest, are the mold-blown historic flasks of one half pint to quart capacity, made for rum and whisky. These are found in so many varieties, and with the faces of so many great and near-great people blown upon them—from Benjamin Franklin to Jenny Lind, and from George Washington to Dr. Dyott—that the collector can assemble a sort of statuary hall in glass. These bottles were made in various colors from pale green to almost black-green; in all shades of blue, purple, amethyst, rose, yellow, amber, and white. Almost every glasshouse made them, and sold them by the hundreds of thousands of gross. Even the list of makers is far too voluminous to include in this primer. But the makers, and what they made, and when they made the flasks, are all in the McKearin book, mentioned as mandatory reading for all who want the entire story of glass in America.

The most valuable of mold-blown flasks are those memorializing events and people. "Success-to-the-Railroad" flasks, in their various types and styles, are all good. The Pike's Peak, Lafayette, Franklin, Jackson, Washington, and other presidential and political flasks are highly

desirable. Kossuth, Steamboat, and Kensington Glassworks flasks also are fine to own. There is also a flask bearing upon its bottom the impress of the mold maker's name, Dolflein, of Philadelphia. That flask is historic in that it gave the late Edwin Atlee Barber the first clue to how these flasks were actually made, and by whom. That was ages ago, in the history of collecting. Since then so much research has been done that we know almost exactly who made every flask ever discovered and who made some of which no examples have as yet turned up. There was a Balloon-Ascension flask commemorating the long flight of John Wise, made in the 1850s. Who has one? Was it suddenly withdrawn from circulation before more than a dozen or so were blown? Nobody knows. Yet Dyott of Philadelphia is reputed, or reported, to have made one.

Generally speaking, a flask in colored glass is more desirable to collectors than a clear, transparent glass flask. Yet collectors who go in for rarity alone will prefer the clear glass flask *if* it is scarcer than colored ones. Today these flasks, and the earlier bottles blown in colored and tinted glass, are displayed at their best against direct lighting which shines through them. Glass shelving placed across deep window openings, or closets with concealed lighting and glass doors, are favored by collectors.

Of the many books and pamphlets written concerning these bottles and flasks, we might perhaps select a dozen for inclusion here as recommended reading. But uselessly. All you need for further study is the McKearin book, *American Glass*. It is the latest. It has sifted the contents of all books that appeared before it, and it contains a wealth of original research material and data which appear in none of the other books. All illustrations in this section appear through the courtesy of Mr. McKearin.

The shapes of glass flasks and bottles, such as the violin, the cornucopia, the log cabin, and the bull fiddle, are variants of the historic blown-flask production. The American glass companies may well have gotten the idea for these blown flasks from early nineteenth-century Swedish glass companies who made the prototype of our historic blown-mold flasks. Several Swedish flasks, reputedly dating as early as 1820, have been found in Early American glass centers. Our makers kept abreast of European production and, conversely, European makers kept informed as to what we were doing. When Owens conceived the idea of a bottle-blowing machine, his idea was born of the urge to make bottle blowing mechanical and thus eliminate the need for so many glass blowers. His first successful bottle blower marked the beginning of the end of our hand-blown glass industry. It made production easier; it removed the occupational hazards of glass blowing (overdeveloped lungs which, degenerating, often caused pulmonary diseases). It doubled and tripled employment in glass factories. And that, as far as today's antique collectors are concerned, is the end of the story.

35

Sandwich Glass

DEMING JARVES, of Huguenot ancestry
(original name Gervais), was born in 1790 and
died in 1869. In his life span he promoted, man-
aged, expanded, and developed the Boston and
Sandwich Glass Company. This, after having
been in the dry-goods business, the crockery
business, having helped found the New England Glass Company, and having acted as factor (sales agent) for the Sandwich Glass Company. His father, John Jarves, had been a successful cabinetmaker of Boston and, it may be
presumed, son Deming, from association with
his father, knew a great deal about design and
the making of fine things. In 1825 Deming
Jarves began making glass at Sandwich, Barn-
stable County, Massachusetts. At that very
same moment he began making American
commercial and industrial history, and the
items of American antiques that are today
collected by thousands of enthusiasts.

Jarves perfected the method of pressing
glass by the action of a plunger in a metal
mold. He derived the method itself from The
Netherlands and from England, but so improved the process that he could press, or
mold, almost any object, including a drinking
glass. In his memoirs he states that when it became known he had pressed a tumbler, he was
in danger of bodily harm from glass blowers,
who felt that he was about to take their liveli-
hood from them. When Jarves succeeded in
pressing tumblers, European glasshouses began

aping his methods and pressed glass became common the world over. But all pressed glass is not Sandwich—and all Sandwich glass is not pressed. In that sentence lies the key to innumerable headaches of glass collecting, and also the cure. Thousands have blithely collected pressed glass, imagining it to be Sandwich. Other thousands have purchased what everyone believed was Stiegel glass of pre-Revolutionary vintage, only to find, after years of research by scholarly glass collectors, that the beautifully blown glass was made by Deming Jarves' Sandwich Glassworks, pontil mark and all.

The first book about Jarves' glass is his own reminiscences, originally published in pamphlet form in 1854, and as a book in 1865. His earliest pressed glass—a tumbler—was exhibited as an antique curiosity at the Centennial Exposition in 1876. The first productions of his factory were inkwells, vials, tumblers, lantern bulbs, lamps, peg lamps, and lamp stems. Also dishes, tulip lamp glasses, pans, bird-drinking fonts, and bowls of all sizes. Heavy glass for cutting, blown objects with writhen ornamentation, figures, and prunted décor—all these came from the Jarves factory in its first few years of successful operation. It made fancy glass, striped glass, threaded glass, mold-blown glass—or blown-molded as it was originally called—in patterns that Frederick William Hunter, the first biographer of Stiegel, believed to be of Stiegel origin because he found so much of it *with* Stiegel glass in Lancaster County, Pennsylvania. Jarves made clear glass and colored glass. He made creamers, decanters, mugs, door handles, newel-post finials, stoppers, pressed-glass drawer pulls. His sapphire blue is a gorgeous color and his sunburst pattern is as good as anything Stiegel ever made.

All this before he began the making of lace

glass: the lacy-pressed glass that is today almost worshiped by its collector devotees. Cup plates, dishes, salt cellars, compotes—everything in the way of odd pieces for the table in glass lace! Of a brilliance unmatched by any other American maker, this glass is now appreciated even by the specialized collectors who sneered at it a score of years ago.

Sandwich blown glass is enough of a subject for anyone's active life as a collector. Lacy Sandwich has enough facets (no pun intended) to keep a collector busy on it alone. If neither of these interests you, there are Sandwich lamps—in this field you can also go as deeply as you please and not strike bottom; Sandwich blown lamps of clear glass; Sandwich lamps for whale oil, camphene, and kerosene; Sandwich lamps in lacy glass; Sandwich lamps of milk-white glass, overlaid glass (in colors and pattern redolent of paperweights, though made by a different technique), and Sandwich candlesticks—especially the dolphin pattern.

What, still no spark of interest? How about pomade jars? Vases? Doorknobs? Spill holders? Toilet bottles? Perfume bottles? Sandwich made all of these things, and made them exceedingly well. For thirty-five years the Jarves glass factory at Sandwich continued, making glass for all America; producing the layer that is today coming to light to make life something of a joy to a veritable army of collectors. Those who fail to study Sandwich and its history are apt to buy Pittsburgh, Wheeling, and Ohio pressed glass, believing they are buying Sandwich. No seasoned collector is apt to make this mistake, but the new collector may fall into error both easily and hard. That is why we reiterate: All Sandwich glass is not pressed, and all pressed glass is not Sandwich. Only Sandwich is the best of all pressed glass—the earliest of note and perhaps the original. The illustrations show in small degree the breadth, scope, and glory of Sandwich glass. Black and white is a poor medium in which to display what should be shown in full color. Also, we are unable to picture Sandwich lacy glass in our medium of illustration. So by all means grasp every opportunity to study this glass at firsthand. To you who wish to pursue the quest for Sandwich glass, or knowledge about it, the volume listed below is earnestly recommended.

Sandwich Glass, by Ruth Webb Lee.

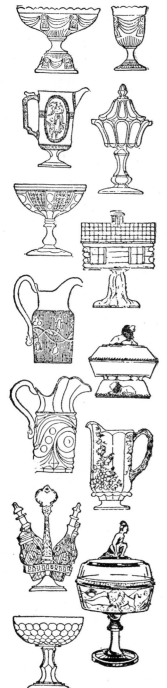

36

Pressed Glass

IF THIS were a midway at a national antique fair, instead of a lowly primer, we might hire a barker for this section who'd cry, "Step this way, ladies and gemmun, and see the two-hundred-ninety-sided 'What is it?' American pressed glass!" Which is as good a beginning for this section as any other we can think of after several months of cogitation. Think of it! Two hundred and ninety known, identified, and listed patterns of pressed glass, with heaven alone knows how many collectors trying to complete some kind of set in each and every pattern! Most of this glass isn't antique when viewed in the same perspective we use in viewing antique furniture or silver. But it is collectible. Like Currier & Ives lithographs, there is enough of it to go 'round, even at a big party.

"Thousands of people who do not know an antique from an aardvark are collecting this stuff—this premium glass—this stuff made late enough to sell over the Woolworth counters of yesterday," wrote a caustic commentator about this glass. He received several hundred letters asking, "*Is* the glass my mother bought at Woolworth's, back in 1895, worth money today? Is it antique?" Whereupon the commentator decided to say no more about pressed glass. Even scathing insults only increase public interest in it.

It may show poor taste to collect it, as some people aver. But poor taste in collecting is always a matter of opinion, and usually the opinion of non-collectors. Certainly it was neither poor taste nor poor judgment to keep pressed glass during the great years of its making, from 1840 to 1900. What if it was a tea-store premium in 1880? What if you could get a barrelful for $10.00 from Sears-Roebuck or Butler Brothers in 1896? There was a time when your remote ancestors could have bought a silver teapot from Paul Revere for $25. If they did, and you have fallen heir to it, you have a $5,000 teapot now. And likewise your grandmother's barrel of pressed glass at $10.00 or less is now worth ten times what she paid for it, and perhaps a great deal more.

To list the makers of pressed glass is impossible in this primer. To show even one piece of every pattern collected is also out of the question. All that we can do with this colossal subject is to select a few examples and say, with our blessing, read the book recommended. Study it. Learn your pressed-glass patterns by heart. It is a no bigger job than learning the two hundred and twenty-six radicals of the Chinese alphabet.

Pressed glass represents a great mass-production effort on the part of some fifty glass manufacturers from New England and New Jersey westward to Indiana and Illinois. It was made for hotels and eating houses, beer saloons, taverns, and ice-cream parlors. For stores, trading posts, and premiums: for the great American home. It was glassware for the people, without reference to size of purse or size of home. It was peddled by pack-on-back itinerants, sold by mail-order houses, variety stores, and tea stores. There were catalogues of it issued by the makers, and these, it should be remarked parenthetically, are collected by the knowing ones with as much gusto as the glass itself. "Try to find one of these catalogues," says Ruth Webb Lee, the historian and biographer of this glass.

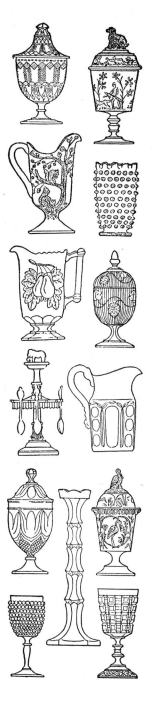

Just as the vogue for Currier & Ives prints led to investigation that revealed other great American lithographers, so did the vogue for lacy Sandwich glass reveal that pressed glass was made by a host of other American manufacturers. Great names are tied up with this pressed-glass production. And while most of the glass is decorative, some of its examples are historic in that they memorialize events and heroes as late as our war with Spain. And in this great mass of glass is also found that grand, typical, all-American pattern, "Westward-Ho!" Lodge emblems, fraternal glasses, famed actresses, Grant, Garfield, Cleveland—American history from 1840 to 1900 is found pressed into this glass. What more do you wish to know? Several thousand dealers have it for sale. It is to be found at every antique exhibition. Great museums are quietly salting it away. There is one book about it, listing all the patterns, and picturing them in their altogether-amazing totality. The book now is in its seventeenth edition. That in itself is something of a record. We know of no other book in the entire field of Americana that has enjoyed, and deservedly, so wide a circulation.

Early American Pressed Glass, by Ruth Webb Lee.
Handbook of Early American Pressed Glass Patterns, by Ruth Webb Lee.

37

Old Glass Paperweights

Tʜᴇsᴇ ᴏʙᴊᴇᴄᴛs, these solid balls of clear glass imprisoning exquisitely composed and designed works of art in colored glass, are a resurgence of fancy glasswork done by Egyptian craftsmen of the twelfth century B.C. and by the Romans who copied from the Egyptians about the time of Cleopatra. In America, fine and even superb paperweights were made independently by workmen at the Sandwich Glassworks, by the New England Glassworks, the Mount Washington Glassworks, the Pairpoint Glassworks, the Somerville Glassworks, all in New England; by the Millville (New Jersey) Glassworks, by the Gillerland Glassworks (Brooklyn, New York), by Doerflinger (in Brooklyn, and at White Mills, Pennsylvania), and the Ravenna (Ohio) Glass Company. The finest of these weights are the Millville rose designs. In New England, millefiori (many flowers) pattern weights were made.

All of these, and perhaps other, glass companies produced paperweights for commercial sale. Certain of the workmen carried off many paperweights in the form of imperfects, or did "government jobs," which was the jovial term they used to designate making something for themselves. Today almost any American-made paperweight is valuable—some of them are so valuable they fall into the class of precious stones.

European factories in France, Moravia, Belgium, Italy, and England shipped glass paper-

weights to America. It requires years of study and expert knowledge to identify the various makes. Only a very few are dated, and marked. The making, while not simple, was not so complex as observation of the finished objects would cause you to think. Most of the flowers, cane sections, et cetera, were assembled in a small nest, the latticinio and bubble work was then worked over and around them. The final step was complete enclosure in a solid blob of fine, clear glass. The paperweights pictured here are all American examples.

Many actual "fakes" of paperweights are now being offered. Some Belgians, familiar with the method of making them, are now working in England. Others are working in this country. None of these makers is in any way to blame for his work being offered as antiques. And only in that act—offering honest, contemporary work as old, and charging the antique market price for it—does the faking reside. It should also be remembered that the Millville rose, the most desirable of all American paperweights, was made as late as 1912. That means most of us now deep in collecting might have had one for a graduation, confirmation, or baptismal gift. Fine paperweights were never cheap items of merchandise. Time, and lots of it, was required to create one, and often three were spoiled for every perfect one achieved. The story of glass paperweights is exceedingly well told in the Bergstrom book mentioned below. There is also much information in the McKearin volume.

Old Glass Paperweights, by E. R. Bergstrom.
American Glass, by George and Helen McKearin.

38

Lighting Fixtures and Lamps

Other than candlesticks, the lighting fixtures of early America ranged from the simplest of iron sconces to brass, pewter, and silver sconces; from punched sheet-iron lanterns to true lanthorns, and from Betty lamps of iron to magnificent creations of silver. The story of colonial lighting has been told once. It deserves a retelling, planned to include all that was not known at the time of the first telling. The real problem posed to our ancestors desiring better light was how to get it. The only answer for many years was "use more and better candles, and use reflectors to amplify the light of whatever candles are used." Hence the sconce to reflect light; the hurricane shade to prevent the flame from wavering in a draught; the multi-candle fixture known as a chandelier; twin-wicked candles; and twin-wicked lamps, some of which were fitted with magnifying lenses.

With the advent of whale oil, turpentine, and other animal and vegetable oils and fats, better lighting came through the use of lamps. The lamp, as we know it today, evolved from various fixtures designed to burn what were known as Palmer candles. The Argand lamp, invented in 1780 by a Swiss scientist, had, as its secret, the use of a circular hollow wick which permitted a draught of air inside the flame. The Argand was an oil-burning lamp. It was a vast improvement over the Betty lamp, the stubby-wick and the flat-wick lamp, all

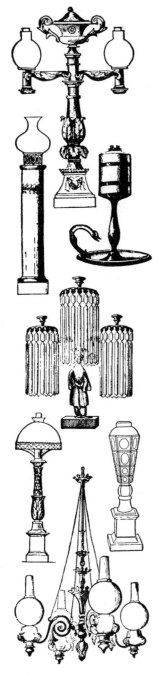

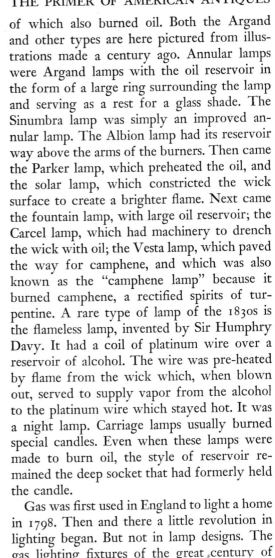

of which also burned oil. Both the Argand and other types are here pictured from illustrations made a century ago. Annular lamps were Argand lamps with the oil reservoir in the form of a large ring surrounding the lamp and serving as a rest for a glass shade. The Sinumbra lamp was simply an improved annular lamp. The Albion lamp had its reservoir way above the arms of the burners. Then came the Parker lamp, which preheated the oil, and the solar lamp, which constricted the wick surface to create a brighter flame. Next came the fountain lamp, with large oil reservoir; the Carcel lamp, which had machinery to drench the wick with oil; the Vesta lamp, which paved the way for camphene, and which was also known as the "camphene lamp" because it burned camphene, a rectified spirits of turpentine. A rare type of lamp of the 1830s is the flameless lamp, invented by Sir Humphry Davy. It had a coil of platinum wire over a reservoir of alcohol. The wire was pre-heated by flame from the wick which, when blown out, served to supply vapor from the alcohol to the platinum wire which stayed hot. It was a night lamp. Carriage lamps usually burned special candles. Even when these lamps were made to burn oil, the style of reservoir remained the deep socket that had formerly held the candle.

Gas was first used in England to light a home in 1798. Then and there a little revolution in lighting began. But not in lamp designs. The gas lighting fixtures of the great century of gas, 1802–1902, were based almost wholly upon earlier candle and oil-lamp designs. Even the electric bridge lamp of today has its counterpart in the iron floor candlesticks of the seventeenth century, examples of which will be found in the section on candlesticks. Words are poor things with which to paint pictures, especially when we have contemporaneous drawings of the lamps and lighting fixtures of America's early days. Therefore, the reader is referred to the illustrations. For the rest of the story, reference is made to the following books which will satisfy the information requirements of the most inquisitive:

Colonial Lighting, by Arthur H. Hayward.
Collection of Heating and Lighting Utensils in the United States National Museum, by Walter Hough.

39

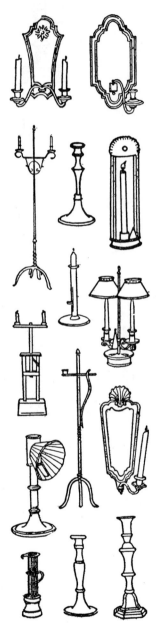

Candlesticks and
Candle Fixtures

ANDLESTICKS, candelabra, chandeliers, and candlestands must, at one time, have been the bane of every housewife's existence. They have come down to us in so many kinds that the wide variety of these items looks, to the amateur, like a page from *Alice in Wonderland*. Then, when you begin collecting them, the field takes on the aspects of a labyrinthine maze. The knowing ones speak about brewers' cask prickets, miners' dagger sticks, soldiers' bayonet sticks, fishermen's spike sticks, ships' sticks, officers' candlesticks, and other variants.

Candlesticks fall into two broad categories of which the socket type is the more common. As the name implies, this type of stick or holder has a socket into which the candle end, or butt, is inserted. The other type is the pricket, so called because instead of a socket it has a spike upon which to impale the candle end. The pricket stick is of oriental origin; the socket of occidental origin. Dutch and Italian traders brought the pricket stick from the East. Prickets were used mostly in churches, but not a few of them were used in homes, from hovels to the halls of high officials.

Iron, tin, pewter, silver, wood, glass, pottery, turned and carved stone, Sheffield plate, and other materials were used in candlestick and chandelier making. Light and its usefulness in terms of application, availability, and portability, was an ever-present problem with our ancestors. Not until the coming of illuminating gas and electricity did this problem stand as solved. Thus we find the multiple candlestick of from two to seven lights for brightness; candlesticks attached to trammels to adjust the light to the place it was required; wrought-iron stands to hold one, two, three, and even seven candles and some of these with branches and arms adjustable as to height on the upright member. Also we find a little gadget made as early as the seventeenth century which converted a pricket candlestick to a socket stick and another gadget which converted a socket stick to a pricket. Still another gadget was a mock candle of white-painted tin which, fitted into a stick, was used as an extended holder in which to burn candle ends. This gadget sometimes had a tiny pricket upon which to impale the butt.

Chandeliers (from chandle, candle) were designed for use in large halls, suspended from the ceiling. It is said that cartwheels were used as chandeliers in both taverns and castles, the spokes and rim of a wheel holding as many as fifty candles. They make a lovely light, undoubtedly, but let who will care for the snuffing and replacing of candles for a fifty-candle fixture. Most collectors seek things far simpler in the way of candlelighting fixtures. The connoisseur will seek bishop's silver or gold candlesticks, the sort held for His Grace after mass by a deacon or priest; or the elaborate silver or brass collapsible sticks affected by travelers and high army and navy officers. The collector of general American antiques will be more than content with examples in silver, pewter, iron, brass, and glass illustrated here. Any candlestick made before 1850 is now close to having antique status. Those made before 1840 are antique officially. The dolphin candlesticks of Sandwich glass; the pottery candlesticks of New England, New York,

Pennsylvania, and Ohio; the glass ones made there and in New Jersey and Maryland; the wrought-iron and tinned sticks, Pontipool (another name for fancy painted tin), turned wood, china, and porcelain candlesticks, either made or sold in America between 1640 and 1840, offer a great variety of collectibles. The niceties of candle use brought forth the snuffer and the extinguisher. The former is a scissors-like arrangement with a flange opposing a snuffing box. These were used to remove excess carbonized wick and to prevent candles from smoking. The extinguishers are cones of metal which, placed over the flame, extinguished it without scattering hot wax, as was often the case when candles were blown out. Rare among snuffers are hurricane-shade snuffers for use in trimming candles in hurricane shades, or globes.

The book here recommended is well worth your study and reference, but there is another publication, *United States National Museum Bulletin 141*, procurable at seventy cents from the superintendent of Documents, United States Government Printing Office, Washington, D. C., that every collector should own. It tells the story of lighting from the earliest days, and is profusely illustrated.

Colonial Lighting, by Arthur H. Hayward.

40

Historic Staffordshire
China and Pottery

A. STEVENSON (ANDREW)
Mixed Flowers.

Cᴏᴍᴍᴏɴʟʏ ᴄᴀʟʟᴇᴅ "old Blue," this now
avidly collected ware is known also in black,
brown, green, pink, mulberry, and several
lighter shades of blue, in addition to that rich
indigo that marks the best-loved examples. The
term "Historic" is well deserved by this ware
for, in spite of the fact that some of it is not
historic in an American sense, and that some
of it pictures the tours of Dr. Syntax and other
fabled moralists, the greater part of it found in
this land of ours is Historic with a capital *H*.
On this china and pottery, made mostly between 1818 and 1848, we find pictured places
and events, circumstances, vistas, symbols, and
signs—all having to do with the United States.
Beyond the historic category this primer dares
not venture. This because the historic aspect
alone involves the work of some sixty-five
artists, many of note, and the use of their
creations to embellish cup plates, platters,
dinner plates, teacups, tureens, and other odd-
ments for the dining and tea table. Six hundred
and eighty-eight separate and distinct subjects have been tabulated by the great and good
historian of this china, Ellouise Baker Larsen.

Historic Staffordshire china and pottery for
the American market were made by the following potters: Enoch Wood & Sons, Andrew
Stevenson, James & Ralph Clews, J. & W. Ridgway, William Ridgway & Co., Joseph Stubbs,

A. STEVENSON (ANDREW)
Flowers and Scrolls.

ENOCH WOOD & SONS
Shells. Irregular Center.

JOSEPH STUBBS
Eagles, Scrolls and Flowers.

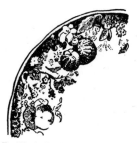

E. W. & S. (ENOCH WOOD & SONS)
Flowers and Fruit.

J. & J. JACKSON
Floral.

S. Tams & Co., Tams, Anderson & Tams, Thomas Mayer, Ralph Stevenson & Williams, W. Adams & Sons, John Rogers & Son, E. & G. Phillips, J. & J. Jackson, Thomas Godwin, Davenport & Co., Charles Meigh, Thomas Green, Joseph Heath & Co., J. & T. Edwards, John Tams, Mellor, Venables & Co., "J.B.," Francis Morley & Co., George L. & Taylor Ashworth (G. L. A. & Bro.), T. F. & Co., R. Hall, R. Hall & Son, Josiah Wedgwood, Podmore Walker & Co., and a few unknown makers.

These imposing statistics on potters, artists, and production should indicate without further ado that the subject of Historic Staffordshire is not to be approached, or its study and collecting undertaken, lightly. It is a profession, almost, to know this ware. And if we can take the smiling countenances of its devotees as an indication, to indulge in that profession is to live a happy life. Few subjects in the category of antiques offer so much of a challenge and so satisfying a reward, as indulgence in the study and collecting of Historic Staffordshire. It has its social aspects and its political aspects. It reflects the growth of our nation. The very act of our ancestors buying it in the great quantities they did is proof that we, as a nation, loved to see our self-esteem reflected in our dinnerwares. Further, this pottery and china did more to recement amicable relations between the United States and Britain than any ten diplomats, statesmen, and politicians. It was the court plaster that healed the sores left by the War of 1812. It soothed the wounded vanity of England's Navy. It erased the bruises of "fifty-four forty or fight." It boomed the wholesale and retail china and crockery business in both England and America. After 1860 new issues of this ware appeared, but collectors disregard this production as modern. They prefer the wares made from 1818 to 1830, which

116

are characterized by the deep, rich—almost royal—blue.

A good many American families still have some of this Historic china salted away in sundry closets and attics. Every year there are new finds and new caches of it discovered. So widespread was its distribution that a Pennsylvania Arms platter might be found in the Panama Canal Zone, carried there heaven only knows when. There is hardly a district or region of America, hardly an important city, town, or county that cannot boast a view, or views, reproduced on this ware. That some unimportant places were favored may today offer some cause for wonder. There is an explanation for this which, to the best of our knowledge, has not yet been given in full in any work on the subject. It is this: The views were pirated from the artists who made them originally. That the piracy was not obnoxious is due to the fact that merely the design or pattern was copied. A new engraving, made especially for the potters' transfer printing process, was required for each pattern or design. The engraver thus re-engraved (and sometimes changed slightly) the print, sketch, or original view as made by the artist. Availability was of utmost importance. Hence view books, collections, portfolios, et cetera, were scanned.

Because Captain Basil Hall had made forty etchings of American scenes, one of which was a view of the little village of Riceborough, Georgia, that village is pictured on Historic Staffordshire. However, most of the views copied are important; that is, they had broader appeal because of fame attaching to the scene and consequently had appeal to a greater number of buyers. Railroads, canals, famed faces, tombs, and scenes—these vie with cities and battles for your interest and favor on Historic Staffordshire.

R.S.W. (RALPH STEVENSON & WILLIAMS)
Acorns and Oak Leaves.

J. & W. RIDGWAY (JOHN and WILLIAM)
Medallions of Rose and Leaf.

ENOCH WOOD & SONS
Shells. Circular Center.

UNKNOWN MAKER (CITIES)
Large Roses in Groups.

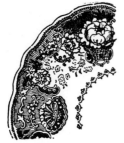

T. MAYER (THOMAS)
Trumpet Flower and Vine.

W. ADAMS & SONS (WILLIAM)
Baskets of Roses and Fan-shaped
Medallions.

According to Mrs. Larsen, the borders on Historic Staffordshire are the keynote to quick identification. No matter how much a potter may have pirated views of subjects issued by another, he drew the line at pirating the other fellow's border. This, then, offers our primer its one opportunity of displaying the main characteristic of consequence in Historic Staffordshire—the border designs of the major potters who made it. Each of the fifteen border sections shown is identified with its maker's name. Within that border appeared most of the historic designs the maker offered. Some offered as many as fifty-seven varieties. Others offered a bare three or four. But all told they total six hundred and sixty-eight picturizations, and that is a lot in any branch of collecting.

Staffordshire was collected in a small way immediately after the Centennial Exposition of 1876. There was a little book published in 1878, titled *The China Hunters' Club* which uttered a prophecy about this ware that should be recorded here. It says: "With whatever disdain the collector of Dresden and Sèvres may now look down upon the blueprinted crockeries of Clews and Wood and Ridgway, the day will come when ceramic specimens showing our first steamships, our first railways, the portraits of our distinguished statesmen, soldiers, and sailors, the opening of our canals, the various events of our wars, and our triumphs in peace, will rank in historical collections with the vases of Greece. And whatever then be the estimate of the art they exemplify, men will say, 'These show the tastes, these illustrate the home life, of the men and women who were the founders and rulers of the American Republic.' "

That is evidence, written before this china had attained a modest fifty years of age, that its charm was appreciated and that its historic significance to a later age was recognized. The

first two decades of the twentieth century saw
the beginning of the fulfillment of this prophecy. The past two decades have witnessed
platters in this ware selling from $500 to $2,500
—historic states platters and views of towns and
cities. In any present-day appraisal of Historic
Staffordshire we should not forget that this
ware was made for everyone. It was not rich.
It was not rare. It was not expensive. It was a
staple, stock item, sold without frills. It appealed not to limited groups, as did the Gaudy
wares after Imari patterns, but to all red-
blooded Americans. No matter whether it was
made three thousand or more miles to the
east, in Old England, it was made for us, and
it is of us. For the types of views shown on
this ware the student is referred to *Forty
Etchings Made in America*, by Captain Basil
Hall, *American Scenery*, with views by Wm.
H. Barlett, and other books listed in the master
work on Historic Staffordshire mentioned below. Of this work, the late Homer Eaton
Keyes, editor of the magazine *Antiques* said:
"It is the standard work on the subject, not
likely to be superseded."

American Historical Views on Staffordshire China,
by Ellouise Baker Larsen.

CLEWS (JAMES & RALPH)
Birds, Roses and Scrolls.

R.S. (RALPH STEVENSON)
Leaves and Vines.

41

Lowestoft or Oriental
Export Porcelain

Quite recently this ware, examples of which by 1840 were in almost every American home, was pronounced by modern antique experts with some ado as not Lowestoft, but Chinese porcelain made for export only—not good enough for Chinese home use. In spite of this modern expert opinion, Lowestoft was announced as being Oriental Export Porcelain in a book much favored by the lady china collectors of 1878 who, stirred by the antiques exhibited at the Philadelphia Centennial Exposition, started the new vogue of collecting, displaying, and using American antiques in their homes. In less than no time these ladies, as determined ladies will, had the men interested. Then it was discovered that most of what had been called—and continued to be called—Lowestoft had been imported directly from Chinese treaty ports by American firms, brought here by clipper ships docking at most ports along the Atlantic coast.

That is how most so-called Lowestoft got here, and why so much of it arrived. It was not expensive. In fact, the ware was bought at ridiculously low prices from Chinese factors. It was low-grade stuff to the Chinese; Chinese "low stuff" if you will. They called it "Ying [long journey] yu [to paint]." Thomas Ormsbee claims it was also called "Yang Stai," but "yang" in Chinese is a six-stroke radical meaning sheep, goat, kid, or lamb. At least so says the Chinese radical dictionary. Yu-ying, or Ying-yu, may well have been the Chinese name for the stuff our clippers carried home by the shipload.

It is evident that patterns for both the design of the pieces and the decoration were supplied to the factors with whom our shipping magnates traded. Punch bowls, lighthouse chocolate pots, handled teacups, coffeepots, and flat service plates are not Chinese shapes. Neither is the floral-banded star-studded décor on much of this ware: the heraldic device, or the Occidental monogram in English script characters. It is a ware decorated after the first glazing in the pottery; a ware probably decorated near the sea and not inland in China where it was made. Overglaze is proof of "after decoration," but it takes more than a superficial knowledge of ceramics to know "overglaze" when you see it. Nor can you grasp the technique of judgment from books. You must handle, feel, and examine the various wares. In fact, to be anything of a china expert you must be an expert indeed.

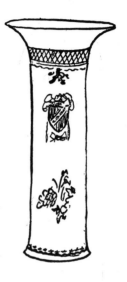

The Lowestoft or Oriental Export Porcelain here illustrated represents the more common pieces which almost everybody in America once owned. The finer armorial and initialed pieces were special orders for which the customer waited often as long as several years. Importation on a large scale seems to have begun about 1800 and, barring the interruption to trade caused by the War of 1812, it continued well into the 1840s. Not until the rage for Historic Staffordshire had swept the country did the trade in Oriental Export Porcelain slacken and finally dwindle to a mere trickle. Not all of the imports were of this ware. Trade in Canton and Nankin wares was quite brisk. But these wares, plus Oriental Export Porcelain, are too specialized a study

for this primer to attempt to enlarge upon. The list of suggested reference books stands ready to enlighten all and sundry who wish to delve either deeply or broadly, or both, into this absorbing subject. And to all who dig—good hunting!

Oriental Lowestoft, by J. A. Lloyd Hyde.
Antiques Magazine, June 1922.
Chats on Oriental China, by J. F. Blacker.
Practical Book of Chinaware, by Eberlein and Ramsdell.

42

Liverpool Ware

LIVERPOOL WARE is as English in body as John Bull, and as American as the Stars and Stripes to a depth of about 1/1000 of an inch. Which is to say the American part of it is only on the surface—the decorated surface. It was imported by shipmasters and merchants from about 1788 to 1830 or even 1840. And during the years 1788 to 1810 and from 1815 to 1825 the decorating must have cost the British potters and workmen a few wounds to their pride. This ware is largely historic—loaded with views of our naval victories over British ships and squadrons, with portraits of presidents, philosophers, and naval heroes, with arms of the United States, memorials, presentation emblems, and many other designs. Creamy in color and fine and satiny to the touch, this lovely ware is transfer printed. An engraved copper plate was made for each design. This yielded prints from a mineral-base ink on thin tissue paper, which, transferred to the ware, stuck to it, and became permanently fixed when fired in the kiln. The firing which fixed the design was the third firing. First the clay ware was fired at high temperature. Then a light firing was given to fix the first glaze. Then it was transfer printed, and fired again. The exemplary illustrations are from the collection of the author of the one book on this ware that every collector should have and every student should read.

Liverpool Transfer Designs on Anglo-American Pottery, by Robert H. McCauley.

123

PENNA.

GAUDY
DUTCH

GAUDY
DUTCH

PENNA.

GAUDY
DUTCH

43

Gaudy Dutch and
Pennsylvania Tulip Pottery

Perhaps more misinformation is current concerning these wares than any other items of general property in the American scene. "Gaudy Dutch" is quite gaudy, but it is not Dutch, or German, either in source of design or place of manufacture. It was made in great quantities by English potters, for world trade. It caught the fancy of American importers, who found ready sale for it in Pennsylvania, New Jersey, Maryland, and Ohio. The source of the design is direct from the Chinese. Much ware, comparable in design but not quite so gaudy in colors, was made for sale in England. The original Chinese pattern was pirated by Japanese potters and called Imari. The English potters pirated the designs from both the Chinese and the Japanese. In turn, and very crudely, the designs were copied by Americans, on fractur, in penpictures, motto cards, certificates, memorials, et cetera. The designs are also found executed in embroidery and cross-stitch. Often they are represented as Pennsylvania-German.

Tulipware is either slip decorated, that is, covered with curlicues and lines made by applying light-colored clay over a red clay body, or "sgraffito," which means the entire surface of dark clay was covered with light clay, and the designs scratched through the light clay coating. This ware of common red clay was made to sell at very low prices. Most of it was ovenware. The finest pieces were made for presentation, or to commemorate some event—a wedding, engagement, birth, or anniversary. Tulipware has been put forward as a distinct Pennsylvania-German creation and achievement.

Most of the tulipware potters appear to have been Swiss or German. Also the vast majority of the ware was made after the Revolution. It was made, in very crude form, up to 1920 by the sons and grandsons of old potters who, inheriting trade, pothouse, and kiln, still carried on. A few of the old potteries turned to making stoneware, clay flower pots, et cetera, and enjoyed a very profitable revival. The designs on tulipware, however, are not German. Nor is the style of ware particularly German. The potters of Switzerland and the potters of Staffordshire were making fine tulipware before 1660.

Much Staffordshire tulipware was once imported to Pennsylvania (1680–1750). So also were Bristol delft tulip chargers, or tulip plates. These two English imports are probably the source of many of the designs used by the artisans of the Ephrata community, near Lancaster, Pennsylvania. Pictured are a pair of Bristol delft tulip chargers, two Staffordshire tulip plates, a pair of Imari plates (Chinese), a group of "Gaudy Dutch" plates and a group of Pennsylvania tulip pottery. Most of the Pennsylvania tulipware is to be found in the form of pie dishes (in many sizes), mixing bowls, baking dishes, pans, and mugs. Gaudy Dutch is most common in the form of dinner plates, cups and saucers, pitchers, creamers, and sugar bowls. All of these wares are now scarce, and avidly collected. It is believed, however, that many pieces must still reside with descendants of original purchasers.

Tulipware of the Pennsylvania Germans, by Edwin Atlee Barber.

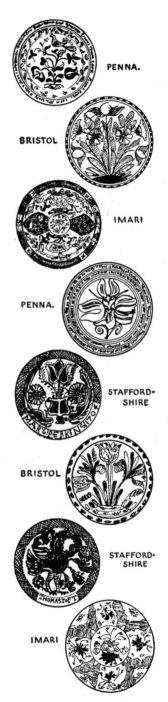

PENNA.

BRISTOL

IMARI

PENNA.

STAFFORD-SHIRE

BRISTOL

STAFFORD-SHIRE

IMARI

44

American Samplers

Almost every girl in America, between the years 1620 and 1860, made a sampler. She made it for just what the name implies: to serve as a sample for initials, numerals, ciphers, emblems, and decorative borders and elements. These she used later in life, to mark her linens, and to embellish her pillow shams (originally "pillowberes" and even called by a contraction of that term: "P'lowbers" as late as 1850), towels, napkins, tablecloths, and doilies. From this we can imagine, if not tabulate, the volume of production that went on in the two centuries, plus forty years, of sampler making. New England samplers of the seventeenth century (1620–1700) follow the traditional English shape and are higher than wide. In fact, many of them are as long as a guest towel. In the eighteenth century the sampler became almost square, and finally wider than high.

Most of the patterns on American samplers come from what were known as pattern or model books. Such books were issued in England from 1591 to 1640. Italy provided most of the designs which she, in turn, received from the Near and Far East. Swiss and French pattern books provided most of the designs on the so-called Pennsylvania-German samplers. Dutch pattern books contain traditionally Dutch designs and not a few from Scandinavia. Very few American samplers show designs from German pattern books even though scores of pattern books were made in Germany.

Samplers fall into many categories, or types. There is the alphabetic, the semi-pictorial, the pictorial, the map, the religious, the openwork (uncolored), the embroidered, and the cross-stitch; the true "sampler," the presentation, and the memorial piece. Many embroidered and cross-stitch "door panels" originating in Pennsylvania and Ohio (1780–1840) are in the early long, narrow shape, have a limited amount of work on them, and were probably wedding-box towels or hope-chest finery made by the hopeful girl. Samplers are collected today in limited numbers by general collectors who seek the unusual, and the early, to be a part of the period decoration of a roomful, or a houseful, of antiques. They are also collected by specialists, and some really monumental collections now exist. One such, assembled by a noted author, is perhaps the world's outstanding collection.

The move of the sampler from the Atlantic seaboard westward is as clearly defined as the movement of any other item of antique interest. Ohio, Indiana, Kentucky, Tennessee, Louisiana, Missouri, and Iowa should now yield the greatest returns in terms of source of supply. Samplers of all kinds have been pretty well "collected" in the East. Those still privately owned by descendants of the original makers are so thoroughly appreciated that flattering offers no longer tempt the owners to part with their treasures. And this, in spite of the fact that it may slow up trading, is as it should be. Collectors' collections are eventually destined for dispersal, or immolation in a museum. The dispersals alone should keep the antique business supplied.

Unfortunately, samplers do not lend themselves to the type of illustration used in this primer. The books listed below should be studied if samplers intrigue your interest. Both are well illustrated and cover all phases of sampler making.

American Samplers, by Ethel Bolton and Eva Coe.
The Development of Embroidery in America, by Candace Wheeler.

45

Floor Coverings

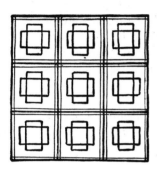

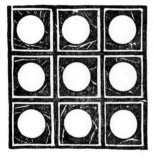

THE FLOORS of the seventeenth-century American home were almost wholly bare. What floor coverings there were in the average home were of rushes, or sand strewn on the floors to catch dirt and to provide insulation. When these were badly soiled, they were tossed out or burned. By 1680 the finer homes began to enjoy what is essentially the great-granddaddy of today's inlaid linoleum: painted floorcloths. These were made, in room sizes, of sailcloth heavily painted on both sides with six to ten coats of filler and then, on the display side, painted in checkered and tessellated marble designs. Such floorcloths persisted until at least 1780. But by 1720 they were imitated for the middle classes by artisans who achieved almost the same end by painting a great variety of designs directly on the floors. Floorcloths were imported in great numbers and were also painted here by various artists and artisans. Any fragment of such original floorcloth is today scarce and highly prized. When Governor Burnet of New York and New England died in 1729, his inventory included a floorcloth "square as the room," valued at £8. This value, secondhand, indicates something of what the price of a new floor cloth must have been at that time.

Many full-length portraits, painted between 1700 and 1780, show the subjects posed upon what have been thought to be marble floors, put there by artistic license. But they are not marble floors: they are floorcloths. Carpets for floors began to arrive about 1750. Shortly thereafter a carpet-weaving loom was set up in Philadelphia. The next loom appears to have been erected at Worcester, Massachusetts. Fine Oriental rugs, when used in the homes of the wealthy, were laid on the painted floor-cloth which in that day was considered as the finished floor. This idea, revived in 1918 by one of America's pioneer linoleum makers, was derided by many decorators who, it appears, did not know their history. The suggestion was—and is—absolutely sound, and in the best American tradition. Since this primer is not concerned with Oriental rugs, or with factory-loomed carpets, this section will deal only with the floorcloth and its high place in the American scene for at least a century. The illustrations are from floorcloths pictured on famous American paintings. Hooked rugs—another important item in the category of antiques—are dealt with in a separate section.

46

Hooked Rugs

Brought to America by Scandinavians—
Swedes, Finns, Danes, and Norwegians—in the
seventeenth century, adapted almost at once by
French, English, Welsh, Irish, and Scottish
settlers, the hooked rug appears to have been
contemporaneous with nearly all seventeenth-
century furniture. Only the rugs were used
as mats for tables and covers for beds, chairs,
settles, et cetera. The craft, or art, consists
of hooking, or pulling, loops of colored cloth,
cut into "strings," through a piece of sturdy
linen. One loop is pulled through every—or
every other—mesh in the weave. Design is
achieved by hooking strips of various colors
along a line or pattern inscribed on the base
fabric.

These rugs are quite long-lasting; in fact,
they might readily last a century or more as
bedcovers and tablecloths. As floor rugs, however, they disintegrate faster than loomed
stuffs. Also, they are not hard to make, and
for at least two centuries their making was distinctly a home craft. Of course those who were
experts at the craft had custom. No doubt a
lot of trading was done over back fences,
across doorsills, and over teacups. But we find
listed no hooked-rug makers among early
craftsmen. We do, however, find advertisements by genteel ladies of uncertain age who
undertook to teach girls the gentle art of embroidery, rug hooking, and crewelwork.

The Swedes on the Delaware, the Finns in

lower New Jersey, the dissenters of Scotch ancestry in New England, were our first makers of hooked rugs. By 1700 almost every housewife in the Northern colonies knew how to hook a rug and did it. The only tools required are wooden or metal hooks to pierce and spread the mesh and engage the loop of rug stuff to pull it back through the orifice; some chalk or marking crayon; and a scissors to clip the rug hooking when done. One would perhaps think that by 1870 this craft would have died of competition with cheap machine-loomed carpets, and rugs. On the contrary, that's when it entered its stage of greatest popularity. A New Englander, Edward Frost, born in 1843, joined the Army of the Union in the war between the states and was invalided home with consumption. Advised to take to the open air as a peddler, he hit upon the idea of adding rug patterns to his stock: pieces of burlap upon which a rug design was traced.

The idea took the fancy of New England housewives. Frost began to seek ways of making patterns faster. He hit upon the idea of metal stencils. These, once tried, worked very well. He could even indicate the colors by varying the paint he used in making his stenciled patterns. By 1876 he had cut no less than four tons of rug stencils out of thin sheets of tin, zinc, copper, and iron. And by then he had also waxed rich, had a factory, and was the source of rug-pattern supply for innumerable peddlers, shops, and stores. Again attacked by tuberculosis, he sold the business and removed to California. There he conquered the disease once more, and by 1890 visited the scene of his hooked-rug pattern works. It was still going strong. It kept going until after the turn of the twentieth century. The stencils were not scrapped, but stored away. Some years ago they were purchased by a discriminating collector who, instead of burying them

in a museum, recopyrighted the entire collection and began to reissue the patterns for rug hookers.

The Frost success engaged the eye of one Pond, of Biddeford, Maine, who, in 1877, began the manufacture of rug patterns by the stencil process. He advertised his wares in religious and national newspapers and built up a sizable business.

According to William Winthrop Kent, author of the two indispensable books on the hooked rug herein recommended for reading and study, certain hooked rugs should never be placed on the floor. Preserve the fine, antique ones on walls—as pictures. These antique rugs, made from rags, tags, and scraps of home-woven, home-dyed fabrics, have a naïveté of design and a quality of workmanship too precious to risk as floor mats. Be wise. Buy Frost patterns and make, or have made for you, the rugs you want to walk on; preserve the antique ones as hangings. Hooked rugs, obviously made between 1750 and 1850, are still to be found, but not always in the neighborhood of their making. These rugs traveled overland in immigrant wagons, along with a few precious sticks of furniture, pots, and pans. They also stayed at home and did neighborhood visiting. They won ribbons at mechanics' institutes and at county fairs. They were made in cabins on the frontier and in the drawing rooms of city mansions. Today they are part and parcel of our antique heritage.

As floor coverings, in their naïve patterns, hooked rugs are best with pioneer, cottage, and country things, but in their more sophisticated patterns are good with any of the classic furniture of the century 1750 to 1850. Don't be surprised at this. There were—and are —sophisticated patterns, after Patna chintzes, *toiles de Jouy*, Pontipool tinware, Oriental rugs, Turkey work, and from embroidery pat-

terns in the seventeenth-century editions of
the great English pattern book *A Schoolhouse
for the Needle*. Even though you have seventeenth-century furniture, and have no hope of
finding a seventeenth-century hooked rug, you
can find an appropriate pattern and have the
rug made. Unfortunately, the hooked rug does
not lend itself readily to reproduction as pictures for this primer. Therefore, we show no
rugs, but show rug patterns as they were originally drawn on the basic linen or burlap pieces.
These are not from either Frost or Pond patterns, but from original rugs made between
1750 and 1850. A variety, or variant, of the
hooked rug is the wool-on-wool coverlet. Instead of rags or strips of fabric, these covers
are hooked with tufts of fluffy woolen yarn,
or dyed wool. They are very effective as wall
hangings and very comfortable bedcovers.
These coverlets appear to have been made
from 1800–50.

The Hooked Rug, by William Winthrop Kent.
Rare Hooked Rugs, by William Winthrop Kent.
Hooked Rugs and How to Make Them, by Anna M.
 Laise Phillips.

47

Engraved Prints and Pictures

Daniel boone, painted by Chester Harding, engraved by J. O. Lewis, is one of the rarest of American prints; only one copy is known." In this manner an enthusiastic amateur (and may there be many more like him) announced in public print what he believed to be a fact. In New York, Baltimore, Boston, and Philadelphia, wise old collectors laughed. They knew seven proofs of the print were in private collections, and also that three others could be had from dealers at a moment's notice. You can always get a copy of Paul Revere's atrociously engraved "Boston Massacre" or almost any other great and important Early American engraving if you are willing to pay the price. The hard things to find are the obscure little prints of events and people no longer important. These are hardly worth search by a dealer because the price is bound to be low. As one canny dealer put it, "I'll sell it to you for a dollar if I find it, but I'll charge $5.00 an hour to hunt for it." Which should be sufficient evidence to all and sundry that the way to collect prints is to go out hunting for them and not sit, after the German manner, in an easy chair, surrounded by champagne and sausages, waiting for yokels to drive the deer in your direction within easy shot.

No less than twenty copper-plate engravers were producing prints in the Colonies before the Revolution. Some twenty-six were at work during the Revolution. Between 1785 and 1850 more than six hundred and fifty were at work, their output dwindling, as far as framing prints was concerned, after 1835. In the company of early men are found names such as Foster, Burgis, De Bruhls, Claypoole, Copley, Dawkins, Emmes, Hurd, and Peter Pelham, the latter our great early eighteenth-century mezzotinter. Any prints by these men are pure and unadulterated history. So also are the prints made by the company of men who worked during the Revolution, recording, as did Revere, the Boston Massacre (but copied from a far better print, publication of which was blocked by Revere's pirating the design), as did Norman in the depicting of the Battle of Bunker Hill;

Doolittle in his Battle of Lexington and Concord; and Inauguration of Washington as First President on the Balcony of Federal Hall, New York City. Our later engravers concerned themselves first with memorials of the Revolution and its famed men and battles and then, after—and even during—the War of 1812, executed plate after plate depicting the exploits of our glorious infant Navy in knocking out many units and squadrons of the British Fleet which showed up in our waters. Only one battle, and that a defeat for our side, went unrecorded. When Jackson turned in the only land victory of that war, in the majestic triumph at New Orleans, that event was pictured in prints made by four different engravers.

Engravings, especially in aquatint, were often hand-colored. Many of the naval battle scenes, land battles, and views, as, for example, the magnificent portfolio of Hudson River scenery, were issued hand-colored. Some few prints were issued printed wholly or partly in colors. These are excessively rare—but not unprocurable. When printed in colors, the colors were rubbed into the engraved plate wherever they were to appear in the print, exactly as the black ink was rubbed in for general printing. Engravings are incised on copper plates. To print from them, the incised lines, or dots, or mezzotint screens, are filled, or charged, with ink. Then the surface of the plate is wiped clean, a sheet of dampened paper laid over it, and the whole thing run through a press that is akin to a huge clothes wringer. This squeezes the paper into the lines of the plate, where it picks up the ink. Thus any engraving is really a mold of the plate, and if the plate were not inked the paper would still have the impression upon its unblemished surface in the form of raised lines, dots, and mezzotint screening.

Generally speaking, Early American engravings depict either town or city views, landscapes, forts, battles (land and sea), and portraits of famous and near-famous men. That most of the events and most of the men retained their fame, and even have had luster added to their names, makes such prints increasingly valuable. Early American prints have never been traded in as freely as lithographs, mainly because they do not exist in sufficient quantities for brisk general trade. But they are to be had and, without prejudice, they are far more appropriate framing prints for one's walls, when used with Early American furniture, than are Currier & Ives and other colored lithographs. Early American prints belong to the age of handmade things; the days of personal craftsmanship. They are in line, stipple, aquatint, etching, and mezzotinting; all artists', or classical, methods, or processes, of reproduction. You are referred to the list of books noted below for further study. Approach them without fear—they're not stuffy, or so scholarly as to befog rather than enlighten. Most large libraries have the rare ones; several are still in print and procurable.

American Graphic Art, by Dr. Frank Weitenkampf.
American Engravers upon Copper and Steel, by D. McN. Stauffer.
American Engravers upon Copper and Steel, by Mantle Fielding.
Early American Prints, by Carl W. Drepperd.

48

Currier & Ives Lithographs

Tʜɪs firm of lithographers was launched on the highway to success by the timely publication of an extra edition of the New York *Sun*, January 16, 1840. This extra was illustrated with a view of the disaster known as the burning of the steamship *Lexington* in Long Island Sound. So many copies of the *Sun* were purchased, not only in and around New York, but all over America, that the fame of the lithographers and the desire for more such pictures were born in the twinkling of an eye. Eighty years later these pictures, single-stone, hand-colored lithographs, regained public attention. This time they enjoyed the attention of collectors. In the decade prior to that resurgence, only a very few wise students and connoisseurs had recognized them and their worth, and had quietly collected sizable caches of them. Then after innumerable trades, sales, and transactions had occurred with Currier & Ives prints as the chattels, Mr. Harry T. Peters ennobled them forever in the American scene by writing not one, but two monumental tomes about them. He annotated the prints; he listed the known production; and he delved into the history of the firm so deeply that his books are, literally, the open book of Currier & Ives.

Nathaniel Currier, born in 1813, was apprenticed to the Pendletons, Boston lithographers, in 1828. Upon achieving craft mastery of the then brand-new craft, he went to Philadelphia, and entered into a working partnership with one Stodart. Prior to that he worked for a while as a master craftsman in the shop of M. E. D. Brown, one of our very early lithographers. The Stodart partnership was not a success. Currier moved to New York and established his own business in 1835. In that same year he issued a print of the catastrophe, the collapse of the Planters Hotel, New Orleans, May 15, 1835. Currier seems to have been born with an eye for the news value of prints memorializing events, circumstances, and disasters—or anything that was enough news to enough people to make a picture profitable.

In 1852 James Merritt Ives was hired as a bookkeeper by N. Currier. In 1857 he was made a partner. These two men, whose names are now household words, made prints for the people. They never dreamed of making them for collectors and connoisseurs. Their product was for the cottage wall, the tack room, the livery stable, the barroom, tavern, and hotel; the shop, the store, the office, the library, and the kitchen. They also made pictures for schoolrooms and Sunday schools; for the nursery; to decorate the saloon and cabin walls of steamboats, river-, and canal-boats. Their production of drawing-room prints was almost non-existent. Sports, though, were their meat and drink. They had the artists who could record sporting events to the King's taste. Hence every sporting and gun club in America (and it is amazing how many of these there were) had something offered them by N. Currier and by Currier & Ives. The prints wholesaled at from six cents to $1.00 or more each. At one time in their career Currier & Ives had 1,100 subjects in stock and listed in their catalogue. Selling by the tens of thousands yearly for every million of population, and to a constantly increasing and print-appreciating people, it is no wonder that Currier & Ives prints have survived in great numbers, and that unique ones—examples of which only one copy is known—are scarcer than the teeth of the proverbial hen. Such a subject is too big even for one book. Mr. Peters required two books, both of which are out of print and now almost as scarce as a Currier "Flying Cloud." But in 1942 Mr. Peters condensed his Currier & Ives history into a volume for the people, and some 500,000 copies were distributed. Look to that volume, and to others listed below, for the pictures you want to see and the further information you seek. No matter what information you seek, you'll probably find it there.

Currier & Ives seem to have made pictures in three general sizes. Large folio, 17 × 24 inches; medium folio, 11 × 15 inches; and small folio, 8 × 12½ inches.

Currier & Ives: Printmakers to the American People, Volumes I and II, by Harry T. Peters.
Currier & Ives: Printmakers to the American People, Special Edition, by Harry T. Peters.
Currier & Ives—A Manual for Collectors, by Jane Cooper Bland.
Best Fifty Currier & Ives Lithographs, Large Folio Size, Foreword by Charles Messer Stow.
Best Fifty Currier & Ives Lithographs, Small Folio Size, Foreword by Charles Messer Stow.

49

Other American Lithographers

THE GREAT COMPANY of lithographic print makers which flourished in America between 1821 and 1880 has been lost sight of in the brilliant aura that has for so many years surrounded Currier & Ives. Yet in this company, numbering no less and perhaps considerably more than 1,172 individuals and firms who made lithographic prints and pictures, are to be found the craftsmen who made many of our finest and rarest examples. Among the really important firms represented are the Kelloggs of Hartford, Pendletons of Boston, the Endicotts and Sarony of New York, and Duval of Philadelphia—to mention a very few. The output of many of these firms is deserving of books every bit as definitive as Mr. Peters' books on Currier & Ives. Perhaps Mr. Peters realized this, and laid the foundation stones for future writers and researchers in his great work, *America on Stone*, in which he lists at least 90 per cent of all the lithographers who ever worked in America, even though their commercial life was less than six months. In this section of our primer we are again hampered by a lack, not of illustrative material, but of facilities to reproduce the pictures in primer style and to the very small size we must use. One other good reason presents itself: there are so many prints made by America's lithographers other than Currier & Ives that any selection of six, or ten, or a dozen would be too much for anything but a jury. Mr. Peters' book about these print makers is now out of print, but I am advised a few copies are still available from dealers at the publication price. By all means treat yourself to a copy if you find one. *America on Stone* is a far more important book to the general student than Mr. Peters' *Currier & Ives*.

America on Stone, by Harry T. Peters.

50

Miniature, Profile,
and Silhouette Portraits

Even though vastly different in social significance, value, and medium of expression, these three forms of popular portraiture were—and remain—examples of the same objectivity and purpose: to have one's visage preserved. In miniatures, the portrayal was in water colors, though sometimes in oils, by the best talent available. In America, about fifty able miniaturists are listed as working between 1725 and 1845. Among these are notable names: Fulton, Theus, Malbone, Hesselius, Copley, Trumbull, Bembridge, Williams, James Peale, and others. Painted upon copper plates, pewter plates (not culinary plates but thin sheets of the metal), upon parchment, paper, whalebone, hardwood panels, but most frequently on ivory, these miniature works of fine art are framed in gold, in silver, and in lockets. Sometimes the framing is jewel set. Collecting such elegancies in the form of portraiture is a pursuit reserved for those willing to spend their all—or their surplus—and in a major key. The sizes of these miniatures vary from $1\frac{1}{4} \times 1\frac{1}{2}$ inches to 4×6 inches. They are known in circular, oval, oblong, and square shapes. They have been objects of collecting interest ever since they became heirlooms. One of the first books about them was published in 1897.

Silhouettes were the cheapest form of miniature portrait. They were cut out with a scissors, from the life, by the better silhouet-

tists. They were also drawn from the life and very elaborately contrived by artists who worked not with a scissors but with hair pencil (fine brush) and plumbago stick (the equivalent of our modern lead pencil). The very cheapest silhouettes were made by itinerants and mountebanks at fairs and bazaars. Their method was to reduce the shadow in an optic machine and then trace the reduced image in black ink, or cut it out of white paper, mounting that over black paper or cloth. The name derives from that of the Royal Intendant of French finances, Silhouette, whose economies soon gave rise to the calling of anything cheap "à la Silhouette." The greatest American silhouettist was William H. Brown. His work is today avidly collected by many specialists.

Augustin Edouart, a Frenchman who came to America and began making silhouettes at a great rate, stands today as perhaps the chief rival of Brown, in both output and quality of workmanship. But Brown and Edouart had at least five hundred contemporaries, both amateur and professional, who would cut or draw a silhouette portrait for a few cents or a half dollar. These fellows toured the country, from village to town, peddling their services.

Armless men and women cut silhouettes with their toes. One lady in this category cut them with her mouth! In their day they were patronized by many and observed at work by many more. They were comparable to those glass blowers who used to tour the country with a gas lamp, some rods of glass, and who made all sorts of gimcracks and gewgaws to sell on the spot for a quarter, a half dollar, or a dollar.

The production of silhouettes in America reached an amazing total. Now collecting them is something in the life of every lover of antiques. Signed, dated, and identifiable silhouettes are the most valuable. Silhouettes of famous people are very desirable. A Philadelphian

named Folwell switched from making hair ornaments to silhouette drawing. He made a silhouette of Washington as the President was at worship in Christ's Church, Philadelphia. It was so good a portrait that Folwell took up painting, and finally became an art instructor. He was not unique in this. Peddlers of tinware took up silhouette cutting. Anyone with the itch to roam the open road found silhouette-cutting ability the sure key to bed and board even if there were no other goods to vend. Silhouettes vary in size from 2 × 3 inches to huge cuttings of events and to full-length portraits drawn on prepared lithographed backgrounds, up to 10 × 14 inches in size. The dates run from approximately 1770 to 1845.

Silhouettes exist in three general kinds: hollow cut, cut and pasted, and drawn or painted. The hollow cut is cut from white paper and mounted on a dark background of black silk, velvet, paper, et cetera. The cut and pasted is cut out of blackened paper and mounted on white mounts. The drawn and painted type is handmade, sketched and darkened by the artists. Many of the peddlers' and itinerants' silhouettes were cut by use of a sort of camera and a pantograph. Full details of the various methods will be found in the books recommended for further study.

Profile portraits stand between the miniature and the silhouette in point of importance and desirability. Most of these were painted, either in water color or oils, on wood panels, metal plates, canvas or paper, or done in crayons (in color) on special pastel-tinted or white crayon paper. J. B. St. Memim, a Frenchman who worked in America in the late eighteenth and early nineteenth centuries, made not only fairly large crayon drawings of profiles in tints, but also for a consideration of some $33 would reduce them to small size by pantograph, engrave them on a copper plate, and deliver a dozen to twenty-five hand-colored proofs. These St. Memim portraits are known as Phisionotraces. This term derives from his method of making the original by tracing the profile through a glass screen. St. Memim also had competition from contemporary profile painters. Several hundred unnamed and unknown painters and sketch artists were at work painting profiles between 1780 and 1845.

Most of the profile paintings and drawings here considered measure between 7 × 9 inches and 9 × 12 inches. They are often framed in wood frames, contemporary with the period of the portrait. As with silhouettes and miniatures, so with the profiles: signed, dated, and identified examples or profiles of famous people are the most valued. Sharpless Washington profiles are quite valuable. So also is any Sharpless drawing of Early American notables of the post-Revolutionary period. But all miniatures and all profiles are good to own; even the lowly silhouette has value. Our illustrations include only two cheap miniatures, as these cannot be done justice, even by photographic reproduction. The silhouettes and the profiles date from 1770 to 1840.

In the 1850s the daguerreotype sounded the death knell for all of these forms of personal portraiture. By that time almost anybody could have had a miniature done chemically, by the action of light, at a low price. Many really good miniature and profile artists, and not a few silhouette cutters, became daguerreotypists and finally operated photographic studios.

Heirlooms in Miniatures, by Anne Hollingsworth Wharton.
American Miniatures, by H. B. Wehle.
Shades of Our Ancestors, by Alice Van Leer Carick.

51

Primitive or Pioneer Paintings

Here is an "antique" which many families still own. Briefly, a primitive or pioneer painting may be a portrait by an itinerant or local jack-of-all-painting, a landscape or genre painting, a seascape, or a fruit, flower, or game piece. It must show an amateurishness that is unmistakable, and preferably some crudity and naïveté. In other words, a painting by one who lacked formal academic training.

Twenty years ago such pictures were begging for someone to buy them for a song, or to take them away, gratis. Now they are the prizes of galleries and shops which display them with pride and sell them for a consideration no longer in the small-change category. The vast majority of these paintings were made between 1820 and 1880. It is a pity the term "primitive" has been applied to them with such emphasis that it seems to be fixed. America's true primitive paintings are those painted by the known and unknown masters who worked here between 1650 and 1710.

Portraits are, of course, the most common in this group of so-called primitive pictures. Almost everybody in America, prior to the advent of the daguerreotype, and in the back country for some years afterward, wanted a portrait or portraits of all or some members of the family. This need was supplied by an army of itinerants some of whom, on occasion, produced a real masterpiece. But, again briefly, any genre subject depicting an event, a circumstance, a trade, or profession, camp scene or other picture of life as it was lived in America, is now of some value. Also any ship picture, railroad view or scene, any sports or games, any picture of a city or town, a circus, a hanging, a balloon ascension, et cetera, is good. So important and worthy of study is this once-minor subject of Americana interest that the reader is urged to follow any spark of interest by reading the recommended books.

Some American Primitives, by Eleanor Sears.
American Pioneer Arts and Artists, by Carl W. Drepperd.
American Primitive Painting, by Jean Lipman.

52

Art-Instruction Books and Drawing Books

WITHIN these items of American antiques, unnoticed up to 1940 except by a few observers, can be found proof that something "new" in the "old" is always coming to light. When, in 1941, my own interests were directed to the subject of what are now called primitive American paintings, I sought for certain of the causes for all these works of art or near-art. I discovered that no less than one hundred different instruction books on drawing and painting had been issued in America between the years 1787 and 1860. These books were printed for amateurs; for all people, young and old, who had an itch to draw and paint. Here are listed some of the most valuable of these books—books now sought by wise collectors and by farsighted librarians:

The School of Wisdom, or Repository of the Most Valuable Curiosities of Art, New Brunswick (N. J.), 1787.
The Artist's Assistant in Drawing, et cetera, Philadelphia, 1794.
Elements of the Graphic Arts, New York, 1802.
Elements of Drawing, New York, 1804.
Elements of Drawing, Boston, 1814.
Thackera's Drawing Book, Philadelphia, 1814.
Progressive Lessons—to Elucidate the Art of Flower Painting, Philadelphia, 1820.
Elements of Drawing, Philadelphia, 1823.
Lucas' Progressive Drawing Book, Baltimore, 1827–28.
Theoremetrical System of Painting, New York, 1830.
Key to Art of Drawing the Human Figure, Philadelphia, 1831.
Young Ladies' Assistant in Drawing & Painting, Cincinnati, 1833.
Vermont Drawing Book of Landscapes, Burlington, 1838–39–40–44.
United States Drawing Book, Philadelphia, 1839.

Your ancestors, or some of them, if they were in America, probably used one or more of these instructors. If you have fallen heir to the books, you have antiques of some value—say anywhere from $1.50 to $150. The most valuable is the Lucas' drawing book with its quite charming small folio hand-colored aquatint views of American scenery.

What the drawing instruction books did to many who owned

them was to motivate the making of drawings in a sketchbook. These sketchbooks are now avidly sought because the best of them can be broken up and the individual pictures sold for exactly what they are: Early American amateur drawings and paintings. Any sketchbook done in the eighteenth century, or the first half of the nineteenth century, is, today, an antique prize. Several, broken up in the past two years, have realized sizable sums of money as pictures for framing. Special value resides in any inscriptions which give the name of the amateur artist, the place of making, and the approximate or actual date. That is the kind of information which adds much to the satisfaction of owning the pictures or the books. Such art is also to be found in the handmade albums of the 1830–50 period. In these, which are smaller than sketchbooks, the pictures approximate miniatures. In 1942 one such album yielded six miniatures which today enrich four important collections. Many girls at boarding schools between 1790 and 1850 made sketchbooks as a part of their training. The great American genre painter, Lewis Krimmel, made "The Return from Boarding School" one of his subjects. At the feet of the girl just home from school are her possessions. Among them are a paintbox and a drawing book. This picture was painted about 1816.

Annotated Bibliographic Check List of American Art and Drawing Instruction Books, New York Public Library.

53

Firebacks

Fɪʀᴇʙᴀᴄᴋs are what a heating engineer would call a limping step toward convection. No matter how much attention was paid to making firebacks decorative or beautiful, the purpose was to provide a radiant reflector which pushed more heat out of the fireplace. Sometimes the firedogs, or andirons, were welded to the fireback, thus providing a sort of open stove. Usually firebacks were pinned in the rear walls of fireplaces. Most firebacks were made of iron, although mention is made of copper and bronze firebacks, and royalty is said to have enjoyed small ones of silver. Most of the firebacks made in the Colonies and prior to the Revolution were cast in New England and New York foundries. Pennsylvania, Maryland, and Virginia foundries are known to have made some.

The true fireback is usually higher than wide and has a cresting on the top. The examples shown are all of iron, and all of American make. They were cast in sand, from the first run of iron, and from molds made of wood and pewter or lead. Firebacks are today scarce and desirable items of interest to the more advanced collectors of American antiques. Most collectors buy firebacks for use in their fireplaces.

The only book dealing with cast-iron stoves, and firebacks, is *The Bible in Iron* by the late Dr. H. C. Mercer, published by the Bucks County Historical Society, Doylestown, Penn-

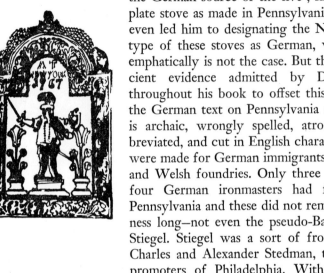

sylvania. Dr. Mercer, a painstaking historian, seems to have had a decided bias in favor of the German source of the five-, six-, and ten-plate stove as made in Pennsylvania. This bias even led him to designating the Norse proto-type of these stoves as German, which most emphatically is not the case. But there is suffi-cient evidence admitted by Dr. Mercer throughout his book to offset this bias. Even the German text on Pennsylvania stove plates is archaic, wrongly spelled, atrociously ab-breviated, and cut in English characters. They were made for German immigrants by English and Welsh foundries. Only three or possibly four German ironmasters had furnaces in Pennsylvania and these did not remain in busi-ness long—not even the pseudo-Baron H. W. Stiegel. Stiegel was a sort of front man for Charles and Alexander Stedman, two shrewd promoters of Philadelphia. With their help Stiegel went up like a rocket and when they abandoned him, came down even more swiftly than he had risen.

The Bible in Iron, by Henry C. Mercer.
Iron & Brass Implements of the English & American Home, by Seymour Lindsay.

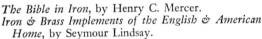

54

Ten-Plate, Six-Plate, Five-Plate, and Franklin Stoves

THE IRON STOVE, in America, was introduced by the Dutch and the Swedes. The ten-, six-, and five-plate stoves of America are made after the pattern developed in Norway, Sweden, and Denmark, and fully appreciated and used in great numbers by the Dutch in The Netherlands. The five-plate stove, often mentioned but seldom explained, was not properly a stove, but a hotbox, projecting from the rear of a fireplace (from which it was shoveled full of hot embers or coals) into a room on the other side. This hotbox heated the other room and eliminated the need for a fire therein. The six-plate stove was a self-contained heating unit, while the ten-plate was a heating, cooking, and baking unit. Thus the five-plate had right, left, top, bottom, and front plates, with the rear open and abutting into a fireplace wall. The six-plate had top, bottom, and four side plates. The ten-plate was simply a large six-plate with four extra plates providing the oven cavity. The outside or exposed plates of these stoves were cast with various designs in low relief, and often bear considerable lettering. Because most of these five-, six-, and ten-plate stoves were made for the German immigrants, they were cast with German (of a sort) text, but cut in English letters. The vast majority of them, made in the eighteenth century, were produced by English and Welsh ironmasters. At first Biblical characters and scenes decorated the plates.

Later a standard tulip pattern superseded the Biblical designs. This tulip pattern is a clean break with the European tradition of décor for stove plates, so it must be assumed to have originated here. Stove plates are collected for their quaintness, their occasional use as a fireback (which is an error), and by advanced collectors in the hope of finding enough plates to reassemble a complete stove.

The Franklin fireplace is the result of our great all-American philosopher considering the wastefulness of big fireplaces and the little useful heat they produced, regardless of their size. The result was his invention of a little fireplace, cast in iron, which not only retained but also radiated heat. It was light enough to be portable from room to room. It could readily be fitted to a flue with a pipe, or connected with fireplace flues by piping which permitted the stove to be set out of the fireplace and into the room. Thus Franklin's stove yielded all the aesthetic joys of an open fire with the creature comfort of more heat and the economic value of less fuel. Some are really beautiful in line and proportion as well as performance. Some are fitted with doors which, closed, make the little open fire an enclosed stove, burning either coal or wood. Collectors, museums, and other enthusiasts, of course, want original and early cast stoves. In spite of the fact that thousands of these stoves have been melted down as scrap iron, it is surprising how many remain—stored away, perhaps forgotten; some even bricked up between the jambs of closed fireplaces! Franklin stoves were also cast with various decorations, perhaps the most famed being the "Alter Idem" and the "Be Liberty Thine" designs.

The Bible in Iron, by Henry C. Mercer.
Forges and Furnaces in the Province of Pennsylvania,
Colonial Dames of America.

55

American Victorian
Period Stoves

Between 1840 and 1880 a most interesting galaxy of "parlor stoves" was produced by American iron founders. These stoves were designed to function as fireplaces when connected to flues, or to be placed inside or outside an existing fireplace, either connected to the chimney flue or to a pipe orifice in a metal shield placed over the fireplace opening. Some stoves were made in hilarious sizes and shapes. Many were embellished with elaborate scrolls, shells, figures, et cetera, molded in low relief. Some were designed for double duty: to use as auxiliary cookstoves, hot-water heaters, and warming ovens. The fuel shortages of 1943–44 seem to have heightened a collecting interest in these stoves. A brisk market has developed for them as useful heating elements for modern homes. Stoves that had sold for little more than secondhand or old-iron value were, by 1944, selling at from $25 to $100. The record price was brought by a lovely model, cast about 1848, and marked "J. BT. CLUTE'S PATENT, MAY 1846." This stove is in the form of an urn on a boxlike member. The decoration is indubitably in Victorian style, but the basic design is taken directly from a stove invented by Benjamin Franklin in 1776. Many of the stoves of the period here considered are also based, in principle and design, upon Franklin's other heating invention, the portable fireplace stove. Marginal illustrations

include the Victorian and the Franklin urn
stoves and several pictures taken directly from
Early American stove catalogues. The reader
is invited to compare these Victorian cast-iron
stoves with those illustrated under section on
"Ten-Plate, Six-Plate, Five-Plate, and Franklin
Stoves," on pages 149–150.

56

Ironwork

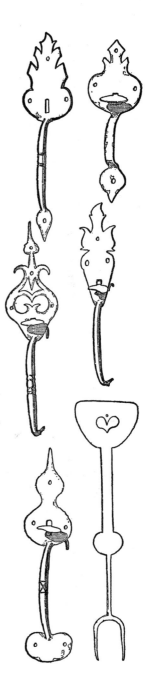

Anything in wrought iron, from a four-inch rattail hinge to a complete iron balcony, has a collector waiting somewhere for it. Similarly, almost any cast-iron eagle, whether of two-inch or twenty-inch spread, and any cast-iron balcony or railing, has a collector of cast iron waiting. Almost twenty years ago the *Mentor Magazine* told a part of this story, pointing out there was gold in our Early American iron. There is. Any early wrought-iron hinge, utensil of charm, or decorative object has its devotees in the collecting world. Even the common H and HL hinges have value, no matter how ruthlessly they have been pulled from their doors. Ram's-horn or cock's-head hinges are on a parity with fine historic china. Marked iron is better than marked pewter. That is, better in the collector's eye and mind. So important is this subject that a really monumental book has been written about it. So varied are the things made of wrought and cast iron that even partial justice to the subject is impossible here.

Not a little of our early wrought iron traveled across the country in a most unusual way. Pioneers had the habit of heading for a new country with a bag of hinges, angles, latches, nails, and spikes. Where they found a likely place they built a cabin and used their hardware. When the itch to move farther came upon them, they burned down the cabin, collected the ironwork from the ashes, and moved on, to use it again. Often this occurred

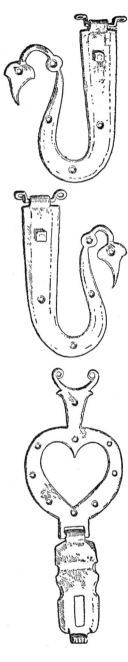

three times in a lifetime. Only when black-smiths kept abreast of the vanguard in population shifts did the era of cabin burning to recover hardware come to an end. That is why Virginia, New York, Pennsylvania, and New England ironwork can be found in Indiana and Kentucky, and why some of it traveled as far as Missouri. Bernard Lagan, Conestoga wagon builder, left the Conestoga Valley of Pennsylvania in 1843, with a trunkful of clothes and two boxes of ironwork. He headed for Saint Louis, then the headquarters for prairie-schooner travel to the West. Ten years later he was in Dubuque, Iowa, doing the same thing: fitting out wagons for the overland journey. It should also be remembered that in every overland wagon there was a box of iron: hinges, brackets, spikes, and nails.

Some of the decorative ironwork on Conestoga wagons is superlatively fine master craftsmanship blended with perfect functioning, whether it was a sheath for the ax blade that was anchored on the wagon's side, or the hinges on the lids of the kitbox and the feedbox. The latter boxes were used by collectors as mailboxes until they became too valuable. More than one collector set out a hundred-dollar wagon box with its elaborate hinges only to go to his gate one morning and find his box gone—stolen by a discriminating and knowing thief in the night!

American iron has been mined, smelted, wrought, and cast since early in the seventeenth century. By 1750 the American iron industry was booming. No less than fifty pre-Revolutionary forges and furnaces were operating in Pennsylvania; New York, New England, New Jersey, Maryland, and Virginia had their complement of forges and furnaces.

Early American Wrought Iron (3 volumes), by Albert H. Sonn.

57

Ship and Other Models

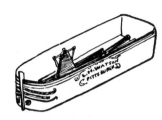

Aʙᴏᴜᴛ five years before the crash of 1929 there was a nationwide revival of interest in ship models. Concurrently with this phenomenon, many books on ships and shipping, ship prints and paintings, and ship models were published. The great romanticist Joseph Hergesheimer did a book about his lovely old Pennsylvania home, and in it pictured a fireplace over which was anchored a model of the steam frigate *Lancaster*. Came a country-wide search for ship models. Every collector's house, almost, had a ship model on the mantelpiece. I found one and did the same thing with it. But my old tutor, watching my excursions into collecting, said to me, "What you need over that fireplace, in this part of the country, is a model of our great contribution to America, the land ship, a Conestoga wagon, and I know where you can find one!" That started me on a hunt, not only for the Conestoga wagon—which I did acquire—but for other models, and to the discovery that models of all kinds were made by our ancestors.

Diligent search resulted in finding models of sleighs, the old high-bowed, paneled eighteenth-century kind, complete with spans of wooden horses; sulkies, one-hoss shays, fish carts, barrows, river boats, paddle-wheel river steamers, threshing machines, railway locomotives, canalboats, hose carts and fire engines. These were not patent models, but

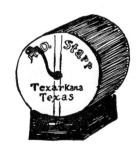

155

labors of love by someone who wanted to imitate and enjoy, in a model, the lines and forms of the original objects. What was made in one county was made in other counties. I have lived in several sections of the country since that time—in upper New York State, in Virginia, in central Illinois, and in Maryland. In all of these sections could be found models of early vintage, standing as replicas in miniature of the machines and inventions of other days.

In this year of grace 1944 the ship model no longer reigns supreme. Furthermore, ship-model collecting is now so refined and specialized a vogue that only scale models, accurately rigged and fitted in minutest detail, bring record prices. "Has it a full complement of eighteen guns, is each gun bored and touchholed, and can it be aimed and fired?" is what a collector said to a dealer who was singing the praises of a thirty-two-inch frigate he had just found. The answer, believe it or not, was "yes." Only one ship model in a thousand is that meticulously made. There is a story of how an early model so made was badly damaged when it was used as the centerpiece for a banquet to Captain Hull of the United States Navy. The little guns were loaded and joined by a fuse mechanism to fire a salute of so many guns to the captain. The works went wrong and all the guns fired at once. The model was considerably damaged.

"Models, and models, and models" is the way the late Homer Eaton Keyes, co-founder of the magazine *Antiques* he so ably edited for many years, summed up the model situation. "I suspect there are more of them than we have thought, and a greater variety than we have dreamed." He was right. Look for them and you shall find them. When you find them, if the price is agreeable to your purse, buy them. They are Americana closer to the people than almost any other item collected today. They are personal, unique, and objective expressions by people who had courage enough to try anything—even to making models of great ships, intricate machines, or fine coaches. If you ever find a locomotive model of machined iron, brass, and steel that runs, or a paddle-wheel steamer that has working boilers, engines, and paddles—you have a joy forever. Lay down the tracks. Build a canal in your back yard, get up steam—and people will travel for miles to see your show. In fact, collect enough interesting models of any kind and you'll have visitors. You'll not need to advertise. They'll find you. Illustrated are a Conestoga wagon model, a ship model, a washing-machine model, a locomotive model, two balloon models, and several others. That locomotive is by a professional model maker of 1845. Its price at that time, off the tracks but ready to run, was $45. It was not made as a toy, but as a philosophical model. That's why it is shown here, rather than in the section on toys.

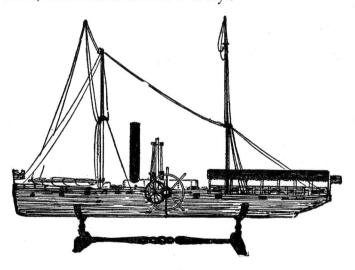

58

Clocks

HOUSEHOLD CLOCKS were not common American articles of furniture until the beginning of the Federal period. In spite of the fact that many so-called grandfather clocks of American make are believed to be more than two hundred years old, the vast majority of these fine old timepieces were produced between 1775 and 1820. Clocks with tall pillar-and-scroll or bonnet-top cases, having hand-painted dials with moon-phase or rocking-ship features, sweep second hands and other refinements, were made largely by individual clockmakers in villages, towns, and cities. Sometimes (but rarely) the clockmaker produced the entire clock. More often than not he purchased certain of the parts, made others by hand, assembled the mechanism, had a cabinetmaker fashion the case, and then delivered the clock to the customer.

In Boston, New York, Philadelphia, Baltimore, Charleston, New Haven, Hartford, Albany, and other big towns there were dealers in watches and clocks who imported a considerable number of movements, cased and uncased, from England and from The Netherlands. Such dealers appear to have been engaged in clock importing for at least the first three quarters of the eighteenth century. Most of the William and Mary, Queen Anne, and Chippendale period style clocks were imported. This influx of clocks did not go unnoticed in England and Holland. Over there, artisans and mechanics in the clockmaking trade put two and two together: if Americans buy so many clocks they must need a lot of clocks, and that means a good chance for a clockmaker in almost any town over there. So, not a few clockmakers and watchmakers emigrated from England and The Netherlands. These, upon arrival, taught American apprentices the craft. Fine workmen were needed not only to produce clocks for the homes but to produce, repair, and keep in order the far-more-precise instruments known as ships' chronometers, which were one of the major requirements for good navigating.

The first efforts to make really good yet inexpensive clocks for the people resulted in the creation of one of the most beautiful clocks the world has ever known—the banjo. This clock, invented and patented by Simon Willard, received so enthusiastic an acceptance that many other clockmakers pirated the design without so much as a thank-you to the inventor. In spite of its beauty, grace, and charm, the American banjo clock is primarily a triumph in functional design.

The banjo is a snugly cased clock: there isn't more than a cubic inch of waste space anywhere in the casing, which fits the movement to perfection. The drum houses the escapement and time train—the "works" of the clock and the dial. The neck provides the exact space needed for the drop of the tapered driving weight, in front of which the pendulum rod swings. The box provides swing room for the bob of the pendulum and the seating of the driving weight. Inside the banjo all is constant activity, with every part as carefully planned as the interior of a submarine. Outside, all is beauty. The shape is lovely; the carving, molding, and gilding are fine and even rich, and the glass panels in the neck and box are painted in excellent taste—often with ships

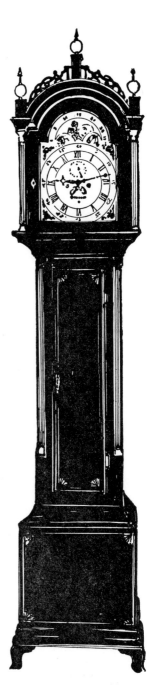

and marine motifs. Surmounting the drum is an acorn finial, an eagle, or some other *epi*. A grand clock. A fine timepiece. By 1925 this type clock in the antique markets was competing with grandfather clocks for top value.

Close upon the heels of the banjo in popular esteem is the Terry clock. This, too, is a well-considered piece of clock engineering. Its exterior presents a broad, frank dial that is easy to see and a case that is a delight to the eye. It has a bonnet, or pillar-and-scroll top, has free standing pillars of great delicacy, a painted tablet or glass panel under the dial, and brass finials over pillars and above the center element of the bonnet top. The Terry clock is a mantel clock; the banjo is a wall clock. Around these two forms, in a wide variety of individualistic designs, revolved by far the greatest number of clocks produced in America. Grandfather-clock production was not enormous and, to the best of our knowledge, was never carried on as a factory operation. That it took the complexion of a factory operation in some districts was due entirely to the fact that in those districts many individual clockmakers were at work.

The grandfather clocks of Lancaster County, Pennsylvania, for example, exist in goodly numbers because so many clockmakers in that county specialized in them. The pamphlet issued by the Lancaster County Historical Society on the clockmakers of that district has been reprinted several times to supply the constant demand of collectors and clock historians. Similarly, the clockmakers of Bucks and Berks counties, Pennsylvania, produced many fine grandfather clocks, as did the clockmakers of many districts of Maryland, New Jersey, New York, and New England.

But the great age of clock producing in America may be put down as the half century

1800 to 1849. In that fifty years the clock-making industry of Connecticut, born in the eighteenth century, reached its full flowering of production in what today we call antique clocks. Ingraham, Thomas, Terry, Boardman, Jerome—names to conjure with—are found among the list of mechanics, inventors, and shrewd producers who made clockmaking an industry instead of a craft. Brasswork clocks, woodenwork clocks—turned out with the aid of water-power machinery, down a production line that led right to the tailboard of clock peddlers' carts, then carried over the countryside and across the nation. Clocks that run for a whole day at one winding—for one dollar! Eight-day clocks with brass works. Weight-driven clocks, spring-driven clocks, clocks with wagon springs for motive power. Banjo clocks with lyre-shaped cases. Shelf clocks with Gothic cases. Pillar-and-scroll-top clocks. Carved-top clocks. A thousand different designs at prices to fit all pocketbooks.

From this pool of New England-made time-pieces we draw most of our antique clocks.

Obviously, if clockmaking the science and clockmaking the art intrigue your interest, that interest is deserving of satisfaction. And satisfaction stands waiting for you in many books—in books of clock pictures, books on clock history, and books on the science of horology. Those listed below will at least start you off on what can be a grand tour of the clock world.

Early American Craftsmen, by Walter A. Dyer.
The Clock Book, by Wallace Nutting.
Old Clock Book, by N. Hudson Moore.
Furniture Treasury (Vol. III), by Wallace Nutting.
Old Clocks and Watches and Their Makers, by Britten.
Antiques Magazine, February 1922 and December 1923.
Connecticut Clockmakers of the Eighteenth Century, by Penrose Hoopes.

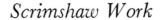

59

Scrimshaw Work

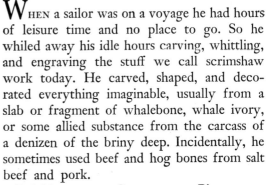

Wʜᴇɴ a sailor was on a voyage he had hours of leisure time and no place to go. So he whiled away his idle hours carving, whittling, and engraving the stuff we call scrimshaw work today. He carved, shaped, and decorated everything imaginable, usually from a slab or fragment of whalebone, whale ivory, or some allied substance from the carcass of a denizen of the briny deep. Incidentally, he sometimes used beef and hog bones from salt beef and pork.

Drinking mugs. Corset stays. Pie cutters. Toggles. Snuffboxes. Inkwells. Pictures of the ship scratched on a slab of peeled whale ivory. Paper knives. Powder horns. Plates. Skewers. Needle cases. Sailors made these afloat and even when marooned on shore between voyages. A knife or two, some sharp sailmakers' needles, and some tar to blacken his cut and etched lines were all he needed for his work. And work he did. There is a great deal of very good scrimshaw and not all of it is anchored to New England. In spite of Yankee supremacy in our early Merchant Marine, sailors got around a lot more than the shipowners.

Scrimshaw has been found in all our Atlantic ports as far South as Savannah, at various Gulf ports, and in San Francisco. Incidentally, no little amount of it may still be found in the Windward and Leeward islands. It has been found in Hong Kong. Then, again,

the lucky ladies who, it seems, were invariably the recipients of this sailors' work, didn't
always marry the sailor but more often a land-
lubber who at least stayed home except on
Saturday nights. Yet the lady cherished the
scrimshaw, and so some of it was carried to
Ohio, Michigan, Illinois, and Indiana. From
there some of it moved still farther westward.
Learning to like scrimshaw enough to collect
it has been compared to cultivating a liking
for olives. You must like the first piece in
order to buy a second piece. Be that as it may,
the pieces here reproduced were liked very
much by the people who owned them.

Most scrimshaw was made between 1790
and 1840, but some dating back to 1720 is
known. With the advent of steam power for
ships, scrimshaw work seems to have stopped.
Jackknife carving and ship-model making took
its place. But some scrimshaw exists that is
obviously of much later date than even 1865.
When it is carved and scratch engraved with
scenes, curlicues, love emblems, initials, and
what not, it is worth collecting, worth owning, and worth keeping.

60

Paper Cutwork

THIS decorative minor art, practiced by both men and women, seems to have had its beginning in the seventeenth century, deriving, perhaps, from attempts to duplicate patterns for linen cutwork in paper. Often a sheet of paper was folded once and the cutting made to form a symmetrical design when opened. Sometimes each element was cut separately and the design assembled by securing the joints with wax or paste. Many valentines and other love tokens were made of cutwork, further embellished with pen drawings and verses. Sometimes these were intricately folded in star, wheel, and labyrinthine patterns. Within the category of cutwork also fall cutwork watch papers: small disks of paper used to "pad" the space between the inner and outer cases of the turnip watches of the eighteenth and nineteenth centuries. Making these cutwork elegancies and conceits persisted as an indoor pastime well into the nineteenth century. There was a revival about 1900.

English designs in cutwork found in Philadelphia include many patterns once believed to be exclusively Pennsylvania-German. The same designs are noted on the fashionable quilted petticoats worn by wealthy women of the Quaker City in 1750. But cutwork was not peculiar to any locale. It was made everywhere. Because of its fragile nature, only a small percentage of the original production remains. But what does remain now has its

devotees; it is collected and cherished by a small company which seems to be increasing in size.

Much cutwork is often found nesting between the pages of old books, particularly Bibles. The several examples here shown as silhouettes are actually made of now faded red, yellow, and green papers. The dates are 1740 to 1840. No commentators on antiques seem to have given this vagary any attention. Therefore, we have no list of reference books to suggest. But we do have this to recommend: hunt out the superlatively fine pieces of cut-paper work in your own community or locale; save it; collect it. One day it will come into its own and you will be none the poorer.

61

Paper Dolls

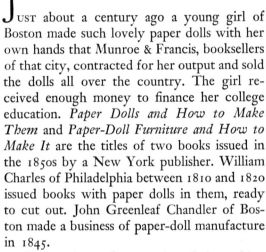

J UST about a century ago a young girl of Boston made such lovely paper dolls with her own hands that Munroe & Francis, booksellers of that city, contracted for her output and sold the dolls all over the country. The girl received enough money to finance her college education. *Paper Dolls and How to Make Them* and *Paper-Doll Furniture and How to Make It* are the titles of two books issued in the 1850s by a New York publisher. William Charles of Philadelphia between 1810 and 1820 issued books with paper dolls in them, ready to cut out. John Greenleaf Chandler of Boston made a business of paper-doll manufacture in 1845.

These various efforts motivated the making of innumerable paper dolls by girls between the ages of seven and seventeen. Not a few rather sophisticated ones were also made by adult ladies and gentlemen—just for fun. Then large-scale production began. Manufacturers sold paper dolls in packs, through variety and fancy-good stores. Now the entire production, handmade and factory-made, is an object of collecting interest. History, as history will if we dig deeply enough, comes up with information. Paper dolls, originally called "*pantins*," were exclusively an adult conceit in the eighteenth century. Everything from the hilarious to the lascivious, from the political lampoon to the ecclesiastic lampoon, was made as a paper doll. Fops and ladies of leisure in-

THE GIRLS' DELIGHT

PAPER FURNITURE

(Number One.)

FOR PAPER DOLLS

sisted upon showing a new one every day. In case you are disposed to say "tsk, tsk," you may be interested to know that a small collection consisting of some hundred American paper dolls made about 1850 was sold in 1943 for the tidy sum of $250. That proves the collecting vogue for them isn't just starting. It is going. Only thus far it has had no publicity.

There is now a monograph being written on the subject of American paper dolls by a direct descendant of America's first paper-doll manufacturer. Of course handmade paper dolls, carefully drawn and colored, with at least three changes of costume, are much preferred. If they are dated, all the better, but quite frequently the costumes are a fair indication of date. The manufactured ones are preferred in the original envelopes. Our illustrations include examples of the handmade and factory-made dolls, a few of the original envelopes used to market the manufactured articles, and a few of the commercially produced dolls.

62

Weather Vanes

THE historical significance of weather vanes appears to have been appreciated for more years than the subject would have you think. Perhaps this is because weather vanes were out in the open, and when the oldest resident of a neighborhood began to tell tales about how the weathercock on such and such a building had been there in his grandfather's time, the people began to reverence these old playthings of the four winds. Weathercocks, so called because they were frequently an effigy of the cock which crew when Peter told his lie about Christ, were used in America, especially on churches, meetinghouses, and town halls, in the seventeenth century. One of the most interesting of weather vanes now preserved was set up by William Penn, Samuel Carpenter, and Caleb Pusey on their gristmill at the former Swede's Settlement Upland (Upsala), now Chester, Pennsylvania, in 1699. This vane is of pierced iron, and is of Tudor pattern.

Bannerets, fish, cocks, lambs, and other objects were formed into vanes during the eighteenth century. But still the chief use was for installation on the church, public building, meetinghouse, or mill. With the ruralization of America, and the development of organized farming, between 1800 and 1875, the use of the weather vane spreads. Barns, stables, mills, as well as the former traditional carriers of vanes, began to sport a wider variety of weather tellers. Famed running, trotting, and racing horses; fire-fighting equipment; horsecars; steamboats; locomotives; canalboats; clipper ships and sloops—all these appear on weather vanes. Then came the age of the really fancy vane—the vane made of sheet copper or zinc, not only in silhouette of the object, but showing the object in relief, and matching on both sides. These fancy vanes ranged in price from $50 to $250.

Today all these vanes are collected by gentlemen farmers who are restoring old estates, by museums, by collectors of metalwork, and by the rank and file of Americana enthusiasts. Our illustrations show the Penn-Carpenter-Pusey vane of 1699, a few eighteenth-century vanes, and at least six of the vanes popular between 1840 and 1880. The latter are drawn directly from the catalogue of the maker, and the maker is perhaps the only producer of what are now antiques who might have cause for disappointment at the prices his wares are bringing. His vanes, as antiques, are still, generally, under the prices he charged for them as new goods.

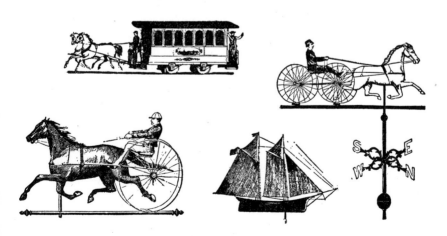

63

Jackknife Sculpture and Carving

Very few people gave a second thought to jackknife carvings as possible candidates for the accolade of antiques until somebody discovered—and promoted—the work of one Schimmel, a German hobo who, after the Civil War, did a heap of drinking and a heap of carving in and around Carlisle, Pennsylvania. Eagles were his specialty: copied mostly from the cast-iron eagles decorating building façades and the bowls of Dutch clay pipes which in those days sold for a penny at all crossroads stores. Then the late Jack Edgette discovered another archaic carver named Mountz who also worked with the jackknife in Pennsylvania. Now these caricatures of carving, these amateurish efforts at expression, are just about as popular, and a great deal scarcer, than pioneer paintings.

Happily, the Schimmel, Mountz, and other discoveries are not taken too seriously as yet. No appreciative twaddle, linking them with Praxiteles or Michelangelo, has as yet appeared. The sanest approach is, of course, the humorous one. They are humorous, these jackknife carvings, and somehow they seem right at home with pioneer and cottage furnishings. Thus they have a real place in the category of collectible Americana. Schimmel and Mountz are not necessarily names to conjure with. They just happen to have had the best publicity to date. Other jackknife carvers must

have worked in every county in every state of the Union, and their work, when as good —or as bad—as Schimmel's and Mountz's, is just as worthy of collecting.

The discovery of other such carvings is an event greatly to be desired. Especially if the name of the carver and his history can be revealed. It is likely that in Ohio, Tennessee, Indiana, West Virginia, and Kentucky, plenty of ne'er-do-wells had the time and the patience to do such carving. Here, then, is another new field of antiquing open to you. Search for curious jackknife carvings, especially of birds, beasts, statues, and busts. Seek, too, far better carvings by carpenters and cabinetmakers. You can have much fun in this field, and it is still wide open. The illustrations of the work of Schimmel and Mountz here shown include also a drawing of a cast-iron eagle copied by Schimmel and a clay-pipe eagle which he may well have used as a model. The iron eagle is about 1850. The pipe eagle about 1875.

64

Daguerreotype Cases

LOUIS J. M. DAGUERRE (1789–1851) was a French artist who all acquaintances thought was crazy. He was attempting, in the 1830s, to make permanent the images in mirrors. He succeeded. And thus the daguerreotype and photography were given to the world. The first daguerreotypes were, literally, mirrors in which the image was fixed by the action of light on silver salts. The real daguerreotype must be viewed at a slight angle in order to see the image clearly. In certain lights it is more a mirror than a picture—a mirror with a ghostly vision of the individual whose clear image is there under different light. Parenthetically, I have always wondered why this mirror picture was not made in large size for use as a mirror *and* a picture. What romantic connotations, and what a business there would have been in them! In fact, there may be a big business lurking in the idea, even now.

There are collectors of daguerreotypes of famous people; there are collectors of daguerreotypes as examples of early photography; and there are collectors of daguerreotype cases. The last-named group of collectors is by far the greatest in number, even though some of them make cigarette boxes and compacts of the cases. What they are collecting is, literally, America's first plastic product as the term plastic is used today. Actually, daguerreotype cases as made in America between 1848 and 1860 are shining examples of fine mold modeling and mighty fine plastic casting, curing, and finishing. The plastic used was gutta-percha (from the Malayan *gëtah*—gum, and *përca*—the tree yielding the gum which, hardening on contact with the air, can again be softened in hot water). This gum, pigmented, fortified with wood flour and other ingredients, became, in the hands of our ingenious craftsmen, the bakelite of that day. Every daguerreotype made in the late 1840s and up to 1855, at least, had its plastic molded case. Daguerrean galleries sprang up like mushrooms all over America. Miniature painters, rather than be put out of business by the new art, learned daguerreotypy and made miniatures on mirror glass for the masses.

Cases in a variety of designs not yet classified, and perhaps not even in process of classification, are now, under the gentle stimulus of collecting, coming to light. Sentiment down through the years has preserved them. Now they are American antiques, and a little boom is due to break in their trade. Historic, sentimental, memorial, political, trade, fraternal, patriotic, baroque, rococo, and other patterns; valentine, Christmas, and Easter designs; designs inspired by popular singers and songs—all these are known. But that is subjective knowledge. What is needed is objective knowledge—just how many different designs of each kind or class were made? You can add something to this subject if you will scout your surrounding countryside for these cases and tabulate your collection. Also, you can do some research into who made daguerreotypes in your home town, or any other town, and record that. If, by any chance, you discover there was a daguerreotype-case manufacturer in your locale, you can delve into that firm's history. Meantime, you can contemplate this single item of Americana; can revel in the fact that every kind of human being, from babe in arms to luscious damsel, from young lad to the cantankerous (and superstitious) grandfather who refused to have his visage captured by any devil's contraption and posed with his back to the camera, is now to be found.

Daguerreotype cases are known in so many patterns that the following are mentioned only to give some idea of the variety: Coming of Saint Nicholas, Capture of André, Washington Crossing the Delaware, Liberty, Masonic, Odd Fellow (a lodge), Hibernian, Heart, Cupid and Scroll, Seashell, Forget-me-Not, Jenny Lind, Eagle, Shield and Stars, and Union Forever. But this, after all, is a primer. If these notes intrigue you, you'll be beyond them in a few weeks and having good fun. You may even help to write the up-to-now-unwritten book about these minor though delightful relics of a day when all America was up and coming, expanding and indulging in free enterprise with a vengeance.

65

Illustrated Merchandise Catalogues

Fifteen years ago these items were almost entirely disregarded except by farsighted historical research workers. There were not enough researchers to keep watch on the entire country, so innumerable early merchandise catalogues and trade lists, with woodcut illustrations, were burned or sold as old paper. This is a great pity, because now we know there is no surer guide to the dating, making, and distribution of many antiques than the catalogues and trade lists of those who made them. Almost all that is known about pressed glass, Bennington pottery, weather vanes, and similar objects derives from data and illustrations in trade catalogues. Several notable collections now exist. The New York Historical Society, Harvard University, The Metropolitan Museum, and other institutions recognize the value of these catalogues and are continually adding to their collections. So also are many private collectors.

Few catalogues and trade lists are known of issue prior to 1790. Button makers and clockmakers then made up trade lists. By 1840 a considerable few makers were issuing catalogues. By 1850 there was fairly general publication. By 1876 it was an epidemic. The most valuable of trade catalogues are of course those dealing with things collected today: pictures (Currier & Ives, Prang, and other lithographers), glass, pottery, china, stoves, buttons, lamps, weather vanes, stable fittings, woodenwares, silverwares, watches and clocks, butter molds, kitchen utensils, cast-iron goods, toys, hollow ware, chairs (fancy, Windsor, and Boston rockers), and stencils.

Type founders' catalogues are particularly desirable because most of them picture more stock cuts for newspaper illustrations than type. Type catalogues date from about 1790 and are collected as of so late a date as 1880. Early catalogues are today obtainable at old bookstores, priced from $1.00 upward to as much as $100 for a fine type founder's catalogue. But the great thrill is to find a basket or boxful of them ready to be thrown out by some old drugstore or specialty shop. There is but one thing to do: grab and run!

66

Trade Cards and Craftsmen's Labels

The importance of labels was pointed with painful accuracy when, at a public auction sale, a very fine piece of Chippendale period furniture sold at a record price. The buyer, upon examination, discovered a label pasted under one of the drawers. On that label, a very nice bit of engraving, was the name and address of the maker. That so accurately identified the piece that the next time it was sold, the auction price made the entire collecting world gasp in amazement. It brought more than three times the high price that had once been paid for it as a fine antique. Therefore, any book, piece of furniture, cased instrument, or cased silver that is labeled with the maker's name or trade card is considered the last and final word in desirability.

Trade cards were distributed by our eighteenth-century artisans and craftsmen for very much the same purpose as trade advertising and promotion by direct mail are used today: to drum up trade; to impress the possible customer. The most highly regarded trade cards are the engraved ones. But printed ones are not ignored. Any eighteenth-century trade card is worth keeping; any billhead, or any label.

In 1850–70, and particularly after the Centennial Exposition at which millions of trade cards and catalogues were distributed to visitors, American women took up a new pas-

time: pasting the trade, courtesy, and compliment cards of shops, stores, and products in albums. Today these albums are collected. Some collectors remove the pages and carefully soak off the cards, refiling them according to types, trades, and subjects. One charming lady has collected a quarter of a million or so, all different, has filed them in huge folios, presented them to a great institution of historic lore, and spends half of every working day with the collection as curator, without pay. Her hobby has given her an interest in life that is a joy to her and to all who know her and who avail themselves of the usefulness of the collection she has assembled. Pictured here are trade cards and labels dating from 1766 to 1876.

U. S. Card Collector's Catalog, by J. R. Burdick.

67

American and European
Pottery and Porcelain

IF EVER there was an avocation so specialized as to verge upon a profession, it is collecting pottery and porcelain. That is, collecting these objects so purposefully as to acquire as much knowledge about the wares as one acquires specimens for the collection. Porcelain was first tried as an American venture by Bonnin and Morris of Philadelphia in the latter half of the eighteenth century. This ware is so rare (and it isn't true porcelain) that only a few marked specimens are known to exist. But by 1825 William E. Tucker of Philadelphia started a porcelain factory that achieved considerable production of what is called soft paste—not the hard-bodied porcelain of China. Tucker cannot be chided for that. Almost all that we have in the way of English china and Dutch delft is just an attempt to imitate the porcelain of China. We do, however, have Tucker's American porcelain, and delightful ware it is. It is mostly in French patterns, richly gilded, and delightfully colored. What we need now is a good book about Tucker porcelain to tell us more about the ware, with several hundred good pictures of it.

Bennington Pottery, made at Bennington, Vermont, by various potteries during the middle years of the nineteenth century, achieved wide distribution and sale. Catalogue-like billheads of this ware reveal that you could buy most anything in Bennington ware, from a birdbath to a butter churn—pitchers, vases, figures, jugs, pots, pans, and jars. Bennington turned out a good Parian ware—pottery that looks very much like marble, and a glazed, mottled ware called Rockingham, after the pottery in England which seems first to have developed it.

Lusterware, from the crushed-strawberry variety that is Sunderland to the platinum called silver and the copper called by its rightful name, has been an item of collectors' interest for many decades. Made originally to simulate gold and silver vessels, it soon achieved general appreciation for its intrinsic merit and beauty. Silver-resist luster is considered the finest, although collecting the pink of Sunderland is said to be the mark of connoisseurship. Luster is probably of Eastern origin. It was introduced into Spain by the Moors about the eighth century, or earlier. Persian lusters dating from the fifth century are known. Gold oxide yields a pink luster; platinum oxide yields silver; and copper oxide yields a gold color, from bronze to bright.

In England, after the advent of William and Mary, the potters of Staffordshire became intrigued by what the Dutch had done in imitation of Chinese wares, and to their knowledge of red-ware making they added attempts at china making. The result was the development of an English china, porcelain, and pottery industry that startled the entire world, and a production of so many kinds and types of ware that, to become a collector, you must first become a student. Therefore, the sole contribution of merit this primer can give is the list of suggested books for further study. If the list looks formidable, take heart—there is fun lurking in every one of them.

Spode and His Successors, by Arthur Hayden.
Artificial Soft Paste Porcelain, by Edwin Atlee Barber.
Bow, Chelsea and Derby Porcelain, by William Bemrose.
Bristol Porcelain, by Frank Hurlbutt.
A Century of Potting in Worcester, by R. W. Binns.
The Ceramics of Swansea and Nantgarw, by William Turner.
Chelsea Porcelain Toys, by G. E. Bryant.
China Collecting in America, by Alice Morse Earle.
Collecting Old English Lustre, by J. R. Hodgdon.
Collecting Old Lustre, by W. Bosanko.
Early American Pottery and China, by John Spargo.
Josiah Wedgwood and His Pottery, by William Burton.
Lead Glaze Pottery, by Edwin Atlee Barber.
Potters and Potteries of Bennington, by John Spargo.
Pottery and Porcelain of the United States, by Edwin Atlee Barber.
Delftware, Dutch and English, by N. Hudson Moore.
Shenandoah Pottery, by A. H. Rice and John Baer Stoudt.
English Earthenware and Stoneware, by A. H. Church.
Practical Book of Chinaware, by Eberlein & Ramsdell.
The Book of Pottery and Porcelain, by Warren E. Cox, Jr.

The magazine *Antiques,* the *American Collector,* and the *Antiquarian* have, in the past, published monographs on certain small American potteries. Students can refer to the cumulative indices of these various publications at libraries having complete files and thus delve into what might be called the byways and lanes of potting in the United States and the Colonies. Certain but by no means all of the small colonial and nineteenth-century American potteries are listed in the Glossary. Not until a complete research undertaking on Americana production is completed will we know just how many potteries were in operation here. A conservative estimate would be 1,000!

68

Early American Packages

A BOUT every five years the American public becomes conscious of some new and interesting accomplishment achieved by Americans of the past. Then there is quite a scramble to collect the relics of the accomplishment. Perhaps it was the fanfare that accompanied the new art of package designing in the booming 1920s that started a few courageous souls peering into our past for early American packages. Maybe somebody got mad at the crass statements made by designers who decried everything old, and decided to prick some so-and-so stuffed shirt. At any rate all this, and more, was accomplished with the result that today it can be said, "There is no dentrifice package, no shaving-soap package, no perfume bottle, no soapbox, or even can or jar of preserved food, packaged so delightfully and artistically as were the perfumes, the soaps, the *crèmes*, the fruits, and vegetables sold in American shops and stores a hundred to a hundred and fifty years ago."

Broad as that statement may sound, it can be, and is, backed up by the packages. As one collector recently said to a modern designer, "Look at these first, then look at your red face in that awful 'modern' mirror you thought was so good last year." Thus far only two short articles on this subject have appeared in print. But collecting goes on ever so quietly. Discreet advertisements are now appearing in popular magazines of the antique

SCOTCH SNUFF

PETER & GEORGE LORILLARD
No 42 CHATHAM·
NEW YORK

field reading "WANTED: Old plugs of tobacco, old bottles and jars; any early packages; must have original labels." Here shown
are a few such packages.

Research in this branch of antiques reveals
that all sorts of shaving soaps and creams, perfumes, toilet soaps, snuffs, tobacco, spices, coffee, tea, salt, herbs, nutmegs, pickled oysters,
brandied fruits, ginger, and condiments were
packed in containers of delightful quality.
Merchants' boxes, in which men's hats and
ladies' bonnets and frocks were packed, were
gaily decorated with wallpaper and tied with
ribbons. Many of the labels were engraved.

There is a turned-wood collar box, for patented
plastic collars, made by A. Goodyear and Son
that has an engraved label showing the seal
of every one of the thirteen original states.
Taylor of Philadelphia packed his shaving
soap in a china box with a cover showing
Washington crossing the Delaware. The round
label on the Hazard Powder Company's brilliant red flask of Kentucky Rifle Gunpowder
is engraved from a sketch by Catlin, the famed
American artist-sportsman.

"Were our early American manufacturers
package-stupid?" is a foolish question. They
employed the best—not vociferous second-
rate—craftsmen to design their packages and
labels. They hired the best engravers. Paul
Revere engraved tradesmen's labels. Kneass
engraved package labels. Artists designed the
stencils used in decorating tea boxes and spice
boxes. And in doing this our early manufacturers and tradesmen were creating antiques
for us to collect. The owner of a chain of

super-markets started collecting early packages a score of years ago. Now he has a complete early store, stocked with the packaged
merchandise of a century ago. When he de-
sires to arouse interest in and boost sales of
present-day products in one of his markets,

he sends over a display of old packages from his antique store.

What happens? You guessed it! Sales go up, and up. Here is another field still wide open to you who would become collectors. For a very small budget you can start right, selecting only the best of packages, and in less than a year, if you are diligent and patient, you will have, if not a collection, at least the nucleus of one. Depending upon where you are, you can collect early packages dating from 1760 to 1860. Your richest finds will probably date in the 1840s and 1850s. No effort has been made as yet to date these packages, perhaps because everybody knows the facts are buried somewhere in the town and county records. It isn't hard to locate a manufacturing concern and date it. You can double the value of your collection if you collect the facts about every old package you find and buy and keep.

69

Cast-Iron Mechanical Banks

Production of these began, in a very small
way, in 1870. More were made by 1880. By
1890 almost all the small-iron foundries—the
foundries casting small things—were either
making mechanical toy banks or making parts
for some other maker. They're not antique in
any sense of the word. Properly, they are toys
of the mid-Victorian and late-Victorian eras.
But they now engage the interest of an enthusiastic crew of collectors which includes
bank and corporation presidents, bigwigs,
stage and screen stars, and just people.

If you are prone to laugh, or even sneer,
go out and buy a Punch-and-Judy bank. Or
try to buy a Harlequin-and-Columbine bank,
made as late as 1910. You'll be amazed, not
only at the price, but at what happens to you
when you start to play with the banks. That's
how the collecting vogue started. Only it isn't
a vogue. It is an exclusive avocation. Seasoned
bank collectors run regular campaigns of
"want ads" in an attempt to collect every
bank ever made. Their correspondence is said
to keep several highly paid secretaries busy
after hours.

It is a great pity that at this point in time
the really definitive book on these banks cannot be listed. It is scheduled for publication
in 1945 or 1946. Louis Hertz is doing it, and
he begins by saying, "No bibliography is given
in this work for the simple reason that no
literature as yet exists on the subject." Mr.
Hertz has corresponded with every one-time

maker of these mechanical banks, whether or not the makers are still in business. He has visited many foundries and done research on the spot, delving in company files and pattern piles. He has listed every bank ever patented and every bank ever made. He has the maker's original pictures of every bank. So you have at least one book to wait for that will be definitive in respect of one subject—Mechanical Toy Banks of Cast Iron.

It is not hard to understand why these banks appealed to youngsters. Each one gave a little show for the penny deposited in it. This proved to be far more effective than moral maxims or stern admonitions. They moved. They did things. And they could be opened with a screw driver in emergency.

With all of these plus factors, it is no wonder so many of them were made, and in so great a variety. Some of these banks are quite decorative as table pieces, notably the Eagle bank (eagle feeding a nest of young with the penny), which is well-articulated and beautifully cast. Even the tiny eaglets raise their heads and open their mouths as the mother bird bends forward, raising her wings. Within the bank there is a little bellows which also "peeps" when the bank goes into action. The Uncle-Sam bank is quite appropriate. So is the one called Atlas, which shows the ancient giant supporting the earth. The trolley-car and sewing-machine banks, of course, reflect a popular interest in inventions; so also the "camera" bank which, it is said, was withdrawn from circulation because several camera companies objected to it. The Independence-Hall bank obliges with a peal from the Liberty Bell when a penny is dropped in it. Scores of comic banks—from the whale swallowing Jonah to a darky doing a somersault in a cabin doorway in order to kick the penny into the bank, are known.

These toys were sold at from seventy-five cents to $1.50 each. Some have as many as fifteen to twenty separate bits of casting, all of which had to be assembled, articulated, and fitted with various levers and springs, then painted, and boxed. Mrs. Ina Hayward Bellows in 1940 wrote a monograph on these banks and what she had learned about them in her experience as a collector and dealer. Mrs. Bellows classes the Harlequin and Columbine, Man-in-the-Chair, Circus Rider, Snake-and-Frog, 49-er (Gold Digger's Mule), Freedman's Bank (darky at a table), Woodpecker, Milking Cow, Little Red Riding Hood, John Bull, and Merry-go-Round (carousel) banks as valued at from $40 to $75 each. Values quoted in any book on antiques or near antiques are a hazardous addition. Information as to prices and values is and can only be current as of the moment they are put down. They may change tomorrow. And almost always they do change, up or down, as the case may be. If the top hundred bank collectors quit collecting tomorrow and put their collections up at auction next month, their action would do two things: (1) set new price levels, and (2) upset the market for some time.

Inflation is easy in antiques because there are just so many. When these little banks were being bought by dealers at fifty cents and sold for a dollar or two, the surface supply was quickly skimmed off. Then the prices went up. The minute they did, and news got around that the banks were bringing five and even ten dollars, innumerable attics were searched for cast-iron banks. A new supply reached the market. New examples came to light. The boom was on.

What are these banks *worth* today? Two prices: what you can get for one from a reputable dealer or collector, and what you must pay for one if you go to buy it. Conceivably

that price may be the same, but it seldom is.
A collector may well pay you what you'd
have to pay, if he wants your bank. But a
dealer? No. He is in business. He will pay the
equivalent of the wholesale price and rightfully expect a hundred per cent mark up.
Until the definitive book on these banks is
published, and it will not quote prices or values, you will do well to study the book listed
below. Mrs. Bellows deserves more than a
round of applause for tackling this subject in
1940 and in making a little book that tells a
good story in words and pictures.

Old Mechanical Banks, by Ina Hayward Bellows.

70

Buttons

Here is a present-day collecting vogue which would have been laughed to scorn a score of years ago. The sniffs from even the most amateurish of collectors would have been loud enough to be heard everywhere. But now there are not even patronizing smiles. Instead, the wise collectors are now, as usual, going after what might be termed the masterpieces among buttons: the silver, gold, pewter, brass, and glass buttons of the seventeenth, eighteenth, and early nineteenth centuries. Buttons of the sort that were made in celebration of Lafayette's visit to America. Gold buttons made by American goldsmiths. Military buttons used on uniforms of Continental troops. Buttons that trimmed the dresses of fair ladies, the somber garb of Pilgrim and Puritan, the gay waistcoats of Virginia and Maryland gentlemen, the rich Quakers of Pennsylvania, the Dutch burghers of New York and Albany.

The rank and file of collectors are content with the brass, glass, pottery, and composition buttons of the late eighteenth and nineteenth centuries, from 1790 to 1901. In that span of years button makers broke the commandments of the Decalogue and the Koran "to make no images in the likeness of anything in the heavens above or the earth beneath." They pictured everything in buttons and on buttons. Birds, beasts, flowers, insects, objects, portraits. An alphabetical list of subjects would fill many pages of a big book. The subvarieties under each classification make one reel. It is believed that a collection of a quarter of a million buttons—all different—is readily within the realm of possibility. Collecting goes on at a dizzy pace. The button booths at antique shows are busier than any other booths. Trade is better than brisk. Supply, apparently, is unlimited. This is largely because women for years have been collecting buttons for household emergency use. Some caches of ten thousand have been found. A string of buttons was in almost every American home when the craze for collecting buttons as antiques began. Now the button strings are revealed as having value.

Buttons that were just buttons in 1936 are today selling at from fifty cents to $5.00 each. The subjects that are most likely to retain their value are, naturally, the historic buttons, or the superlatively beautiful ones, such as the small ones made in the same manner and style as glass paperweights. These are now being fashioned into ear ornaments. Wedgewood buttons are highly desirable. Any button with a ship, a locomotive, a balloon, the portrait (painted or sculptured) of a famous man or woman, is really good. But button enthusiasts need no guiding, by primer or otherwise. They, as a group, follow their own inclinations, and if they derive suggestions from others, within a few days the suggestion is their own discovery. Therefore, the best service this primer can render is to advise the owner of any string or collection of old buttons to study what you have and separate the wheat from the chaff. Hold your good things as minor valuables and be glad that another one of your seemingly worthless possessions has been given value by the flight of time and collecting vogue. Unfortunately primers are not dictionaries, guidebooks, or encyclopedias. Therefore, we cannot illustrate the "1000 Best Buttons" nor have we the courage to attempt a showing of what, in our opinion, are the best twenty-five buttons. Here we can give only the quick facts and the directing impetus. There are several books listed for your further study if buttons appeal to you as something to collect. Each of these books is well illustrated.

The Button Collector's History, by Grace Horning Ford.
Button Handbook, by Florence Zacharie Ellis Nicholls.
A Button Collector's Journal [Vol. I and II], by Lillian Smith Albert.

71

Theatrical and Circus Posters

Y ES, these, too, are collectors' items of some
importance and have generated no little enthusiasm among a fairly wide group. One of
our famed university libraries has a rare collection of theatrical posters. A collector in
Texas now owns some twenty-four-sheet circus posters of the late nineteenth century.
The most desirable pieces, however, appear
to be single-sheet posters, varying in size from
small folio to elephant folio (see paper sizes in
the Glossary section) within these categories:
woodcut and engraving-illustrated posters of
1760 to 1850; lithographed and color-printed
posters of the 1850–80 period.

The first category was produced by the
printers selected by the theatrical company
or troupe and were filled in, either with type
or in longhand, for notation of the time, place,
and admission fee. The second category was
stock posters, made in great numbers by
poster printers for a wide variety of popular
pantomimes, playlets, dramas, et cetera. They
were sold at so much per dozen, or per hundred, to all comers.

George W. Childs of Philadelphia (1850-
80) seems to have been the great poster producer in the latter category. In 1869 he issued
a large catalogue of his posters, reproducing
all of them in miniature. This book is today
selling at from $75 to $150 per copy as an
antique of theatrical interest.

Houdini, who was an avid collector of

theatrical material, owned a copy of this book and prized it highly. Most poster collectors want it because it represents perhaps the first American catalogue of such material. The illustrations here shown are reproduced from the Childs' catalogue. If you locate, find, or own any such posters and have no personal interest in them, you can at least be sure that somewhere someone will want them, and consider them American antiques.

72

Local, Provisional, and Carrier's Postage Stamps

Mᴏʀᴇ ᴅᴏʟʟᴀʀs have been lost owing to disregard of these little items than any other objects of common possessions. Similarly, many owners have almost cut values to one quarter by soaking or cutting early stamps off the original envelopes or folders. Any early local stamp—stamps issued by private carriers of mail or to and from post offices to offices and homes—is worth twice to fifty times its value on the original envelope or cover. "On the cover" is proof of use, especially if there is some overlapping of the official cancellation.

Local stamps were issued and used from 1842 to 1882, in so many places and by so many companies that this primer lacks space to list them. Let it suffice to say they were in use in more than fifty cities and towns, and issued by more than one hundred concerns carrying mail. When the Federal Government decided to use stamps to indicate prepayment of postage, the duly-appointed postmasters were permitted to issue a semi-official or provisional stamp pending issue of the Government's own stamps. This was done by some twelve postmasters. Any letter or paper carrying one of these stamps is worth from $70 to $10,000. The first official carrier stamps were the Government's attempt to charge extra for carrier service to the door instead of the post office. There were two of them, the Eagle and the Franklin. They are worth from a few dollars for the Eagle to a good few hundred dollars for the Franklin. Provisional carrier stamps were also issued. Their value today makes a Queen Anne lowboy blush.

Missionaries from New England who settled and did very well in the Sandwich Islands or Hawaii instituted a postage system between the Islands and the United States. They issued stamps, some of which bear the legend H.I. & U.S.POSTAGE. Those stamps on original covers are worth a two-story house and lot. In fact, you could buy some New York City real estate with one of them. That should be enough from this primer on stamps. All that need further be said is that local, provisional, and carrier stamps are but a drop in the bucket of stamp knowledge and stamp collecting.

The annual Bible of stamp collecting and stamp values is Scott's *United States Stamp Catalogue*. This is recommended as required reading for all who have old stamps, or any United States postage stamps, used or unused. Even some of the quite late United States postage stamps are valuable. By study of Scott's catalogue you may well avoid the grievous error made by a Pennsylvania woman whose husband had collected entire sheets and blocks of postage stamps as an investment hobby. When she looked through his property after his death, she found a number of blocks of unused two-cent postage stamps with a card clipped to them, stating "these are good." She smiled sorrowfully. Anybody could see they were good. There was gum on them and everything. And they weren't old. She used them up. It was a great pity. They were blocks bearing pairs of five-cent errors, now worth from $15 to $30 each! So don't make a killing on some antiques and throw away a fortune by disregarding others. It pays to *know* that stamps, and especially United States postage stamps, are rare antiques.

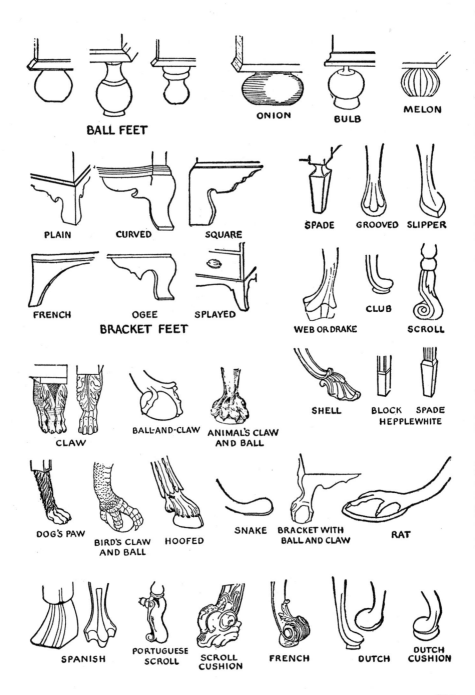

BALL FEET

ONION

BULB

MELON

PLAIN

CURVED

SQUARE

SPADE

GROOVED

SLIPPER

FRENCH

OGEE

SPLAYED

BRACKET FEET

WEB OR DRAKE

CLUB

SCROLL

CLAW

BALL-AND-CLAW

ANIMAL'S CLAW
AND BALL

SHELL

BLOCK
HEPPLEWHITE

SPADE

DOG'S PAW

BIRD'S CLAW
AND BALL

HOOFED

SNAKE

BRACKET WITH
BALL AND CLAW

RAT

SPANISH

PORTUGUESE
SCROLL

SCROLL
CUSHION

FRENCH

DUTCH

DUTCH
CUSHION

Glossary and Index

THE FOLLOWING Glossary of antique terms and Early American names for objects and services includes also entries referring to the various sections of this primer. Therefore, the Glossary also serves as an Index. Terms referring to antiques are usually defined in their accepted, present-day meaning; terms for things, services, et cetera, as used by our ancestors are defined in their contemporaneous meaning, current when the word was in common usage.

ACETARRE: A salad of herbs and cresses. Seventeenth century.

ACHAUFFE: To warm. Hence achauffing dish; warming dish, heating plate.

ACHAT: Agate.

ACORN CLOCK: Nineteenth-century clock in a case of acorn shape.

ACOSTA'D: Mended china and glass. Term derives from Jacob D. Acosta, eighteenth-century china and glass mender of New York, who also invented the cement he used.

ADAM, (Robert, and Brothers): Mid-eighteenth-century English architects and designers who achieved high place and who established the furniture style which supplanted Chippendale in England and from which Hepplewhite got his inspiration. See section on Adam-style furniture, page 21.

ADAMANTINE, ADAMITE: Of the earth, hard, rocklike; a sort of hard composition plaster used in making decorative furniture, clock and mirror mounts, in eighteenth century.

ADEC: Vinegar of milk; soured whey.

ADOBE: Clay plaster. From the Arabic at-tob. Used in monolithic (solid) walls and in form of bricks, as well as coating over wickerwork, wattles, et cetera.

AGATE GLASS: Brownish-purple glass streaked with milk white, imitating rock agate.

AGATEWARE: Pottery veined and mottled to resemble natural agate.

AGUE TREE: Sassafras. Bark and leaves used medicinally.

AIR TWIST: Spiral formation drawn out from bubbles of air in stem of glassware.

AJOURE: Pierced, as carving, modeled pottery, and porcelain, silver, et cetera.

ALABASTER: Sulphate of lime, a translucent mineral used in carving forms, boxes, vases, statuary, et cetera.

ALAMODE: A kind of taffeta.

ALAY: To mix; to reduce.

ALBATA: Alloy of nickel, copper, and zinc, yielding a silvery white metal.

ALBESPYNE: The white hawthorn.

ALBURN: A whitish brown, taupe, or pale tan color. Alburn tree is viburnum.

ALCHEMY: Alloy of copper and tin; used in the sixteenth and seventeenth centuries for making spoons and plates.

ALCOVE BEDSTEAD: Bed in a box or cupboard; bed in a recess or niche.

ALEBERRY: Ale boiled with spices and bread sops, sugared.

ALE FIRKIN: Eight gallons.

ALE YARD: Excessively long, tubular drinking glass, thirty-six inches long.

ALFORD & Co. CHAIRS: Hitchcock chairs made by Alford & Co., successors to Hitchcock. Fancy chairs, factory-made. Rush-seated, painted, and stenciled. Made after 1844.

ALGATE HOLE: Small recess in walls of fireplace to hold tinder, matches, unguents, tobacco, et cetera.

ALKANET OIL: Early furniture polish made of linseed oil in which alkanet root had been boiled.

ALLENDALE: Variety of bedspread or counterpane, imported from England. Early nineteenth century.

ALL FOURS: A card game. ALL-FOURS TABLE: A table on which this game was played.

ALLISON FURNITURE: One of Duncan Phyfe's peers in New York, 1800–33. Much Allison furniture is so fine it was once attributed to Phyfe. Allison marked some of his work with a punch stamp.

ALLSPICE: Jamaica peppercorns.

ALMODZA: Tin. Tinware.

ALTO-RELIEVO: Figures in sculptured friezes, et cetera, projecting at least one half of their diameter, or normal, relative thickness, are called alto-relievo.

ALQUIFOU: Potter's lead ore which provided a green glaze.

ALYZ, ALYCE: A kind of cloth. Once a very rich cloth, with threads of gold.

AMADOW: Touchwood, tinder. Made from fungus boiled in lye and dried with saltpeter. Quickfire was another name. Used in tinderboxes, fire mills, et cetera.

AMATORII: Portrait-decorated plates given as love tokens.

AMBRIE, AMBRY, AMRY, ALMERY, AUMBRY, ET CETERA: Shelves with doors; early cupboards. Any closed or closable piece of furniture. Name appears to have been synonymous with almonry.

AMBRIE CAUL: A cover piece (textile) for cupboard.

AMBROTYPE: Similar to daguerreotype, the picture being on thin film, floated on the glass.

AMELCORN: All edible grains were once called corn. Amelcorn was of a size between wheat and barley, but "faultie, like unto spelt." Spelt was the "corn" of European peasants. Brought to America by German immigrants. Amelcorn is believed to have been once called camel corn; grain fodder for camels.

AMERICAN KINGS: Name given to the lithographic portraits issued by Doggett of Boston (lithographed by Pendleton), size 19¼ × 16¼, of Washington, Adams, Jefferson, Madison, and Monroe, from

paintings by Gilbert Stuart. Stones were prepared by Maurin of Paris. Also name given a set of playing cards in which the first four Presidents were pictured as the kings.

AMIANTHUS: Mineral flax; asbestos.

AMPELITES: Candle coal; cannel coal.

AMPULLE, AMBOLLY, AMPULE: Small glass or pottery vessel for holding ointment.

AMYDON: Starch deriving from fine wheat flour, steeped in water, strained, sun-dried, and rerolled. A sort of early cake flour and thickener for broths.

ANAPES: A kind of fustian cloth.

ANATTO: Yellow color obtained from alumina or alum. Later obtained from pulp of the seeds of anatto tree. The vegetable kind used in coloring butter and cheese, as well as cloth dyeing.

ANCHOR: A measure of ten gallons.

ANDERSON CARPETS: Hiram Anderson (1840), dealer in carpets, marked his stock with his name. He sold Brussels, ingrain, and other carpets at 99 Bowery, New York, but was not a maker of carpets.

ANDIRONS, AUNDIRON, ET CETERA: Ornamental and utilitarian irons to hold logs in burning. Earliest ones are joined with a hooped, serrated band, the dogs, or standards, facing in opposite directions. These were used on the round hearths placed in center of room and logs were rested on the crossbar from both sides. When the hearth with direct flue connection to chimney was introduced, andirons were made in pairs and the logs placed across them. Early andirons of this type were huge pieces, generally of wrought iron. The seventeenth and eighteenth centuries marked the advent of brass, white metal, and even silver decoration of andirons, and the cutting down of fireplace sizes.

ANGEL: A seventeenth-century touch mark on pewter of fine quality and workmanship.

ANGEL BED: Open bed without posts; a day bed. Also a trundle bed.

ANIMATED TOY PISTOLS: Cap pistols of the same era as the cast-iron mechanical toy bank. Pulling trigger exploded cap and set cast-iron figures into some kind of action. Now collected by specialists in cast-iron toys. Many types. Period is 1880–1910.

ANNULAR-RINGED: A kind of clock in which a ring or band contains the chaptering (the hour numerals in order) and which revolves to place the proper hour under a fixed pointer. Movement usually cased in a globular housing, mounted upon supporting figures. A luxury clock. Scarce.

ANTHEMION: Honeysuckle forms used in cabinetwork, carved, inlaid, et cetera. It is a classical form, deriving from Egypt and Greece, revived by Adam, used by Hope, Sheraton, and others.

ANTIMACASSAR: Doily, tidy, or scarf, crocheted, knit, embroidered, et cetera, for placing on chair backs over upholstery, to protect the fabric from Macassar oil used by many men and women as hair dressing, 1825–75.

APOCRYPHAL: Classical term for designating a fake; anything spurious or of doubtful authenticity. Apocryphal mark (silver and pewter) is a mark of an old smith applied to unmarked silver in an effort to increase value.

APOSTLE SPOONS: Sets of twelve spoons having effigies of the Apostles on handles. These were made early in the seventeenth century and in almost every decade down to 1850. Since then they have been made as spurious early ones. Should never be purchased by amateurs without the unbiased opinion of experts. *Apostle Spoons*, by Charles G. Rupert, is recommended for study.

APOSTLE URN: Octagon-shaped water cooler or water urn, made by Bennington pottery (United States), on which was wrought or impressed a series of effigies of Apostles. Said also to exist in Staffordshire and other English pottery in form of urns, pitchers, et cetera.

APPLETON FURNITURE: Made by Nathaniel Appleton, of Salem, Massachusetts. Early nineteenth century. Fine furniture of Federal styles.

APPRENTICE'S DESK: Narrow desk on square or turned legs, with sloping front, surmounted with a closet section.

APRON: See Skirt.

ARABESQUE: Literally, an Arabian figure or pattern which, according to the Koran, is not made in likeness of anything in heaven above or earth beneath. Interlaced curves and intricate geometrical patterns. Name is also given to non-Arabic forms which include human figures, animals, birds, et cetera.

ARCADE, ARCADES, ARCADED: An arcade is a series of arches. Any border, rim, front, balustering, et cetera, characterized by a series of arches, is arcaded, no matter if under an inch high or if monumental in size.

ARCHITECT'S TABLE: A drawing table desk, having a flat section which lifts up from rear forming a slanting board, fixed by ratchets and adjustable. Made in prevailing styles from 1680 to 1840, and even later; 1750–1820 periods are most desirable.

ARGAND LAMP: Invented by Argand, a Swiss, 1783, having a round wick which provided for introduction of draft of air inside as well as around outside of wick. See section on lamps, page 109.

ARGYLE: Vessels of silver or other metal, similar to teapots, having an internal pocket into which a heated iron element was placed to keep contents hot.

ARK: A chest; specifically a large chest for meat and provender.

ARMENIAN STONE: Blue ocher; a paint pigment.

ARMILLARY: Skeletons of orbs; a series of rings arranged as a sundial.

ARMOIRE: Wardrobe, or portable closet. Often very elegant in style.

AROMATIC CANDLES: Early nineteenth-century tallow candles, the tallow impregnated with lavender, thyme, rosemary, et cetera. Perfume released when burned.

ARROW BACK: Refers to the spindles of Windsor-type chairs when having flattened section formed into arrows or arrow points.

ARSEDINE, ASSADEN, ORSADAY: Ornamental tinselwork. ASSAD: The same. Used as early as fifteenth century.

ARTICULUS: Articulated paper toy assemblies picturing crafts, trades, et cetera, and tasks of homely significance, sports, et cetera. Parts which move are connected with wires to the axle of a warm-air flywheel or spinner. When toy is placed over a warm-air register or beside a stovepipe, the current of warm air spins the wheel and the toy goes into action, running as long as the current of air is active. 1840–90.

ARTIFACT: Anything made by human hands, especially of stone, bone, metal, or clay; of great antiquity. Cycladian artifacts; Mayan artifacts; Amerind artifacts.

ASHBURTON GOBLET: Goblet pattern pressed in bold scalloped and other designs. Pressed by Sandwich and many other United States glass houses of nineteenth century.

ASH TRUG: Coal scuttle, coal hod.

ASS'S SKIN: Parchment made of ass's skin, used in tablets, pocket memo books, et cetera. Writing could be erased.

ASTRAGAL: Small convex or torus molding or beading, used as muntins to form a pattern for placing glass panels. The strips are rabbeted and glass is fixed with brads and putty. Known in a wide variety of curvate, saltire (x), and mathematical forms. Often seen on bookcase and cabinet doors. ASTRAGAL MOLDING: A small torus molding.

ASTRAL LAMP: Invented by Count Rumford. Oil from a central reservoir is conveyed to tubular arms holding Argand-type burners. Thus the arms could be brought over a book or other object and a bright light obtained without interference by lamp base.

AUBERGINE: A small upholstered sofa.

AUDUBON PRINTS: John James Audubon, naturalist, artist, taxidermist, who executed the magnificent series of birds of America, quadrupeds, et cetera, and who had his works published as colored prints in several editions which now, broken up, are collected as pictures. The first edition of the birds is in elephant folio.

AX MORTISE CHISEL: Name given by the late H. C. Mercer, of Doylestown, Pennsylvania, to the angular-handled mortising chisel brought to America by the Swedes (c. 1650), who used them in their mortised wooden (log) house construction. Very early type tool.

BABY CLOUT: Rag doll.

BACHELOR'S CHEST: Any chest of drawers for a man's use, and having in addition to its complement of drawers a sliding board under the top which, drawn out,

almost doubles the depth of top and provides space for making the toilet. Some such chests had folding tops.

BACKBOARD, BAKEBOARD: Thin board about twenty inches square, the surface cut crosswise in kerfs or grooves. A rather thin dough, or batter, was arranged on these boards, the kerfs preventing its slipping.

BACKBRON: Backlog.

BACKSTONE: Iron for cake baking, suspended over the fire. Hence the saying "walk like a cat on a hot backstone."

BACON DISH: Covered oblong or oval dish of silver or Sheffield plate, et cetera, fitted with a turned wood handle, for serving grilled bacon. From eighteenth century.

BACTILE: A candlestick.

BADGER: A peddler or huckster.

BAG SEWING TABLES: Sheraton-, Empire-, and Directoire-influenced Federal sewing stands with a fabric bag suspended from lower drawer to hold the work.

BAIL BRASS: Any drawer pull having a handle that is a "bail" or loop, affixed to two bosses on an escutcheon or plate. This type brass seems to have been first used on late William and Mary and early Queen Anne style furniture.

BAILE: A wooden canopy frame of bows, or bowed elements.

BAIL HANDLE: Drawer pull having a loop or bail affixed to two bosses without escutcheon or plate.

BAIN: A bath; a bathtub. A basin or pan for bathing.

BAIZE: Open woven cloth of serge family. Usually green.

BALEEN: Whalebone; also the knife used in splitting whalebone.

BALL-AND-CLAW FOOT: A talon or claw grasping a ball; a form used as a footing for cabinet furniture, tables, and chairs, of Chinese and early Roman origin.

BALL COVER: A large glass ball (hollow) used as cover for milk bowls. It is doubtful if these balls were so used, as they would penetrate deeply into any wide mouthed vessel they covered.

BALL FLOWER: Ball-shaped elements, ornamented with floral forms.

BALL FOOT: Any foot, or leg, ending in a ball, whether turned or carved. Many varieties. Term very loosely used except by meticulous experts.

BALTIMORE CHAIR: A spool-turned chair assumed to be peculiar to that city.

BALUSTER: Any turned, carved, or shaped element of vaselike form used as a leg, stem, or architectural member. Term said to derive from *balustra*, the pomegranate flower. INVERTED BALUSTER: Any standard form of baluster used invert, or upside down. BALUSTER BACK: Baluster split or sawed in half lengthwise, the flat sides used in chair backs and showing outline of the baluster form.

BAMBOO-TURNED: Turning of late type, in imitation of natural bamboo. Also used in a very refined form by Chippendale.

BAMBURY: From the French *bain-marie*, a large pan, used for hot water, in which other vessels were kept to keep contents warm. Also used as a bathtub.

BANDANA: Corruption of Bandhana, an Indian printed fabric in a repeat pattern of squares. These were cut apart and used as 'kerchiefs. Seventeenth to nineteenth centuries.

BANDBOX: Originally a box of thin band-sawed wood. Later of cardboard. Oval and round, painted, plain, and paper-covered.

BANDING: Veneer strip in contrasting color or pattern around table rims, drawer fronts, et cetera.

BAND KIT, BEN KIT, BOW KIT: Woodenware. A large vessel for pickling, storing grain, cheese, honey, et cetera. A utility piece.

BAND, BAND-DOOR: Hinge.

BANDY-LEGGED: Literally, bowlegged. The cabriole leg is often called bandy-legged in old inventories.

BANISTER: Same as Baluster.

BANISTER ROUNDABOUT: A master-type, two-decked back roundabout or corner chair, characterized by split banisters or balusters from seats to rail, and above rail in center to a supplementary top rail. Turned legs and posts. 1710–40. Quite scarce.

BANJO CLOCK: Simon Willard's patent timepiece, and imitations by other makers. An eight-day movement, weight-driven, very accurate, and beautifully cased in a banjo-shaped casing, embellished with side brasses, acorns, and eagles on top

of case, and painted tablets or panels of glass. See clock section, page 158.

BANKER: Ornamental cloth cover for a bench, chair back, or stool, cushion; a tapestry piece used as a cover, et cetera.

BANQUETTE: In 1824 day beds were so designated by Ackermann, the art publisher, in a directory of cabinet styles.

BAPTISMAL BOWLS: High, footed sugar bowls by Stiegel, Amelung, and other early glass blowers seem to have achieved this name because they were so used at times. It is extremely doubtful if baptismal bowls, as such, made of so fragile a material, were sold for family use. More probably syllabubs, which see.

BAQUET: Woodenware; a tub.

BARBOTINE: Thinned potter's clay used to decorate pottery. A kind of slip.

BARJIER CHAIR: Bergère chair. Farm chair.

BARLEYCORN: A measure; one third of an inch.

BARLOW KNIFE: A jackknife of early, sturdy type.

BARREL STOVE: Potbelly stove.

BARREL TABLE: A drum-type table with a deep drum, footed on four legs, or on tripod pedestal. Name is a variant of drum table.

BARTHOLOMEW: A gaudy doll.

BASALT WARE: Vitreous black pottery imitating the mineral basalt.

BASIN STANDS: Square, round, or triangular table frames, with galleries, drawers, and a place for holding a washbasin. Also stands commonly called wig stands, having a circular rim poised on three uprights, over which a round-rimmed washbasin was placed. Also called ewer tables and washstands.

BASKET SWIVEL CHAIR: Infant's school chair in late Windsor style, with seat mounted on a single iron support. Fitted with a basket at side for holding books, slates, et cetera. 1845–55.

BAS-RELIEF: When figures project less than one half their normal thickness from a carved or molded surface they are said to be in basso-relievo or bas-relief.

BASS: Inner rind of basswood tree bark used as rushes for seating chairs. BASS-BOTTOMED: Any chair so seated. A good soft wood of fine grain.

BASTING SPOON: Large spoon or ladle to gather melted fats and meat juices to pour over roasting meats.

BATH BRICKS: Soft fired clay bricks which, crushed into powder, were used to scour and polish.

BATSTO IRONWARE: Batsto furnace in west New Jersey, after 1776, made fishpots, cookpots, skillets, Dutch ovens, superior to those imported from Great Britain.

BATTER JUG: Spouted jug for pouring batter. Used in preparing the delicacy known as "cowlines." Batter was poured into hot fat in a continuous thin stream for baking or cooking in the hot fat as one long line. This was served up in lengths, with butter, sugar, and syrup.

BATTERSEA ENAMEL: Made at the short-lived factory of Stephen Janssen, Battersea, England, 1750–55. Jewel and patch boxes, knobs, lids, et cetera, of exquisite enamel work. Much enamel made after 1760 is called Battersea but the true Battersea was made for only six years at most.

BATTLESHIP TRAYS: Pressed-glass boxes or covered trays in the form of ironclads of the United States Navy of the 1890s, and made after the Spanish War. The *Oregon*, the *Wheeling*, and other great ships were so honored. Sold in cheap stores as novelties.

BATWING BRASSES: William and Mary period scutcheons for handles in a bat-wing shape that is essentially Chinese in design and may well be Dragon Wing.

BAUDEKIN: A rich textile fabric with a web or warp of gold thread and a woof of silk.

BAXTERS: Wide boards strapped on feet for walking over loose sand and muddy ground. Mud shoes. Heavy shoes.

BAYS, BAIES: Baize.

BEAKER: Drinking vessel of tall shape with slightly flaring sides.

BEALL FURNITURE: Gustavus Beale or Beall, of Georgetown (Washington, D.C.), made furniture (1810–20) in the manner of Phyfe.

BEAM: A wax candle.

BEAU BRUMMELL: A gentleman's vanity table; a dressing table for a man. Usually with fold-back top, having mirror, and with fitted drawers. Known in many styles, and in Adam, Chippendale, Hepplewhite, and Federal (Sheraton influence) periods. Also name given chests of drawers when fitted with mirrors, compartmented drawers, et cetera, for a man's use.

BEAUFAT, BEAUFFET, BUFFAIT, BUFFET: For a corner, as a cupboard, a chair, a chest. Beaufat, without any other designation, meant a cupboard for the corner, often built in the room and not portable, or a portable corner cupboard. Never a sideboard. BEAUFAT TABLE: Corner table. BEAUFAT CHAIR: A corner chair.

BECKER: Woodenware; a dish.

BECKET: Rope grip, or rope handle. Found not only on utensils but also on pioneer furniture, on doors, et cetera.

BEDASSHED: Adorned, covered, trimmed, colored.

BEDDER, BEDDINGER: An upholsterer.

BED POLE: A long wand for smoothing sheets in making a bed.

BEDPOST CLOCK: Not a clock to affix to a bedpost but an early brass-cased clock standing on or affixed between a set of posts as a bed. Designed for hanging on wall. A bob-pendulum-type clock. Seventeenth and eighteenth centuries.

BED REAFE: Bedclothing.

BEDSIDE CARPET: Section of heavy, woven stuff of wool laid by the bedside to protect feet against cold floors. Also bearskins, deerskins, lambskins, so used.

BED STEPS: Portable three-flight sets of steps for getting into high beds.

BED TOP: Canopy for bed, various types being field, Venetian, waggon, dome, et cetera.

BEECH BED: A sack or mattress stuffed with beech leaves.

BEECH MAST: Beechnut.

BEEHIVE CHAIR: A chair woven of rushes in the manner of a beehive. The prototype of modern wicker- and basketwork lawn and porch chairs. Seventeenth and eighteenth centuries.

BEER FIRKIN: A measure of nine gallons.

BEETLE: Iron wedge used in splitting logs.

BELDAM: Generally, a grandmother, but also term for a fair lady (*belle dame*).

BELLARMINES: Large, potbellied drinking jugs with the face of a bearded man. Caricatures of Cardinal Bellarmino, champion of the Roman Catholic hierarchy. Made by and for the Protestants of The Netherlands.

BELL BRACES, BELL JANGLES: Straps studded with button-type bells having loose clappers. Harness bells. Not to be confused with horse bells, which were mounted in twos and threes in arched frames fitted over horse collars.

BELL TURNING: A variety of trumpet turning looking more like a bell shape, used on chair and table legs, stems, pedestals, et cetera.

BELLY FLAGON: A barber's vessel held across belly by customer as a catchall.

BELSIRE: Grandfather; an ancestor. BELSIRE'S CLOCK: Grandfather's clock.

BELZNICKLE: Claimed to be a Germanization of Belle Nuit. A Santa Claus figure who cut capers on Christmas Eve.

BENGER: A chest for grain; a corn chest.

BENNINGTON POTTERY: Rockingham-type flint-glazed pottery made at Bennington. *The Potters of Bennington* by John Spargo tells the story. Reading is recommended.

BERGÈRE: Deeply upholstered and cushioned chair, more heavily padded than a fauteuil.

BERLIN WARE: Tinware made at Berlin, Connecticut, 1740–1850. The story of Berlin and the Pattisons, who started the industry, is told in *Hawkers and Walkers in Early America* by Richardson Wright. Reading of the entire volume is recommended. Mr. Wright is editor of *House and Garden*.

BERMUDIAN BROOM: Stick broom, or besom, of Bermuda straw or cane.

BESOM, BEESOM: Originally a red-colored hearth broom. Finally, any broom of cane, rush, corn, et cetera.

BESPOKE: Trade term, applied to craftsmen who made goods to order, as a bespoke hatter, a bespoke shoemaker, a bespoke cabinetmaker. They carried no stock for sale.

BETTY: A cruse for oil.

BETTY LAMP: Small lamp with vertical handle, short or long, which, on occasion, was lowered into cookpot to note condition of contents as they cooked.

BEVELED GLASS: This glass, when old, has a very low bevel; in fact it is almost flat. Made after 1676. When the bevel is acute, or readily noticeable, the glass is not old, that is, "antique."

BEZOAR: Any antidote for poison. In early days the bezoar most prized was the gallstone of a ruminant.

BIBLE-BACK TABLE, BOOK-BACK, BARREL-BACK: A table made (1790–1870) of two leaves resting against a cylindrical section. When raised the two leaves rise around this cylinder and cover it, meeting in a tight joint. When down, the leaves, and this cylinder (only half of which is exposed to view), look like the back and two covers of a book.

BIBLE BOXES: Plain or carved boxes, sometimes with sloping but usually with flat lid. Never made with a lock. If there is a lock it is not a bible box. The Bible was never kept locked. This is a fact developed out of research by Mrs. Edna Greenwood. The desk box, closely allied to the bible box was, usually, fitted with lock and key; hence the confusion.

BICHE: Furred doeskin.

BICKER: Woodenware; a small wooden dish made of staves and hooped. A miniature shallow tub for table and kitchen use. Also BECKER.

BIDDERY WARE: Made in India, at Biddery, near Hyderabad, of an alloy of sixteen parts copper, four lead, and two tin. Inlaid with silver and blackened with salt, this ware was brought to America after the Revolution by clipper ships.

BIDET: A wall lavabo; a wall-bracketed washbowl or stand, usually, accompanied by a fountain or tank holding water for use in bowl.

BIEDERMIER: A German middle-class comic-strip character who was always trying to keep up with and imitate his betters. Second quarter nineteenth-century German attempts to meld French Directoire, Empire, and English Victorian fashions resulted in a furniture given this name, and deservedly so. It is a caricature of its betters, yet thousands of pieces of it have been imported by decorators who attempted to start a vogue for it as a high style. It has no place in the American scene.

BIGGIN: An early type of coffee percolator, in pint size. Known in silver, brass,

Sheffield, tin, pewter, pottery. Biggins were designed for individual use at "biggin time"—9 to 10 A.M. and 4 to 5 P.M.

BILBAO MIRROR: Wooden frame mirror veneered with real or imitation sheets of marble from Spain. Made in France and imported C. 1790–1830.

BILSTED: Wood of the American sugar gum tree (sweet gum) used as a substitute for mahogany and often mistaken for true mahogany.

BIRCH BROOM: Made from a six-foot section of birchwood three to five inches thick, split fine to a one-inch core, core cut out of one end and the shredded, split wood folded down over the others and tied. The uncut core became the broom handle. Invented by the native American Indians.

BIRD-BACK: Type of chair back so scrolled and cut that when standing against a light background there is a silhouette of a pair of birds, facing. These have been called eagles, parrots, lovebirds, et cetera. Probably an accidental achievement.

BIRD CAGE: Name given the structural elements by which a tilt-top table with revolving top can be either tilted or turned.

BIRD-CAGE CHAIR: A type of Windsor chair with very thin spindles, sometimes of iron wire instead of wood. In some the seat is round, not saddle-shaped, and is mounted on an iron rod which in turn is seated in a pedestal base, permitting the chair to "swivel" or turn. Ancestor of the stenographer's swivel chair. Nineteenth century; 1820–50.

BIRD-CAGE CLOCK: A spring-driven table clock or weight-driven wall clock, with a filigree-work domed top (housing the gong, or cloche) and usually with a dial extending beyond the sides of the case, and fitted with only one hand. Very early type clocks which, unfortunately, have been faked or reproduced in great numbers.

BIRD WOMAN, BIRD WENCH, BIRD LADY: See Lady bird cage.

BISCOTIN: Confection of flour, sugar, jam, eggs, milk, and spices, baked.

BISHOP: A grand punch made of roasted oranges and lemons steeped in wine.

BISHOP'S FINGER: A signpost.

BISQUE DOLL: Kidskin or wooden doll with a bisque (or parian) head, but sometimes of all bisque parts, articulated or rigid.

BITTLIN: Woodenware; a milk bowl. Also in china, pottery, glass, and pewter.

BLACKJACK: Leather drinking pot with metal rim. Also called BOMBARD and GISKIN.

BLACK METAL: Cheap pewter. Ley metal and iron were designated by this term. Not a trade name but a colloquialism of derogatory quality.

BLANKET CRANES: Long tapering arms swinging from sockets placed beside doorways and at firesides, singly or in pairs. Used for drying coverlets and blankets on rainy days, also to drape similar stuffs over them and serve as draft stoppers.

BLEEDING CUP: Basin to catch blood in bloodletting; silver and pewter. English name for what we call a porringer.

BLESSING OUT THE FIRE: A cure for burns, out of what is called hexerei or witchcraft. Really a form of faith cure; a prayer with personal symbolism.

BLEW PAPER: Paper from the warehouse of Blew, in Aldermansbury, London, established 1689, which sold small-size sheets of decorative papers for book decoration and for papering walls. Finally issued wallpapers in rolls or sheets up to twelve yards long in wide variety of designs, many of Chinese influence. Also flock papers and others. Imported and sold in America during eighteenth century by many Boston, New York, and Philadelphia shopkeepers and artisans. Student is referred to *Historic Wall Papers* by Nancy McClelland.

BLIND DOOR, BLIND DRAWER: Sham drawer or door on tables, chests, et cetera. Put there for symmetry, or to divert attention from a secret drawer or compartment.

BLOCKED LINEN: Any linen, the surface of which is block-printed—that is, decorated with a design impressed from carved wood blocks dipped in dyes. "Blocked" applies to the manner of application and not to the form or style of decoration. Method was used as early as 2500 B.C.

BLOCK FOOT: Square-shaped foot of spade type, but without taper, hence terminating in a block. Earlier than spade foot.

BLOCK-FRONT: The Townsends and Goddard developed this distinctly American style of cabinetwork in the Georgian manner, similar to but not *in* Chippendale styles. A masterpiece of American designing. See examples illustrated in block-front section, page 17.

BLOCK TINWARE: Table and cooking ware of block tin (pure tin), next to silver plate in value. Rare. Advertised in American papers 1790–1830.

BLOOM OF ROSES: The first "won't rub off" rouge made in America. Could be removed only with lemon juice or vinegar. Made by Hunt, perfumer of Philadelphia, 1850.

BLOWN SALT: Careful scanning of the true usage of this word is recommended. Today the word connotes a saltcellar of blown glass. From 1790 to 1830 it meant the finest table salt procurable, imported from Liverpool.

BLUE SPATTER WARE (Spatter Blue): Made at Staffordshire for American market, 1815–50. The spattering of blue begins at outer rims and shades into natural tone of the ware toward centers where additional décor is applied. Birds, fruits, scenes, et cetera.

BLUES SONGS: Properly bi'you or bayou songs sung by Negroes of the bayou country peddling wares in New Orleans. "Confitures Cocos," "Touts Chauds," "Pralines Pistaches et Pecanes," are among the original blues songs. Street calls of plaintive nature.

BLUNDERBUSS: Gun or pistol having a slightly flaring mouth on barrel. Such arms with exaggerated bell-shaped mouths, as pictured in many nineteenth-century paintings of Pilgrim or early pioneer life, never existed. But excellent fakes were made for gullible collectors who wanted guns like those shown in the pictures. The genuine blunderbuss has but little flare.

BOARD CHEST: Boxlike chest made without pretense of quality.

BOARD CLOTH: Cloth to cover shelves or boards of cupboards, often with a valance which hung a few inches below the shelf.

1680–1750 and later. Often very fancy. Shelf paper is the modern counterpart.

BOBBIN-TURNED: The elongated bulb-turned stretchers of Windsor chairs and cottage furniture are sometimes called bobbin-turned.

BOBECH: Upcurving but shallow drip cup of glass, pottery, silver, tin, et cetera, placed on candle sockets, having a hole in center for passage of candle. When edges are pierced it indicates use of prisms or pendants.

BOCASIN: Early type of buckram.

BOGY, BOGIE RUGGE: A lambskin.

BOHEMIAN GLASS: Seventeenth-, Eighteenth-, and nineteenth-century Czechoslovakian glass of which the rich ruby red is best known, but made in other colors. Also overlaid or flashed with color over white transparent glass, cut, etched, and gilded. Believed to be of Oriental rather than Venetian influence. Much German glass is in imitation of this Moravian or Czechoslovakian ware.

BOLDER BOTTOMING: Rushing of chair seats.

BOLECTION MOLDING: Literally the molding which follows the outer edges of a panel. Now often used in reference to the heavy molding used to frame fireplaces.

BOLTS HEAD: Glass vessel with a long neck tapering to a cone shape.

BOMBACE, BOMBAYS, BOMBAST: Raw cotton. Stuffing. Hence bombastic: stuffy, stuffed.

BOMBAZET, BOMBAZINE: Plain twilled and unglazed fabric of cotton.

BOMBÉ: To bulge, jut, or swell out. Kettle-bottomed chests are bombé.

BONBONNIÈRE: A sweetmeat box; comfit box; any container for candy.

BONCOURS: A seventeenth-century tapestry fabric.

BONE LACE: Lace made with bone bobbins, or bobbins called "bones."

BONNET TOP: The broken-arch and pedimented top; a curved or scroll top converging upon a decorative element in the form of a flame, urn, acorn, eagle, busto, or other figure. HOODED TOP. SWAN-NECK TOP.

BONNIN & MORRIS CHINA: The Southwark pottery of Philadelphia, founded by

Bonnin & Morris, to produce imitation porcelain wares, and to make porcelains as good as "Bow" (English). White glazed earthenware decorated in blue. Excessively rare. Pottery seems to have operated only a year or so. Known mark is small capital letter P.

BOOK-BOTTOMED: Said of toilet stands or dressing cases and mirror stands when the cabinet section or base has a rounded form like a book lying on its side. One or two drawer fronts make up the book back.

BOOK DESK: Reading desk or stand with sharply sloping surface, too steep to write upon. Very early fifteenth-, sixteenth-century.

BOOK MATCHES: Now collected by several million children and grownups, book matches exist in so many varieties and coverings that a listing is impossible. They were invented, actually, in the 1850s, when issued as sheets of thin wooden matches in a cover. Patented as a new idea in 1892 and produced by Diamond Match Company about 1897. The first one issued was an advertisement of Mendelssohn Opera Company; second, Pabst Brewery; third, American Tobacco Company. Since then at least one million different advertisers, local and national, have used them. The feature match (with matches in form of tube of toothpaste, a banana, a chef, et cetera) was patented on the notching of the top to provide for a row of the matches to lie flat. This, too, was a feature of early matches. These flat-lying notched-top sheet-type matches were issued in the 1860s and are known with printed advertising impressed on the sheets of wood making up the rows of matches. The only book on the history of matches in America now current is that issued by the Diamond Match Company about ten years ago.

BOOK MIRROR: Vanity mirror cased in a book of small size. Sixteenth-, seventeenth-, and eighteenth-century conceits.

BOORSLAPS: Coarse linen.

BOOT BOTTLES: Novelty bottles in form of boots, high shoes, and ladies' high shoes. Pottery. Made at Bennington and also in England.

BOOZ BOTTLES: Log-cabin bottles, used by E. G. Booz, liquor dealer and rectifier of Philadelphia. Often thought the term "booze" derives from this man and his whiskies. A pint of Booz'.

BORDE: A portable, knock-down table; a board and trestle table. Hence "bedde and borde": sleeping and eating place.

BORDESLY: Tapestry made in Warwickshire, a branch of the Barcheston works.

BOREL: Coarse woolen cloth of lowest class.

BOSCAGE, BOSC, BOSKY: Wooded; woody; woodlike, reference being to growth; a bosky view; a wooded view.

BOSOM BOTTLES: Tin, pewter, horn, brass, glass and silver bouquet holders in miniature, for pinning to buskin or inserting in V of breasts on high occasions. Filled with water, they kept a bouquet of flowers fresh. Glass ones advertised in Boston, 1756.

BOSTON ROCKER: American mass-production rocking chair, 1820–90. See section on rocking chairs, page 58.

BOTANO: Blue linen cloth.

BOTTLE MOLDING: A round molding.

BOTTLE SLYDER: A movable tray for bottles; a wheeled tray for sliding across a table. Advertised in America, 1773.

BOTTLE TICKETS, BOTTLE TAGS, BOTTLE LABELS: Silver, pewter, ivory, enamel, and tin labels, engraved or painted with "Geneva," "Rum," "Sherry," "Port," et cetera, and hung around neck of bottle on chains. Bottle ducket and decanter ducats are also names for these objects.

BOUGH POTS: Decorative china and porcelain pots with lids or tops perforated in large and small holes, to hold boughs of flowering shrubs, leaves, et cetera. Pussy willow, hawthorn, witch hazel, forsythia, apple and peach blossoms, almond and orange blossoms were "forced" in bough pots.

BOUGHY: A small candle.

BOUL: An iron hoop.

BOULLE, BUHL WORK: Inlay in tortoise shell, brass, silver, et cetera, as practiced by André Charles Buhl, French cabinetmaker.

BOULTING: A cloth or hair strainer.

BOULTING HUTCH: Woodenware; a hutch into which flour was boulted through the boulting temse. Fine cloth used in bolting flour in "bolting mills."

Bow: Fine English porcelain, 1744–60. Later known as Derby.

Bower, Bure: Bedchamber, especially a woman's bedroom.

Bow Kitt: Large can with cover.

Bow Shanks: Bowlegged; particularly a bowlegged woman.

Bowtel: A convex molding.

Box Comb: A hair comb fashioned of boxwood.

Box Iron: Smoothing iron with metal drawer to hold hot coals.

Box on Frame: Rare piece of pioneer furniture of the seventeenth century; a carved box of good proportions and size, placed on a turned, separate frame, having a drawer and often carved.

Boxman: Early sandwich men who paraded the streets encased in a conical box from shoulders to knees, bearing advertising signs and posters. Typical on streets of American cities and towns 1840–60.

Bracket Foot: A chest or cabinet foot projecting slightly beyond body of piece, offering flat sides and a straight edge to view but often shaped with curves and scroll cutting on the flange.

Brackle: To break bread or cake or crumble into pieces; to add such to tea, coffee, chocolate, and milk.

Brades: Pendant ornaments; necklaces.

Braid Loom: A small loom for weaving braid and narrow fabrics generally, as tape.

Braken: Fern. Also a hemp dressing tool, a bread trough, and a mortar.

Braket Rules: Trivet for holding bread for toasting.

Bramage: Heavy cloth used in making bed carpets.

Brandreth: Tripod for supporting a pot, kettle, or caldron over the fire.

Brandy Warmer: Miniature saucepan, usually of silver, but known also in copper.

Braseros: Brazier-shaped jardeniere with handles. Brassware.

Brasil Wood: Dyewood yielding a red color. Also used in cabinetwork.

Brass Buttons: Used on men's clothing up to 1825. Made in New England, New Jersey, and Pennsylvania. Many of our early inventors were brass-button makers. Certain of the brass-button shops of the eighteenth century became great manufacturing concerns, some of which survive to this day. The output was enormous, even in colonial days.

Brasses: General name for cabinet hardware such as drawer pulls, escutcheons, et cetera.

Brass Foot, Brazen Foot: Ornamental cast and finished footings for leg terminals on cabinetwork. Federal furniture of Phyfe and his peers, Sheraton, and some Directoire furniture is brass-footed.

Brasswork: When applied to furniture may mean brasses, brass legs or feet, hinges, et cetera.

Brawdery, Brawde, Brawdry: Sculptured work was once so called; also raised needlework, embroidery.

Brayer: Roller in a two-pronged holder for rolling paint, ink, et cetera, on various surfaces.

Brazier: A footed frying pan for braising, or browning.

Brazing Tongs: Wrought-iron scissorsshaped tools ending in stubby blocks of iron.

Break Front: Not to be confused with block-front. A break front is a cabinet piece, the façade or front of which either has two recessed and one projecting section, or two projecting and one recessed section. Known also in five alternating projecting and retreating sections. Many variants. Many also are of English origin.

Break-Front Wardrobe: A wardrobe made in the break-front manner with two wings flanking a forward-standing central section.

Brewster Chair: Named for Elder Brewster, one of the pioneer settlers of New England. See also Carver Chair. Both are pictured on page 3.

Brewster Clocks: Made at Bristol, Connecticut, 1833–62. Brewster and Ingraham, 1843–48.

Bridgeport Knockdowns: The Furniture Manufacturing Company of Bridgeport, Connecticut, made furniture in knockdown form for ease in shipping either overland or by water. Nineteenth century.

BRISTOL: English glass noted for its sapphire-blue and milk-white (in imitation of porcelain) glass. Stiegel, Amelung, Zanesville, Pittsburgh made glass in the Bristol manner and style.

BRITANNIA METAL: An alloy, once called Prince's metal, composed of three hundred and fifty pounds block tin, twenty-eight pounds antimony, eight pounds copper, and eight pounds brass. This is a recipe of 1840. Almost every maker had his favorite formula.

BRITANNIA WARE: Rolled sheets of Britannia metal spun into shapes on a lathe. Sometimes silver-plated, but also sold in its native state. Commercial production seems to have been general by 1860. Sheet Britannia metal was made about 1830–35, perhaps earlier.

BROCATELLE: Coarse brocaded or figured fabric of silk and wool, linen and wool, linen and cotton.

BRODENAIL: Hand-forged building nail.

BROKEN SWIRL: A form of swirling or ribbing, used especially on glass on which it is achieved by swirling or twisting the hot, plastic glass formed in a ribbed mold.

BROWN'S WASHINGTON: Henry Brown, of Boston, 1861, issued a facsimile of Stuart's Washington in fine proof form at two dollars.

BRUMMAGEM: Colloquial or cant term for Birmingham, England, cutlery and metal wares.

BUEROW (BEAURO, BUREAU) TABLE: Flat-topped case of drawers, as distinguished from the slope-fall case of drawers, the true bureau, or scrutoire.

BUFFET CHAIR: Triangular-seated chair with many variations in structure, said to be the ancestor of the corner chair.

BUFFET STOOL: Flat-topped low stand or stool with slots cut in top to serve as handles or handholds.

BUFF JERKIN: A leather jacket.

BUGASIN: Calico buckram.

BULB STRETCHER: Stretcher having an enlargement in the center, whether turned on a lathe or achieved by shaving away from the center toward either end with a spokeshave.

BULLDOG PITCHER: Container in the form of a squatting bulldog made by the Haig pottery of Philadelphia about 1825–35.

BULLION: The thickened section of a crown of glass to which the pontil was attached after blowing the bubble and from which the spinning into a crown was achieved. The pontil of a crown of glass; the bull's-eye.

BULLIONS: Dress fastenings; hooks, buttons, clasps, frogs, et cetera.

BULL'S-EYE: See Bullion.

BULTINGARKE: Bulting ark; a chest or tub for sifting or bulting (bolting) flour.

BUMALADY: By my lady! An expletive.

BUMPING GLASSES: Heavy-bottomed or heavy-stemmed and footed glasses used in drinking at table and as applause makers; that is, glasses bumped on the table top. Hence a bumper was not always a large glass. Bumping glasses were called firing glasses in England.

BUMROLL: Cushion or bustle used to swell out petticoats in place of more costly farthingale.

BUNTING: A fine linen.

BURATO: A woolen cloth.

BURBECK: Wood carver of Boston, c. 1765–70. He carved capitals for Faneuil Hall and made mirror frames, sconces, et cetera.

BUREAU: (*Espèce de Table à plusieurs tiroirs et tablettes*—Bayer's French-English Dictionary, 1699.) A chest of drawers with scrutoire; the slope-fall desk.

BUREAU À CYLINDRE: Tambour-type desk with the tambour rolling upward in rounded grooves. Ancestor of the modern roll-top desk.

BURET: A drinking vessel.

BURGOIN: That part of the headdress covering the hair.

BURGOMASTER CHAIR: An ornate carved chair with slanting tub-shaped back and sometimes with revolving seat. Early form of swivel chair affected by the burgomasters, or petty village officials of Europe.

BURL, BURR: Wood from or of the knotty excrescences growing on hardwood trees: the maple, walnut, ash, birch, et cetera.

BURL ASH: Knotty excrescence of the native ash tree, sliced into thin sections and used as veneer. Used on fine William and Mary furniture.

BURL BOWL: Woodenware. Bowls of all sizes from a few inches to several feet in diameter, wrought from burls. Made by native American Indians and by early and late settlers and, parenthetically, still made. See also Maser.

BURLET: A hood or headpiece.

BURNET: Brown woolen cloth.

BURNWIN: A blacksmith.

BURRAGE: Thomas and Thomas, Jr., joiners, of Lynn, Massachusetts, 1718–50.

BURYING A WIFE: Feast given apprentice when term expires and he enters the craft.

BUSK: A stay of whalebone or steel to keep corseting straight. The frontal piece of corsetry. BUSK POINT: The lace and lace tag securing the free end of busk.

BUSS: To kiss. A large pitcher.

BUSTLE: A small crinoline worn over the nates; a frame of wire or fine wicker, fastened at waist and worn to accomplish a hump at back over which elaborate skirting was draped.

BUSTOS: Statuary busts of any kind or material.

BUTLER'S SERVING BOARD: A high, footed chest of drawers with closets as ends and with four to five linen drawers and a flat top for service and carving of meats. Many varieties. Federal period.

BUTLER'S SIDEBOARD: Small sideboard with top or center drawer fitted as a desk, and having a falling front. Hepplewhite, Sheraton, and other style influence. Federal period.

BUTLER'S TABLE: Folding table with X supports or other collapsible struts, and when set up offering a table with hinged leaves. Similar to folding service tables used in restaurants today. Late eighteenth and early nineteenth century.

BUTTER BOARD: Woodenware; a small trencher or board for serving butter at table, often accompanied by a glass dome or a bell of pewter, tin, or silver.

BUTTER CUPBOARD: Used to store butter, cheese, et cetera. Usually with pierced doors to supply circulation of air. Often quite elaborate in fifteenth, sixteenth, and seventeenth centuries in England and on the Continent. Also in America in seventeenth and early eighteenth century. Offered as a commercial product as late as 1880.

BUTTERFLY TABLE: See section on tables, page 1.

BUTTER MOLDS: Woodenware (usually, but known in pottery, slate, and tin) molds to give a design to a pat or pound of butter. This "print" or impression is responsible for the term "print butter." Good, or the best, butter was so impressed to make it engaging in appearance. Many designs of molds are known. Usually round, from three to five inches in diameter, with a turned wood handle. Deep-cut carving of tulips, hearts, geometrical patterns, loops, swirls, cows, hens, et cetera, embellish the molds. Seem to have been used from 1750–1880 and later. Molds are still made and still used by farmer-dairymen producing their own butter.

BUTTERY BAR, BUTTERY HATCH: The lowest half of the so-called Dutch door.

BUTTON BED: A spool-turned bed.

BYLIG: A bellows.

BYSSINEL: Fine silk.

C., CIRCA: Around or about. As a date; c. 1780 = around 1780.

C SCROLL: Any scroll with its major theme or pattern similar to letter C. Found on Restoration, or Charles II, chairs.

CABARET: A set of drinking cups. A tea, coffee, or chocolate pot with cups and tray.

CABBAGE ROSE: A gaudy blue, red, and green decorated china by Adams and other English potters about 1840. Akin to so-called Gaudy Dutch, but later production.

CABOCHON: A convex, oval section enclosed in ornamental border, as in cabinetwork on the knees of legs, and as in jewelry.

CABRIOLE: Bowlegged, bandy-legged, bent-legged. Gracefully curvate legs of Queen Anne style, carried into Georgian and Chippendale and revived in the Victorian period.

CACHEPOT: Not catch pot, but cache—a hoarding. Bulbous, cylindrical pots of china and porcelain seven to twelve or more inches high in which to cache or momentarily hide things.

CADDIS: Woolen ribbon; woolen cloth.

CADNAT: A canopy.

CADOGAN TEAPOT: Lidless teapot with vent in bottom, made by Spode and others. Also called puzzle teapots, Mortlocks, and Rockinghams. Made c. 1780–1820.

CAFÉ AU LAIT: The color of coffee with milk.

CALASH: A folding bonnet of cloth over collapsible wire stays. A wheeled vehicle.

CALATHUMPIANS: A set of noisy serenaders beating on pots and pans. Jug music. Cacophony by thumpery. A sort of sharivaree used in town to serenade newly-weds.

CALDRON: Globular cooking pot, with bail handle and one or two spouts or pouring lips. Copper, iron, and brass.

CALICO PRINTING: Block printing in colors on calicut fabrics; printed cotton.

CALIMANICO: Glazed linen (or cotton), printed or plain.

CALLOPYING, CALLOBYING: Mending, repairing, brazing, soldering, fixing.

CALLOT, CALLET: A plain coif, or skullcap.

CALSONS, CALZOONS: Close-fitting trousers of linen.

CAMAK, CAMOKA. Fabric of silk and camel's hair. Seventeenth century.

CAME: H-shaped lead strips used as muntins to hold small panes of glass. The glass fitted into both sides of the H section.

CAMEL-BACK CHAIR: Chair with a top rail having two humps downward or three humps upward (the center being more pronounced) as a part of the curvate top section. Hepplewhite and late Chippendale.

CAMEO GLASS: A late revival of Greek and Roman glass techniques; a layer of white or colored glass is laid over the base color or white glass and the coating cut away. The "Portland" vase which defied the experts for years as to what it was made of was this sort of glass, discovered when it was shattered by a madman. The copy of the Portland vase by Wedgwood is, of course, not in glass.

CAMLET, CAMBLET: Textile of wood, silk, or hair; fabric of animal flax.

CAMPANA VASE: Bell-shaped and bell-mouthed vase with bulbous bottom and thick stem on square base. Krater vase. Usually with two handles.

CAMPHENE: Explosive lighting fluid of turpentine and alcohol. Used 1835–75. Proportions were one and a quarter pints turpentine and six and three quarters pints alcohol to gallon. CAMPHEN LAMPS, CAMPHENE LAMPS: Any lamp to burn this fluid.

CAMPHOR GLASS: Frosted glass having the appearance of gum camphor. Made at Wheeling, Pittsburgh, and other glass centers, first half of nineteenth century.

CAMP MUG: Silver or pewter drinking cup carried by soldiers.

CANAPÉ: A sofa or couch.

CANBOARD: Rack to hold handled mugs, beakers, cans, drinking cans, et cetera.

CANDLEBEAM: Chandelier.

CANDLE CHANDELIER: Unnecessary term; tautological. Candle and chandle mean the same thing. Hence "chandelier" tells the story. Electric chandelier and gas chandelier are also errors; these are electroliers and gasoliers respectively.

CANDLE CONE: Extinguisher of conical shape used to douse candles instead of blowing them and scattering hot wax. Not a snuffer, but an extinguisher.

CANDLESHEARS: Snuffers; wick trimmers which catch the clipped wick in a small box.

CANDLE SHIELD: Shield-shaped shade in metal pincer mounts which grip the candle. Known in horn, tin, parchment, mica, and decorative paper, embroidered fabrics, et cetera. Used from about 1770.

CANDLE TROW: A candle tree; a candlestick of many branches. Some students believe a treelike form to hold many candles for Christmas illumination gave rise to the practice of using an actual tree at Christmastime.

CANDLEWOOD: Slivers of pine rich in natural oil and resin, burned as lights, and usually in or on the hearth.

CANE CHAIR: Any chair with seat and/or back of woven cane or rattan. Used generally by seventeenth century. Original weave or pattern is still in use.

CANNON HANDLE, CANNON GRIP: Used on early flat silver; the handle in the form of a cannon, often with a knobbed projection on the breech of the cannon handle.

CANNON STOVE: A tall, round stove, in the general form of a cannon standing upright on its breech end. Not potbelly or barrel stove. An eighteenth-century stove.

CANOVA: Italian sculptor (1757–1822) who made the Roman gladiator statue of Washington for the state of North Carolina. His portrait (Canova's) appears on Staffordshire china by Mayer, Clews, Wood, and others. A classic revivalist in sculpture.

CANTEEN: Any reservoir or container with a spigot or faucet for dispensing contents.

CANTERBURY: Ornamental stand with divisions or compartments for holding papers, portfolios, envelopes, periodicals, et cetera.

CANTON CHINA: The original blue-and-white ware of commerce. Known in seventeenth century and imported up to 1938. Importation of same ware will be resumed after end of Sino-Japanese War. Canton ware is a traditional staple in Chinese ceramic history.

CANT SPAR: Fire pole.

CANT WINDOW: Bow window.

CANVASSE: Prior to 1650 this name was used for the materials of linen used for bed sheets, bolsters, and biers.

CAP CASE: Bandbox, hatbox, traveling case. Bag or wallet.

CAPHA: A variety of damask.

CAPITOL COVERLETS: A pattern in woven coverlets displaying the Capitol at Washington in a large repeat pattern. Known in prison coverlets and in signed and dated coverlets. 1835–55.

CAP PAPER: Coarse, cheap brown paper. Butcher's wrapping paper. Cartridge paper.

CAPSTOCKS, CAPGALLOWS, CAPTREE: Clothes stocks, costumers, clothes tree, hanging rack for clothes, hats, and caps. Eighteenth-century name.

CAPTAIN'S CHAIR: High-legged Windsor, or similar-type chair used as a seat on the bridge or quarterdeck, in wheelhouse, et cetera. Also in gazebos (glass-enclosed cupolas on tops of houses near riverside or seashore).

CARBERRY: The gooseberry.

CARCENET: A necklace. Also CARQUENET.

CARD GAMES: To list the various games played with cards would be to extend this item to a page or more. Piquet, lanterloo, loo, hazard, basset, écarté, et cetera, are names sometimes used in connection with tables. Thus the table so designated can be established as a card table.

CARDINAL: A punch similar to Bishop except that claret wine was used.

CARD TABLE: Usually a table for four people, with narrow side leaves or with a fold-over top. Known in styles from William and Mary through Victorian.

CARECLOTH: A square held over the bride by four men. Seventeenth and eighteenth centuries.

CARER: A sieve; same as Temse.

CAROLEAN: Of or pertaining to the styles, habits, and times of the reigns of Charles I, Charles II, and James II. Also the Jacobean period.

CAROL WINDOW: Bow window.

CARPET: Originally a hanging, or garniture, for table or a bedcover. Carpets began to be used on floors after 1750.

CARPET CUTTER: A kind of rocker, perhaps the original form, with the shape of a pair of curved chopping blades. They were narrow (less than an inch thick) but very deep. Some extended half the length of the leg toward the chair seat.

CARTEL: Drum-shaped clock in ornate mounting.

CARTOUCHE: Ornamental emblem or form (heart, oval, star, oblong, label, et cetera) carved, painted, inlaid, and stenciled on furniture, woodwork, and various wares.

CARVER CHAIR: Named for Carver, the Pilgrim Father. First chair of this type said to have been brought to America by him.

CARVING TERMS: In eighteenth century carving was a fine art practiced by the gentry. They did not say "carve, halve, or slice," but had special terms for each kind of meat or game as "break" a goose, "thrust" the chicken, "spoil" the hen, and "pierce" the plover.

CASE BOTTLE: Any bottle designed for use in a case of bottles; thus four bottles in a circular case may be found blown in form of a quarter circle. Others are square, oblong, triangular. Of Swedish, Dutch, and English make; 1600–1800.

CASED GLASS: Glass composed of two or more layers of contrasting colors, cut to expose underlayers. OVERLAID GLASS.

CASE FURNITURE: Cabinet pieces; any furniture of the nature of a case, or having the general characteristics of casemaking, as a wainscot chair, settle, hutch, table, et cetera.

CASHOES: Dutch term for mahogany.

CASSIE PAPER: Imperfect paper, sold cheaply. Soiled or wrinkled paper.

CASTING BOTTLE, CASTING GLASS: Bottle for sprinkling (casting) perfume on person. Used in seventeenth century.

CASTOR: A beaver; a beaver hat.

CATHEDRAL CLOCK: Made in the 1840s during the so-called Gothic revival; characterized by steeples, peaked fronts. Some were expensive but most were cheap clocks.

CATMALLISON: Cupboard placed in or near a chimney to hold dried and smoked meats.

CATSKILL MOSS WARE: Light blue painted earthenware by Ridgway of Hanley, made about 1844 and marked CC. American views by Bartlett appear on this ware. Late Historic Staffordshire.

CATTAILS: Bulrush heads used with flocking (raveled woolen cloth) to stuff bed sacks in seventeenth and eighteenth centuries.

CAUDLE CUP: Cup or dish of earthenware, china, silver, et cetera, to serve caud or caudle, a hot drink of wine, eggs, sugar, milk, rum, et cetera. A sort of syllabub, or Tom and Jerry. From "calidus" (warm); not from "caudal" (tail).

CELLAR, BED CELLAR: A canopy; celure.

CELLARET: A case, cabinet, or portable chest for holding bottles, decanters, and glasses.

CELURE: Boxlike frame fastened to wall at head of bed, with rods of metal to carry the tester curtains. Any roofing, any canopy fastened to wall over a bed. Earliest form of bed canopy, before the canopy was supported on bedposts.

CENSER LAMP: Globular lamp, the lower half of which was fuel reservoir and the upper a pierced cover and shade for flame. Hung on chains, these looked like censers; hence the name. Also burned perfumed oils. Silver, brass, and Sheffield plate. Eighteenth century.

CEREDO PIKE'S PEAK: Flask of some fame, made at Ceredo, near Huntington, West Virginia. See *American Glass* by McKearin.

CERUSE: White lead used as a cosmetic by women.

CHAGRIN: Shagreen.

CHAINED (GUILLOCHE): Heavy threads of molten glass applied in form of a chain.

CHAIR FIRE SCREEN: Flat willow or rush mat made to hang on the back of a chair to screen same from fire, from seat to about two feet above top rail. Usually fitted to backs of dining chairs when placed near the fire, or on the chairs of anyone seated near fire in any room.

CHAIR TABLE, HUTCH TABLE: Four legs, joined by a seat section, and with arms across upper sections of legs, forming an armed high stool. Arms are drilled at ends and to them is pegged a broad top (round, square, or diamond shape) which tilts forward to serve as a table top resting on the arms, or tilts back to become a chair back. The hutch table is not properly a chair table but a dual-purpose piece that is a hutch when the top is uptilted and a table when down. Both of these date from seventeenth century. The chair table is still made.

CHALDRON: (Not to be confused with Caldron.) A measure of thirty-six bushels. Sea coal and charcoal were once sold by the chaldron.

CHALK SILHOUETTES: Silhouette portraits painted or mounted on slabs of chalk.

CHALK WARE: A misnomer; it is not chalk but plaster, and "gaudy plaster" would be a far better name. Cast in pewter, tin, and wax molds in imitation of Parian ware Staffordshire figures, and porcelain, most of this ware is painted. It was made mostly by "Portygees" (foreigners) in New England, and by Italian immigrants in other states. It was vended from trays and barrows in towns and from wagons in the country. A cheap ware; ornamentation anybody could buy. Since it has become an item of collectors, it is being faked in huge quantities, most of which seems to come from Pennsylvania. This, perhaps because it was once considered a ware peculiar to that state, when, as a matter of fact, it was sold everywhere. Only, in the back country of Pennsylvania, the original buyers seem to have kept the stuff, while elsewhere it was generally discarded after a few years. Lions, parrots, birds, dogs, hens, ducks, figures, watch holders, castles, and many other forms were made. Sold up to 1890 by vendors.

CHAMBER CANDLESTICKS: Candleholders with broad, shallow bases, often fitted with cone extinguishers, for use in bedchamber. Usually stood in group on table in lower hall, by a burning chandle, where individuals, upon retiring, would light their chamber candles and retire to their rooms. It is quite correct to display these in groups on hall tables. Brass, tin, silver, Sheffield plate. Seventeenth and eighteenth centuries.

CHAMBERLAIN WORCESTER: A fine decorated porcelain made by the Chamberlain plant, a competitor of Dr. Wall's Worcester works. Chamberlain was founded 1786; Wall's works 1751.

CHAMBER TABLE: Eighteenth-century meaning was dressing table; nineteenth (early), a night stand with closet to hold chamber crockery. Term used as early as 1690 for what we call lowboys.

CHAMBLET, CHAMELOT, CAMELOT: A variegated fabric; same as Camblet or Camlet.

CHAMFER: To bevel off an angle, as the corners of a square column or leg. To bevel edges. To pare down the edge of a surface; to flatten an angle where two surfaces meet. Also CHAMFRET, CHAMFRETTED.

CHAMPLEVÉ: Enameling done in engraved or cut surfaces.

CHAMPNOINE POTTERY: Made at or near Boston, Massachusetts, prior to 1738.

CHANDELIER: A candle (chandle) holder of many branches and tiers, suspended from ceiling. As many as fifty candles were socketed in some examples.

CHANDRY: Candle closet or storage box.

CHAPMAN: Contraction of cheapman or cheapener man.

CHARGER: A large dish; a voyder.

CHARIVARI: Mockery in good nature; mock serenade, as a "shivaree" or calathumpian party.

CHARLES II CHAIR: Finely carved stately chair of Flemish and Dutch style with caned seat and back. Also richly carved wainscot chair of same period.

CHARLESTON SMITHS: The ironwork of Charleston, South Carolina, is in many respects older and finer than New Orleans; especially the wrought iron. Early nineteenth-century ironworkers of Charleston were MacLeishe, Werner, Thibaut, Ortman, and Justi.

CHARR POTS: Shallow earthenware pans or dishes (Staffordshire) in which the small salmon called charr were baked. The charr is often mistaken for a trout. Fine distinction exists between a pot for cooking fresh charr and the pot in which preserved charr are packed for market. The latter are commercial pots of standard form; the former are shallow panlike vessels.

CHATELAINE: A cliplike element of silver or gold jewelry, sometimes engraved or enameled and jeweled, to which a chain is attached. This chain in turn was fastened to one's purse, etui, et cetera.

CHAUFERE: Hot water basin.

CHECKERED DIAMOND: Blown-mold glass design of four small diamonds enclosed in large diamond (checker) shape.

CHEESE BRIG, CHEESE LADDER: Poles of wood with crossbars to support skimming bowl over a pan of cream. CHEESE DISH: A sleigh-shaped dish (silver, Sheffield, pottery) made to hold a round of cheese at table. The cheese, set edgewise, rested in a conforming cavity in the sleigh-shaped dish.

CHEESEQUAKE POTTERY: Stoneware in the old English manner, made on the Cheesequake Creek, New Jersey, during and after the Revolution. It was again made early in nineteenth century. *Antiques Magazine*, March 1944, gives some data of interest.

CHELSEA GROUPS: Chelsea toys, or figurines, said to have been made under the direction of Nicholas Sprimont, 1750–69.

CHEMINÉE: Chimney or fireplace screen of tapestry or needlework. Sixteenth-century term.

CHESTER SPICE CABINET: A miniature highboy with cupboard top made in Chester County, Pennsylvania, to serve as a spice cabinet. Excessively rare. Made also in Lancaster County, Pennsylvania; 1740–60.

CHEST JOINT: Hinge.

CHESTNUT URN: Graceful curved funnel-shaped urn with cover, used to store freshly gathered chestnuts for aging. Made as items of decorative character and kept standing on mantels, tables, and chests. Eighteenth and nineteenth centuries; of tin, tole, iron, wood, pewter.

CHEST-ON-CHEST: A chest of drawers, or chest of doors and drawers, mounted upon another chest. A simpler form of tallboy. Usually in two pieces. Lower member should be a complete chest of drawers and not a frame with but one or two drawers.—WITH CABINET: When the upper member has a secretary compartment it is so called. Both types appear to have been made 1730–50.

CHEST-ON-FRAME: Any chest or cabinet standing upon a separate base that is essentially a high or low table (with or without a top). Known from seventeenth century.

CHEST TABLE: The frame of a chest-on-frame has been so called.

CHEVAL FIRE SCREEN: Standing fire screen, supported on two pillars, or a standing screen with adjustable frame and folding wings. Pole screens are not properly cheval screens.

CHEVAL GLASS: Literally "horse mirror," a full-length toilet mirror big enough to reflect a horse. A pleasantry in nomenclature for a full-length mirror.

CHICKEN-COOP CHAIR: Colloquial for Windsor, or Philadelphia stick chair.

CHICLATON, CHICLATTEN, CICLATOON: A rich fabric with gilt threads· gilded leather. Probably brass foil covered and brass threaded.

CHINESE EXPORT PORCELAIN: See page 120.

CHINESE TABLES: (1) Teak and other rare-wood tables exported from China to England, The Netherlands, and America. These are the ones copied by Dutch in seventeenth century and later by Chippendale. (2) Simple tables in the Chinese style. (3) Nineteenth-century importa-tions in richly carved mandarin fashions. (4) Bamboo-turned tables.

CHIOLLAGH: An all-wood stick chair from Isle of Man, contemporary of the Welsh stick chair, which is said to be prototype of our Windsor.

CHIPPENDALE SIDEBOARD: A side table, that is, a side "board," a table for use on the side in a dining room. There are no "Chippendale" sideboards in the same category as Hepplewhite, Sheraton, and Federal pieces so designated.

CHIPPENDALE TRAY: A pattern deriving from the papier-mâché trays having scalloped or gadrooned edges and called Queen Anne Gothic or King's Gothic. Date from about 1759.

CHITTENDEN BED: Iron bedstead made by S. Chittenden, of New York, c. 1850.

CHOCOLATE: Introduced in seventeenth century as a drink; sold as chuchalette in Boston, 1678. Since the Dutch were masters at its preparation it was known very early in New York, also in what was later Pennsylvania.

CHOPPINE, CHAPIN: High clog; pattens of cork on a light framework, covered with cloth or leather.

CHRINSIE: Drinking vessel of any kind.

CHROMOTYPES: Pictures and maps partially printed in colors and finished with color-ing by stencil.

CIERGE: A wax taper.

CIGARETTE PICTURES: Pictures of stage favorites, ball players, pugilists, and others enclosed in packages of cigarettes 1880–1900.

CIRCA: About, or around. Abbreviated as "c."

CISTERN: Metal or pottery water con-tainer, usually for a bedroom.

CLACKET: A rattle; a toothed wheel turn-ing against a piece of hickory. Used to drive birds from corn and grain fields. Used by watchmen on rounds.

CLAP DOOR: Lower half of a Dutch door.

CLAPHOLT: Boards for cask making. Clap-board derives from this term.

CLAP STILE: A stile with movable hori-zontal ledges.

CLARET JUG: Ewer for serving claret, known with narrow necks and wide necks, both types having handles and pouring lips or spouts. Eighteenth and nineteenth centuries. Usually of glass.

CLARICORD, CLARICOL, CLARISHOE: Spinet-shaped musical instrument of from thirty-five to seventy strings.

CLARKE FURNITURE: Made by J. Clarke, 46 Broadway, New York, c. 1845.

CLAVEL, CLAVEY: A mantelpiece. CLAVEL-PIECE: The fireplace; the beams or cheeks of the fireplace. CLAVEL TACK: The beam or shelf over the fireplace.

CLAVEL PAGE: A fireside figure, usually as tall as the cheeks of the fireplace, placed as a decorative element; made of painted wood, or wood forms covered with embroidery work.

CLAVICHORD: The seventeenth-century ancestor of the piano, known in Carolean, William and Mary, and Queen Anne styles.

CLAW AND BALL: Animal paw or claw grasping a ball or pearl; claw dominant, the ball secondary (as opposed to ball and claw, in which the ball is dominant and the claw secondary).

CLAY WARE: Henry Clay, of Birmingham, England, invented a method of laminating sheets of porous paper saturated with glue size. Up to ten sheets were so treated, formed into shapes over a mold, and baked in an oven. To these forms—dishes, boxes, trays, fire screens, et cetera—japanning was applied. Clay's wares were not papier-mâché. They had great strength and toughness.

CLEAT BOARDS, CLEE BOARDS: Another form of mud shoes; flat boards strapped on regular shoes for walking over mires and bogs.

CLEOPATRA'S BARGE CHAIR: See section on fancy chairs, page 56. Cleopatra's Barge was a private yacht afloat in Salem Harbor in the 1820s. It was furnished with fancy chairs.

CLEW: A ball of yarn for making into warp on a loom.

CLEWKIN: A strong twine or cord.

CLINQUANT: Brass foil; brass leaf, hammered as thin as gold leaf. Used instead of gold leaf on cheaper products, frames, japanning, furniture, et cetera.

CLOCHE: Dome of glass fitting over a wood base, with dust ring, to preserve artificial flowers, waxworks, et cetera,

from dust. Also early name for Clock ("cloche," to strike) when clocks were primarily hourly alarums. CLOCHE GLASS: A combined hourglass and clock (sixteenth century).

CLOCK LINE, CLOCK LEAD: Cord running around power drum and attached to weights in weight-driven clocks. Catgut, cord, woven wire cable, et cetera.

CLOME PAN: A milk pan (sometimes in woodenware).

CLOSE BED: A press bed.

CLOUT: Cloth used in making a poultice.

CLOVE: Seven pounds of wool.

CLOVE BOARD: Clapboard.

CLUM-BUZZA: An earthen pan.

COACHING CHAIR: A folding chair of any period, Queen Anne to Federal, carried on journeys to provide seat when viewing a hunt, shoot, race, or fete. Some are very ingeniously contrived.

COACHING TABLE: A table with a two-leaf top about twenty inches square, mounted on two light pillars having arched folding feet. This contrivance folded into very small space, but when opened was a table for use in a coach.

COACHMAN BOTTLE: China or glass bottle in form of a coachman in a stovepipe hat. Seems to have been made in late 1840s in pottery at the Fenton works. Sometimes called BISHOP'S BOTTLES.

COB: Mud plaster mixed with straw and thatch. Used as a plaster and as a wall material tamped in forms. The plastering of the exterior and interior of the Ephrata Cloister walls, Lancaster County Pennsylvania, are cob, or cobbed. COF was also name for a seed basket.

COBBLER'S BENCH, CORDWAINE'S BENCH: Shoemaker's bench with seat, last holder, bin, and various peg and tool compartments. Now much favored as a piece of pioneer furniture but not so; it is tradesman's furniture.

COBBLER'S CANDLE: Double-wicked candle, said to have been invented by B. Franklin.

COB IRON: Originally the one-piece andiron in the form of a broad, humped iron fastened to two dogs, the dogs with high pillars supporting a spit over the iron. These were used on the round, hoodless and flueless hearths of ancient England. Later, any andiron, especially any iron supporting a turnspit.

COCKADE: A hat ornament. The fan-shaped cockade is military, the round (like a bulrush) type is naval or civilian. Used from George I–III and during Revolution. Used also by Army and Navy to about 1850. Still used on some full-dress hats in services.

COCK-BEADED: Round, raised, projecting bead as around drawer fronts, in shaped sections of William and Mary furniture, et cetera.

COCKFIGHT CHAIR, PITSIDE CHAIR: Actually reading and writing chair used by straddling the seat and facing the back, which had a pair of high arms to accommodate this posture, and a slanting shelf with book ledge. From Queen Anne period to Chippendale. May have been used at cockfights but this term is probably modern.

COCK'S-HEAD HINGE: A wrought-iron hinge looking more like the silhouette of a leaping frog, each of the four "legs" of which terminates in a cock's-head outline.

COCOANUT CUPS: Silver-mounted cocoanut shells used as cups. Very fashionable. Sixteenth and seventeenth centuries.

COD: A pillow. CODPIECE: Gusset in the crotch of breeches; stuffed gusset worn at the breast as pincushions.

COFFEEPOTS: Mentioned in New England as early as 1686. Coffee dishes (similar to bouillon cups but without handles) mentioned 1683. COFFEE STAND: A pedestal table, tri-footed, having a galleried tray for a top (to hold a coffee urn) and a sliding shelf under the tray to hold cup and saucer while filling from the urn. Rare. Known in Queen Anne, Georgian, Chippendale, and Sheraton (Federal) styles.

COFFEE TABLE: General name for small tables, larger by a few inches than general run of tea tables.

COFFEE TREE: American forest tree, native to Kentucky and Mississippi Valley. The nuts, roasted, yield a drink tasting like coffee.

COFFERED: Refers to shape. Coffered lid means in forms of a coffer, rounded at sides and ends.

COFFIN TRAY: Octagonal-shaped tin tray, painted and stenciled over japanning. Deep, narrow-edged, and coffinlike in form. Distinct American shape.

COILTE: Quilt.

COIN CHINA: Designs from coins (busts, emblems, et cetera) impressed, in relief, or transfer printed on china. Eighteenth and nineteenth centuries.

COIN GLASS: Any glass object but particularly a drinking glass or goblet with a silver coin blown in the foot, stem, or bowl bottom. Also American pressed glass with coin replicas pressed in glass bosses around rims.

COIR: Cocoanut fiber from the kernels of the nut used instead of horsehair in mattresses.

COIRBOULLY: Molded leather.

COLBERTINE: A kind of lace.

COLD FIRE: Any fire laid but not set alight.

COLESTAFF: Heavy bar of wood carried from shoulders of two men walking tandem, and supporting a huge bundle.

COLLA: Glue.

COLLAGE: A picture, partly painted and partly made up of cut paper and tinsel work. Glued picture.

COLLEGE BOWL: Covered bowl, the cover of which is a smaller bowl, used inverted when used as cover. Seventeenth and eighteenth centuries.

COLONIAL: Actually anything used prior to erection of the federal government or the Republic.

COLOPHONY: Brown resin, residue from turpentine distilling.

COLORS (INTERIOR) 1650–1800: White and ivory were not favorite or generally used colors during the colonial and early Federal periods. Medium and pale blue, green, gray, Indian red, vermilion, rose, lemon yellow, ocher, coffee and milk (café au lait), with parcel gilding, were most popular.

COMB: A measure; four bushels.

COMB-BACK ROUNDABOUT: An English-type Windsor chair of roundabout shape, with a comb back.

COMBED WARE: Pottery crudely akin to scroddled ware, effect deriving from combing colored slip after applied to ware as a wash. A form of slip ware.

COMMODE TABLE: Same as bureau or buerow table.

COMPASSED WINDOW: Circular bay or oriel window.

COMPO: Hard plaster believed now to have been made of sawdust, wood flour, plaster, shellac, and alcohol. Often molded in intricate decorative forms and applied direct to wood and other surfaces. Used in molded filigree by Adam, Chippendale, and other designers.

COMPON-COVERT: A kind of lacework.

COMPORT: Salver.

COMPOSITION ORNAMENTS: As used on some furniture, on chimney breasts, et cetera, made by casting a mixture of whiting, resin, and linseed oil in molds, or pressing papier-mâché into molds, or by applying red-hot metal branding irons to wood sheets, the branding irons having the designs cast in them. By last-named method the charred parts were removed by brushing and the burn stains covered with a priming coat of paint. Such décor was usually glued and tacked to surface destined for ornamentation.

COMPOTIER: A compote; a vessel for serving stewed fruits.

CONCH HORN: Dinner horn made from a conch shell. Also Bell Horn.

CONDRACK: A kind of lace.

CONESTOGA WAGON: Finest freight wagon the world has ever known. A combination of the English road wagon and the high-wheeled cart of the Huguenot. Developed in the valley of the Conestoga River, Lancaster County, Pennsylvania. Characteristics are curved, boat-shaped body, lowest in center, with high bow and stern; arched bows over body to carry cover. Used in substantially its original form 1740–1880. Prototype of all heavy road wagons and prairie schooners. Old ones had very fine hand-wrought ironwork; were pulled by six horses of Conestoga breed. Seems to have been called a Dover wagon in Ohio. Not a German wagon, as some historians seem to have thought.

CONE SUGAR: Loaf sugar; the loaf was cone-shaped, cane or barley sugar.

CONE TABLE: A reading table, the top of which is of conical shape with a ledge around lower rim. The cone revolves.

Student or scholar could arrange many books around this type table and pull them to him as required.

CONFORMING SEAT: A saddle seat; any seat contoured to fit the person.

CONJURER: Cooking utensil for quick and easy use, advertised but not described by Crawley, tinsmith, 1802.

CONNE, CONNATES: The quince; a marmalade of quinces.

CONSOLE: Originally a bracket table, without legs, and suspended from wall. Later forms retained the wall jointure but had two legs to the front. The long side tables called consoles are not consoles in fact.

CONSTITUTION MIRROR: Name given scroll-top mirrors of Georgian and Chippendale periods, generally surmounted with an eagle. Frames of mahogany and walnut, usually parcel gilt (partly gilded).

CONVERSATION CHAIR: S-shaped chair designed to seat two people side by side but facing in opposite directions. Also called INCROYABLE CHAIR. Eighteenth century and nineteenth through to late Victorian fashion.

CONVERSATION PIECE: A genre or story-telling picture, dealing primarily with subjects in conversation or in familial attitudes.

CONVERSATION ROOM: Parlor or parlay room. Often spelled Plor in Early American inventories. The P with crossed descender is a Domesday character meaning pl, or par.

CONVEX MIRROR: Round mirror in decorative frame, gilt, burnished, and surmounted with acorn, eagle, vase, basket, or other finial. Fitted with convex mirror glass. Only when having brackets for candles are such mirrors GIRONDOLES.

COOKLE: Prong for a meat spit to turn in.

COOLER: Woodenware; a large open tub.

COPPERED QUEENSWARE: Copper lusterware.

COPPROUS: A syllabub; mixed hot drink made foamy with eggs and milk.

CORBEL: A shoulder, or shouldering piece, set in a wall to carry a beam; any stone-, brick-, or timberwork projecting as a shoulder to carry a burden, as a corbelled chimney, corbelled fireplace sides (to hold the chimney breast), corbelled beam seat, et cetera.

CORBET: Wall niche to hold images; popular in fine American homes of Georgian period.

CORDEVAN, CORDEWAYN, CORDWAIN, CORDOVAL: Spanish leather and workers in same, as a saddler or shoemaker.

CORDIAL CHEST: Cabinet in period style designed to hold anywhere from four to sixteen bottles in compartments.

CORINTHIAN CANDLESTICKS: From designs by Robert Adam using the classical Corinthian column with traditional cap and base, on a broad foot. Known in silver and brass. 1760–1800.

CORK GLASS: Fine Irish glass rivaling Waterford and not infrequently marked "Cork Glass Company" by blowing in a marking mold. Made latter half of eighteenth and first half of nineteenth centuries.

CORLETS: Raised cork-soled shoes of sixteenth and seventeenth centuries; a sort of wedgie.

CORNER BOARD, CORNER SIDEBOARDS: Hepplewhite and Federal (Sheraton) style sideboards with bow, serpentine, and undulating fronts, made to fit in a corner. Very practical, yet not popular; all examples appear to be a special-order production of local cabinetmakers; a style well worthy of revival for modern homes. Made 1780–1835. Not common but not unique.

CORNER CHAIR: See page 61.

CORNER CONSOLE: Bracket table with quarter-round top for placement in a corner. Buffet table. True console only when hung on brackets.

CORNER STANDS: Corner furniture is very worthy of the book now in preparation on this subject alone. Corner stands or bedroom corner stands are known in quarter-round, right-angle triangle- and square-topped examples, but made to face outward from a corner position even when square-topped. Made in Hepplewhite, Adam, and Federal (Sheraton) styles with tambour slides, doors, shelves, et cetera. Many are fine pieces. All corner furniture is of the space-saving variety. It is significant that more attention was paid to this in the eighteenth

century, when homes were spacious, than today when rooms are smaller and most dwellings have seven rooms or less.

CORNER TABLE: Right-angle triangle-topped table on three legs, sometimes with drop leaves. Various styles, 1750–1850.

CORNICE: See Entablature.

CORONAL: Original spelling of "colonel," which still carries its original pronunciation.

COSEY CHAIR: Upholstered wing chair.

COSSART LINEN: Colonial merchants sold much of this linen damask made by J. Cossart et Fils, France, 1720–40. Early advertisements carry mention of it.

COSTER: Tester; bedside hanging. Table drapery.

COSTREL: Woodenware (or pottery) vessel with ears to attach cordage for carrying. A bottle.

COUNCIL TABLE: Oversize ovoid, oblong, or round table with falling leaves supported on swinging legs. Rare. But known in Jacobean, Queen Anne, and later styles. Not to be confused with console table, often called "council" by uninitiated.

COUNTERFEIT: Portrait or statue of a person. "Yesterday finally counterfeited by Master Lily" means "Yesterday Master Lily finished my portrait."

COUNTERPANE, COUNTREPOINTE: Shaped or divided into squares of diamonds; lozenged. Any fabric so needled took the name counterpane.

COUNTRY-MADE: This term should not connote crudity or poor craftsmanship, any more than the term Provençal should mean provincial. The latter term is applied correctly to the furniture of Provence, a very sophisticated furniture of France more often than not ahead of Paris in style. Country-made in America simply means made in this country by cabinetmakers who clung to styles long after city cabinetmakers abandoned them.

COUPE: A basket; a coop.

COURLAND SPOONS: Funeral spoons engraved "Courland" and bearing a date in the 1680s, made by American silversmiths, have been noted by experienced collectors on several occasions. Several collectors have, justifiably, associated them with the Courtland or Van Courtland family. This attribution appears to be correct. It is alleged that Olaf Svenson, a Swedish volunteer in the Dutch West Indies Company, was from the province of Courland, Sweden, now Latvia. He came to New Amsterdam, served out his time, and because all his fellows called him the Courlander or Courland, he assumed that name, which became Van Courtland.

COURT CHIMNEY: A portable fire; a very small fireplace movable from room to room and known in sixteenth century.

COURT CUPBOARD: "A kind of movable closet or buffet to display plate and other luxuries" is a sixteenth-century definition. See page 6.

COURT DISH: Fine drinking cup, of glass, china, silver, gold.

COURTING MIRRORS: Brought to America by clipper ships in the China trade. Small mirrors in frames made up of inlaid, painted glass. Frames have embryonic crestings and are redolent of finer types of same mirrors from which the Dutch copied the William and Mary and Queen Anne style mirrors.

COURTING PITCHERS: Pitchers bearing love tokens and sentimental verses or scenes, especially depicting pairs of lovers. 1790–1830. Earlier courting pieces are known in form of posset pots, tygs, puzzle mugs, et cetera.

COVERCLE: A potlid.

COVERLET: Properly, any bedcover, but generally used to designate the pattern-woven wool, wool and linen, and wool and cotton bedcovers made in early nineteenth century by hundreds of weavers, some of whom developed into large weaving mills devoted to making these covers. Best (or most desirable) items are signed by the weaver, dated, and have initials of customer or name of customer woven in them.

COWLSTAFF: Short staff to thrust through the ears or bails of a basket or tub to provide a handle for carriage.

COWNTEREY, COUNTERY: A writing desk; an office desk, shop desk, counter.

CRAB: Iron trivet for use over the fire.

CRACKER: Small baking dish; small stuff; a small piece. May be origin of "cracker"

as used in South to designate persons of small importance, the yokelry.

CRADLE SETTEE: See section on rocking chairs, page 58.

CRAFTS POTTERY: Made at Troy, New York, Portland, Maine, Whately, Massachusetts, and Nashua, New Hampshire, by a family of potters named Crafts. Stoneware. Nineteenth century.

CRANE PLATE: Flat iron pan having a gooseneck handle over it, affixed to one side of the plate.

CRAP: Buckwheat; darnel.

CRATCH: Woodenware; a manger; a pannier; a dish; a clothes pole.

CREAM POT: Earthen vessel of urn or pot shape, with cover, for serving thick (clotted) cream.

CRÈCHE: Nativity scene in miniature, composed of wood, plaster, china, or composition puppets, posed around hut or stable, with animals. Often very elaborate. An ancient religious custom of lower Danube Valley, and deriving from Nestorian Christians or Greek Church. Favored by Moravians as a Christmas custom and carried to America by Moravian (Czech) settlers.

CREDENCE TABLE: Very early fold-over top table, legs arranged in a half-hexagon pattern, standing on a shelf that was flush with the floor. Back legs swing out to support folding-top section. Mentioned as early as fourteenth century.

CREEL: An osier basket; a butcher's stool; a ball of worsted yarn.

CRESCENT SIDEBOARD: Designed to fit in a semicircular alcove, having a concave frontal and round back section, akin to a kidney-shaped table. Usually six-legged in Hepplewhite and Federal styles.

CRESSET: Night lamp. Also a four-pronged cuplike arrangement of iron, affixed to a rod. A ball of inflammable material was placed within the prongs and lighted to serve as torch for lighting both indoors and out.

CREST: Heraldic term for the ornamental designation of rank on the top of a helmet. Ladies (the Queen excepted) did not have and therefore could not display a crest.

CRESTED MIRROR: Any ornament surmounting a toppiece is a crest, or cresting. Queen Anne and William and Mary mirrors having such ornamentation are said to be crested. So also any mirror having fretworked, carved, or applied ornamentation above the top frame piece.

CREWEL: A needlework technique of coarse embroidery stitch, using silk or woolen colors and yarns called crewel.

CREWEL MIRROR: Mirror frame covered with crewelwork.

CRIB: A collander or strainer.

CRIB CRADLE, LULLABY: A crib for infants placed on rockers as a cradle.

CRICKET, CRICKET STOOL: Jointed stool with short legs, often placed on the hearth and used as a footstool to warm one's feet. "Cricket on the hearth" probably derived from this little piece of furniture.

CRICKET TABLE: A stool table; a table made as a large stool. "Cricket" derives from Anglo-Saxon "crice," a crutch.

CRIMMLE: To plait or pleat.

CRIMPING: Glass decoration done while glass is soft, imparting a series of dents and flutings similar to hair waving.

CRINOLINE: A fabric of "crin" or horsehair, used for making the bell-shaped stiff petticoats over which dresses were draped. Finally any under form, such as hoops, et cetera, was called crinoline.

CRINZE: Woodenware; a drinking mug. Also any drinking cup.

CROCHON: Fuel for cressets; made of pitch, tar, resin, and other substances.

CROOK CHAIN: Chain fixed in chimney to hold boiling pots.

CROSS-BAITED: Checkered.

CROSS-GARNET HINGE: Any hinge, the leaf of which is a long horizontal strap and the stile a long vertical strip. Looks like a large, spidery T lying on its side.

CROSS LYRE: A table pedestal made of a pair of lyres, crossing at right angles. Scarce vagary in cabinetmaking, used in Federal period.

CROTCH WOOD: Any timber cut from a forked section of the tree; valued for the pattern and often used in veneering. By reversing the crotch pattern in veneer, many beautiful effects were obtained.

CROUKE: Earthenware pitcher.

CROWEN DESKS: Made about 1840–55, of rosewood and mahogany combined with papier-mâché. Named for the maker.

CROWFOOT: Simple ball-and-claw or claw-and-ball foot.

CROWN GLASS: Window glass made by blowing a heavy bubble of glass, affixing the pontil rod, cutting from blowpipe and then spinning the pontil until the bubble flattened out in a huge disk of glass. These ranged from three and one-half to five feet in diameter, and were then cut into window-glass sizes. The piece having the mark of the pontil rod on it was the bull's-eye. This was sold cheaper than any other piece because it was not clear, transparent glass. Sometimes a complete round "crown" of glass was sold for a skylight or attic window light. These are miscalled "large bull's-eyes," as they are complete crowns and should be so called. The crown method of making window glass and other flat glass was used up to 1860. Glass from crowns almost always shows circular wavy lines on its surface. Old framed pictures, cheap mirrors, cabinet glass, and window glass show this method of blowing and spinning flat glass.

CROWN JUG: A pottery or china vessel surmounted by four pipelike spouts which join into one orifice over the vessel and thus form the outline of a crown.

CRUMB MORTAR: Woodenware; a mortar for crumbing stale bread. Also used to pound dried herbs.

CRYBE: Original term for bed.

CUBIT: A measure of one and a half feet.

CUCKING STOOL: Stool with a locking bar, affixed to a long beam on a pivot. Public scolds and minor offenders were placed in stool, and rolled to the side of a pond or wallow, in which they were ducked so many times. Hence the term "ducking stool" for "cucking stool."

CULVERTAIL: A form of building construction (also cabinetwork) in which all joints are so fitted that they cannot part; dovetailing on a complete scale. Often noted in early cabinet pieces.

CUPBOARD TABLE: Table with very deep skirt and fold-over top. The true top is fitted with a lock, actuated by key through an escutcheoned keyhole on the front of the deep skirting. When unlocked and lifted this top reveals a cupboard section. Quite scarce. Usually in Queen Anne or early Georgian style.

CUPID'S BOW: Any cabinet section, such as the top rail of a chair, or the cut of a valance or skirting, in the form of a cupid's bow or the upper outline of the human lips.

CURD KNIFE: A "gang" of four (or more) flexible steel blades arranged parallel, set one-half to one-quarter inches apart, fixed in a handle. Often with the name of a Herkimer County, New York, cutler or maker; used for cutting curds in cheese making.

CURFEW: Conical cover of pierced iron or brass, placed over a raked-up pile of hot coals on the hearth to hold the fire overnight. When the master raked the coals and set the curfew on them it was bedtime.

CURULE CHAIR: Chair having curved X-shaped supports. An ancient style. Sometimes called Dantesque chairs after Dante, the Italian poet.

CUTTOES; CUTTEAUX: A small sword, or a toenail knife. Advertised in 1759.

CUTWORK: (1) Embroidery or fancywork in which certain parts were cut out to form a lacy pattern. (2) Paper cut into fancy designs to form patterns and pictures.

CYLERY: Ancient dictionary gives this definition: "Draperies worcks of cylerie is a kind of carvynge or paintynge." Probably "ceilery," or the decoration of a ceiling by cut plaster, molding, and painting.

CYMA: The double curve; the curve of beauty. Similar to italic S in which the concave and convex curves are joined as one. CYMA REVERSA is the S backward; CYMA RECTA the S in proper position.

DADDICK: Touchwood; tinder.

DADE STRINGS: Lead strings.

DADO: The longitudinal panel at the base of a wall; the facet of a pedestal; often carved, painted, or otherwise decorated.

DAFFER: Small crockery in general.

DAFFLE: An oven mop.

DAFFLER, DAFFLING IRON: Oven hearth scraper.

DAGSWAIN: Rough textile for bed coverings.

DAGUERREOTYPE: First photography invented by Daguerre, 1839, obtained by the chemical action of light on silver salts. See section on daguerreotype cases, page 172.

DAMASK: A rich figure-woven textile from Damascus, imitated in Flanders, in linen, and achieved with high success.

DAMASKEENED: Inlaid metalwork; also lathe-turned engraving on metal, as the steel and brass parts of watches. Much early armor was damaskeened.

DAMNIFY, DAMNIFIED: To damage; damaged.

DARBY-JOAN SETTEE: Late, imaginative name given the two-chair back settees of William and Mary, Queen Anne, Georgian, and Chippendale periods.

DARLSILK: Damask cloth.

DARNEX: From the Flemish dornick; coarse damask from Tournay.

DAVIS, JOHN: Cabinetmaker and joiner of Lynn, Massachusetts, about 1703.

DAVIS TINWARE: Made by Henry Davis, Isaiah Wood, and Nathan Broughton, of New Bedford, Massachusetts, about 1843.

DAWNS: A kind of lace.

DAY BED: Long chair, canapé, lounge, or couch, characterized by a headpiece that is a chair back (sometimes adjustable as to angle within its posts) and a bedlike body on from six to ten legs. Made as early as 1600.

DECALCOMANIA, DECAL. Designs printed on a thin film of gelatine, mounted on paper. Transferred from the paper, by moistening, to any other surface.

DECOYS: Wood or tin effigies of birds (usually game birds), used as lures.

DEERFOOT SPOON, HOOF-HANDLED: Used as terminals on very early silverware; seventeenth century. The form is a very good modeling in miniature of a deer foot or hoofed foot.

DELFT: Tin-glazed earthenware made in The Netherlands, Flanders and France, in an effort to duplicate the porcelain imported from China.

DEMILUNE: Half-moon.

DEMILUNE TABLES: Pairs of half-round tables, also called half-moons, often accompanied by a drop-leaf table with square leaves. This, when leaves were up, was ended by the half-moon tables and a long dining table was achieved. Many such ensembles have been broken up and individual half-moon tables are discovered in lonely splendor. Usually Hepplewhite. A pair of them, back to back, naturally provided an exact round table.

DENTELLE: Tooth, toothed, as a dentelled border.

DENTIL: A toothlike block, usually used in series, as in a cornice or border.

DERBY (CROWN DERBY): English porcelain of fine quality, 1785–90, when the Derby works achieved royal patronage.

DESK BOX: Box with sloping lid, used on a table or stand, to serve as a desk. Often with carving and most frequently fitted with lock. Sixteenth and seventeenth centuries.

DESK-IN-TABLE: Late eighteenth-century table with very deep skirt, sometimes with false drawer fronts or very shallow drawers, and a sliding panel in the top. This, when opened, reveals a complete desk compartment, or a desk box. Uncommon if not rare.

DESK-ON-FRAME: A frame that is essentially a table, usually turned, or cabriole-legged, made especially to support a separate section that is a slope-fall desk box of generous proportions. The desk section usually has drawers under the slope-fall top and smaller drawers, cabinets, closets, and compartments within. No longer common and now verging upon scarce as items of Americana.

DESK TABLE: A desk-on-frame "frame" that has lost its desk section.

DESSERTE: A serving table having one, two, or three tiers.

DEVENPORT: Desk box on a cabinet of drawers; the desk section, in a box, slides forward for use. This part of the piece is usually fitted with a gallery. Not to be confused with davenport.

DIAPER: Actually to paint in colors, but usually meaning a decorative geometrical pattern in several colors. Diapered linen; printed linen. DIAPER PATTERN: cut or painted in imitation of textiles.

DIBBLE: A pewter plate.

DICK POT: Petticoat stove. A brown earthen pot pierced with small holes, filled with hot embers and kept under the skirts of women to warm feet and legs.

DIMITY: Stout linen from Damietta. Finally the term was applied to finer fabrics.

DINANDERIE, DUNANDERRY: An alloy of the fifteenth century, in which copper, tin, and some lead were used. Forerunner of pewter.

DIPPED SEAT: Chair seat having a dip or curve in its center for sitting comfort.

DIPTYCH: Book or tablet of two leaves.

DIRECTORY, DIRECTOIRE: See Federal furniture section, page 28.

DISBROWE, NICHOLAS: Joyner of Hartford, Connecticut, 1639. See seventeenth-century chest section, page 8.

DISH CROSS: Adjustable and folding X section of metal, footed and having extendable arms, used as trivet. Adjustability and conformability enabled its use under many dishes. Sometimes fitted with a spirit lamp to serve also as a warming dish. Iron, Sheffield plate, silver, pewter, et cetera. 1700–1850.

DISH RING: A high ring of metal (silver or Sheffield plate) in form of a capstan. Designed to hold a dish. Sometimes called a potato ring because baked potatoes, wrapped in a napkin, were served in such rings. Last half of eighteenth century.

DISH TOP: Table top, usually round, and turned or carved with a raised rim all around, giving the top the contour of a shallow dish. Scarce.

DISTAFF: The holding staff for flax or wool on a spinning wheel. Anything pertaining to the female line or side of the family; the distaff side.

DISTEMPER: Opaque colors used in painting and printing.

DISTEYNE: To dim (ancient English; compare with modern "disdain").

DISTLEFINK: Any vividly colored bird, painted, or carved, pottery, et cetera. Colloquial Pennsylvania Germanic term for any small or singing bird.

DITTEN, DITTLE: Any block used to stop up the oven opening.

DIXON GRATE: Mid-nineteenth-century invention; an improved living-room hearth fire with grate for coal burning, a concave fireback to reflect heat, a drop ashpit and supply of air for combustion obtained through flues from cellar. Controlled by a damper lever sunk in floor in front of hearth. Endorsed by Oliver Wendell Holmes, Ike Marvel, Dr. Hall, and other notables.

DOCKERY: Furs of weasels' skins.

DODECAGON: See Polygons.

DOG'S FOOT, DOG'S PAW: Brass footing for furniture, usually chairs, in the form of the foreleg and paw of a dog.

DOLLY: Woodenware; a washing tub. Also the staff of a butter churn.

DOLPHIN CANDLESTICK: Glass candlesticks in the form of coiled dolphins, made by Sandwich Glass Company in vaseline (yellow), clear, milky white, and bi-colored glass.

DOLPHIN CONSOLE: A true console table, the brackets of which are curvate dolphin forms.

DOLPHIN PIER TABLE: A monstrosity; a folding-top card table with carved dolphin supports and a footed base.

DOMED STRETCHERS, RISING STRETCHERS, TENTED STRETCHERS: When saltire, criss-cross or X stretchers curve upward to meet at the central crossing point they are said to be domed, tented, or to rise.

DOMESDAY CHARACTERS: When the Norman conquest of England was achieved a complete inventory of real property and taxable assets was attempted. To do this job of listing everything of importance owned by everybody in the nation, a sort of Anglo-Saxon, Norman-French, and Medieval-Latin was made into shorthand characters. Certain of these remained as special characters used by the people, especially in writing of their property and inventorying it. Not a few Domesday characters were used in America. Those most commonly used were:
Þ = par; ƀ = bere; Đ = th; ħƀ = had; ñ = now; Ᵽ = pro, or for; Ꝗ = when; ƀ = a little; ł = that; ꝙꝙ = whosoever; ℟ = required; ẏ = ely, or eli. & = and; m̄ = all.

DOMINO PAPERS: Sheets of colored paper, broadsides, imagerie populaire, papiers peinte; decorative papers. All these names denote fancy papers in sheets, printed, stenciled, floated, and blocked. Sold by vendors originally called Dominotieres, the most famous of whom was Jean Papillon (seventeenth century, France) and next his son, J. M. Papillon. Domino papers mark the beginning of wallpapers.

DONARKIEL: Scandinavian legend carried on mostly in Pennsylvania where round stones are recognized as sacred to Donar. To this day in some parts of Pennsylvania round stones, when found, are set atop fence posts, on tree stumps, or collected in piles.

DOOR KNOCKER: Metal assembly of a pivoted hammer or knocker engaging a fixed anvil or striking block. Various styles, especially in Queen Anne, Georgian, and Chippendale, in brass, white brass, silver plate, et cetera. Also known in heavy wood (pioneer type) and in wrought and cast iron.

DORFER: Same as "banker."

DORFLINGER GLASS: Made by Christian Dorflinger, a French glassmaker who came to the United States about 1846 and had glass furnaces at Brooklyn; Plymouth, and Greenpoint, Long Island, and White Mills, Pennsylvania. He had a store on Broadway, New York, where his cut and gilded glass was sold. Mostly mid-Victorian, but fine glass.

DORMAND TABLE: Any table with a permanently attached top. DORMAND BEAM: The main beam of a house. DORMAND: Anything fixed or permanent.

DORROCK: A coarse diapered linen fabric; coarse damask.

DORSERS: Hangings of tapestrylike fabrics. Cushions for the backs of chairs.

DOUBLE-BEADED: A drawer molding featured by a double line of beading all around the drawer front. William and Mary and early Queen Anne furniture often so treated.

DOUBLE CRUET: Glass, stoneware, china, and metal cruets in pairs, fused together, with spouts or necks bent in opposite direction.

DOUBLE GATE TABLE: Gate-leg table with two swinging gates or leaf supports on either side. The rarest type of gate-leg. 1650–1750.

DOUBLE STRETCHER: Pair of stretchers used instead of a single one, either for added strength or decorative effect.

DOUGH TRAY: Deep, slope-sided boxes for kneading, setting, and "raising" bread dough. Sometimes on separate frames with canted turned legs and stretchers.

DOVETAIL HINGE: The butterfly hinge, the wings of which look also like a pair of dovetails, joined at the narrow ends.

DOVETAIL KEY: Double fan, butterfly, or dovetail key block fitted into conforming cuts in the surface of boards or planks to make a tight, fixed joint. Table tops are often so joined (on underside of table); so also chest tops and other cabinet tops. Floor boards are found so treated.

DOWEL: Wooden peg fitting into a bored hole, used to join and fix parts in cabinetwork.

DOWLAS: Coarse linen fabric.

DRAGEOIR: A dish for dragées or bonbons.

DRAISIANA: The pedestrian hobbyhorse; the two-wheeled ancestor of the bicycle. An assembly of two wheels of same size, spanned by a frame, over which the straddled "rider" walked or ran and then lifted his feet and coasted. Made at Philadelphia, 1818.

DRAKE FOOT: Large-size duck foot.

DRAP DE LAYNE: A woolen cloth; dress fabric.

DRAWING TABLE: Extension table of the sixteenth and seventeenth centuries. See section on seventeenth-century furniture, page 1.

DRAWNWORK: Fancywork made by drawing threads from warp and woof, crossing and tying.

DREADNAUGHT: Thick, long-pile woolen cloth; overcoating; sometimes called bearskin.

DREDGER: Metal or turned-wood box of circular shape with perforated top for dredging any food with contents; flour, sugar, salt, pepper, et cetera.

DREDGE SALT: Salt tempered with spices and seeds for belly cheer; smoked salt, onion salt, leek salt, celery salt, parsley salt, peppered salt, cloved salt—all these were dredge salts and known to our ancestors. Salt for the table shaker.

DRESDEN CATGUT: A kind of fancywork, done on gauze, muslin, silk, and drawnwork.

DRESSER: (1) Board to hold plate and china for dressing the dining table. (2) Bureau-height chest of drawers or toilet table.

DRESSING BOX: Small slope-fall desk box compartmented for cosmetics, mirrors, et cetera, with slide struts supporting a large mirror adjustable as to angle. William and Mary, Queen Anne, and Georgian periods.

DRESSING GLASS: A vanity or shaving mirror, pivoted to tilt horizontally and mounted on a base with drawers. Seventeenth, eighteenth, and nineteenth centuries.

DRESSING TABLE: What we call the lowboy was called a dressing table. So also small kneehole desks. Also any vanity table of Hepplewhite or Federal style. Usually the later examples (after 1760) are fitted with compartmented drawers, bottleholders, et cetera.

DREW BELLOWS: John Drew, and Drew and Hixon, near the Warren Bridge, Boston, 1836–50, made hearth bellows in fancy japanned styles.

DRILL: Twilled linen.

DRILLING: Porcelain saucer or dish of seventeenth century often so called.

DRINKEL TOWEL: A dessert doily; a table towel for guests; a long, narrow serviette.

DRINKING TABLE: Rare. Semicircular horseshoe-shaped table, fitted with wine cooler, fire screen, and other gadgets. A company of drinkers would have such a table arranged at a fireplace or window and seat themselves around the outer side.

DROP-LEAF DUMB-WAITER: Two- or three-tier dumb-waiter on a central pedestal, the table-top sections of which have falling leaves. Rare.

DROPS: Applied decoration in egg, pear, tear, and turtle-back shapes, also acorn; applied in half sections to flat surfaces and in the round as pendants. Pieter Koeck, architect and painter, is said to be the inventor of this décor.

DROWSEND LIGHT: Tallow light, tallow candle.

DRUGGET: Heavy silk or wool fabric; any heavy fabric; used as bedcovers and as bedside floorcloths. Later in very cheap form it was used as a floor carpeting generally.

DRUM TABLE: Rare. Round table, with deep skirt, fitted with drawers all around. Known mounted on pedestals and on four legs. DRUM TOILET: A drum table fitted as a toilet table.

DRUNKARD'S CHAIR: Wide-seated chairs for lolling at one's ease. Also LOVERS' CHAIR.

DUAL-PURPOSE FURNITURE: See page 49.

DUCHESSE: A chaise longue or long chair made up of two or three sections.

DUCK BOX: Ducks, chickens, hens, hares, turtles, and other animal forms made into boxes. Early ones are fine; some imported from China are of crystal and jade.

DUCK FOOT: Three-toed, webbed foot usually found on Dutch or Queen Anne furniture.

DUDLESOCK: The bagpipe.

DUDGEON: Burl wood of the boxwood tree or root. Rare.

DUMB-WAITER: Round trays of graduated size, arranged in a series and turning on a central post, on a pedestal or tripod-footed base. Lazy Susan.

DUNCAN PHYFE STYLE: There is no such thing. See page 38.

DUTCH FOOT: Various footings of cabriole legs: pad foot, slipper foot, grooved foot, drake, webbed, or trifoil foot, club foot, et cetera. See page of furniture footings in this Glossary.

DUTCH GOLD, DUTCH GILDED: Copper, brass, and bronze leaf made in The Netherlands was so called and the work done with it so named.

DUTCH OVEN: A heavy iron pot with cover and stubby feet; set among coals and used for baking and roasting. Also name given an open-faced tin or sheet-iron box with platform and small spit; set before fire.

DUTCH STOVE: Five-, six-, and ten-plate iron stoves. See page 149.

DUTCH TEA TABLE: Flat-, dished- and galleried-top tea tables on pedestals, with three cyma-curved legs (Queen Anne style).

DWARF CANDLESTICK: Low, stubby candlestick of silver.

DWARF TABLE: A table having incurving legs which end in a heavy base. A relic of Directoire styling.

EAGLE-AND-STAR INLAY: On any piece of furniture this pattern of inlay is indicative of American origin. The number of stars is a clue to probable date of making.

EAGLE CONSOLE: A true console in which the brackets are in the form of eagles' wings.

EAGLE'S FOOT: The ball-and-claw foot and the crowfoot are sometimes so called.

EARED BACK: The top rail of a chair back meeting the upright in an outflaring joint is said to be eared, as opposed to rounded.

EASTER CROSSES: Crosses covered with glue, plaster of Paris, and other material, decorated with flowers of paper and wax, often displayed under glass. Not memorials but Easter displays comparable to Christmas trees.

EAST INDIAN FABRICS: Innumerable names were given to East Indian fabrics during the eighteenth and nineteenth centuries. These usually refer to the place of weaving, but in some cases are coined names. Examples: allejars, atlasses, addaties, allibanies, allibrowhas, bafraes, brawles, betelles, bafts, beguzzees, chintzes, chelloes, coopees, cherriderries, cushlahs, dorcas, deribands, elatches, emerities, gorgohans, gurrahs, ginghams, hummadees, izzarees, jamware, luchurries, moorgees, mulmuls, mickbannies, pallampores, ponabuguazzees, rehings, rumalls, seersuckers, ssofays, sannoes, soosays, seerpands, poonahs, tepoys.

EASTLAKE: Styles of furniture advocated during the Victorian age by Charles Eastlake, an architect. His "style" was a grafting of Jacobean on Victorian. Golden-oak sideboards redolent of seventeenth-century court cupboards, but made in the 1890s, are of Eastlake provenance.

EGG AND DART: A molding made up of what looks like half sections of eggs with a series of arrow or spear points between them.

EGLOMISE: Gold-leaf painting on glass. After Glomi, a French decorator who used this technique.

EGRE-DOUCE: Anything sweet-sour; sugared vinegar; honey and lime, et cetera.

EIDOPHUSICON: A rapidly moving diorama which, in displaying a succession of scenes, gave the illusion of motion. William Dunlap, American artist, was the proprietor of such an exhibition. See also Zoetrope.

EIGHT-LEG TABLE: Descendent of the gate-leg in Queen Anne style; a four-legged table with a pair of swinging legs on either side, pulled out to support the drop leaves. Usually very large tables. Rare.

ELL, ENGLISH: One and one-quarter yards. FLEMISH: Three-quarters of a yard. FRENCH: One and a half yards.

ELLBOE CHAIR: Armchair.

ELMEN: Woodenware made of elm.

ELMWOODROOT, ELMROOTWOOD: Root timber of the elm used in fine cabinetwork.

ELMSEAT, ELM BOTTOM: Chair seat woven of the twisted inner bark of the elm tree.

EMBOSSED CALICO: Dudding and Nelson, of England (eighteenth and nineteenth centuries) had a machine for imparting a raised design on calicut fabrics.

EMBOWED: Top rail of chair back bowed; embowed chair. Anything arched.

EMPIRE MIRROR: Name given the tabernacle mirrors of Federal period (1800–40). They are not Empire but a very definite American production.

EMPIRE PERIOD: The period of Napoleon's great power, especially 1804–10. The furniture style which, in France, replaced Directoire and which came into general favor in the United States about 1840. It is coarse, heavy, unimaginative, and at times stupid.

ENCABOCHON: In the form of a gem uncut but polished.

ENCAUSTIC: A form of painting with wax colors, applied hot to walls. Very durable.

ENCOIGNURE: Low corner cupboard or cabinet, finely made. French.

EN FACE: Full face, head on.

ENTABLATURE: A platform; also a protecting frieze or border; the uppermost section of a classic column.

ENVELOPE TABLE: Triangular-topped table of Queen Anne style with falling triangular leaves. Often with a locked compartment in skirting or valance, accessible only through the top, which is movable on hinges or pivot. Also a square-topped table with four triangular leaves, on a square base. The main top is pivoted on a center pin and can be turned. When turned, it brings the falling triangular leaves over the corners of the table frame and thus makes a table almost twice the size. The same kind of a table but with triangular leaves folding over main top.

EPERGNE: A centerpiece, usually for dining table; an ornate assembly of metal, glassware, pottery, et cetera, including dishes and plates for fruits, condiments, and sweetmeats, together with containers for flowers, fernery and boughs.

EPROUVETTE: A powder tester, made with a pistol grip, flint, steel, frizzen, and having a firing chamber with indicating disk or dial.

ESCUTCHEON: Heraldic; the field (shape) upon which the coat of arms is emblazoned (painted). Escutcheons in cabinetwork are the keyhole covers of brass, iron, silver, pewter, bone, ivory, et cetera.

ESCUTCHEON LIFT: A Norfolk-type latch with escutcheon movable; a trick latch of the eighteenth century. Sliding the escutcheon upward operated the latch.

ESTAMIER: French for pewter.

ESTERLING: The beginning of sterling, as a silver of high grade and purity. Silver of the Easterlings.

ÉTAGÈRE: Ornamental stand with shelves. A whatnot.

ETRUSCAN MAJOLICA: An American ware made (1870–90) by Griffen and Smith Pottery at Phoenixville, Pennsylvania.

ETUI: Pocket box for comfits, dragées, perfume, et cetera, of silver, gold, tortoise shell, malachite, pewter, and other materials. Richly decorated, carved, etched, and sometimes jeweled.

EWERY: A basic cupboard.

EXCELSIOR DESK: Empire style with front and top folding back as did the keyboard covers of pianofortes. Has sliding writing board and mounted on two fancy cast-iron supports. Made for college girls about 1850 by R. Paton, furniture maker of New York.

EXTENDING TABLES: Pairs or threesomes of tables; useful single, and joinable with special hardware in each, making extension tables of unusual length. Adam period to late Empire.

FAILLE: A dress fabric.

FALDESTOOL: Turned wood chair of very early date; a chair of state, usually draped. From the term "faldestool" derived "fauteuil," French term for upholstered elbow chair.

FALDING: A rough cloth.

FALDORE: Trap door.

FAMILLE ROSE: Delicate rose-pink color; Chinese porcelain in which this color predominated.

FAN-CRESTED: Fanlike carved element in the cresting of chair rails or cabinet furniture.

FARTHINGALE: Early padded and wired skirt. FARTHINGALE CHAIR: Armless chair to permit a woman wearing a farthingale to be seated comfortably.

FAUTEUIL: Upholstered armchair. —DE BUREAU: Upholstered desk chair. —DE TOILETTE: Upholstered toilet table, chair, or bench.

FEDERAL STYLE, FEDERAL PERIOD: See page 28.

FEET, FOOTING: See page of illustrations in this Glossary.

FELYOLES: Endpieces, holders, curtain hold backs, et cetera.

FEMERAL, FUMAROL: Turret or vent to permit escape of smoke or vapors.

FESCUE, FESCULE: A pointer; a wand.

FFLOCK, FFLOCKING: Raveled carpeting, tapestry, or heavy cloth used instead of feathers, wool, et cetera, to stuff "beds." Note that in early days the "bed" was the bag slept upon, plus covers, and not the frame upon which it stood. That was the bedstead.

FIDDLE BACK: Chair back with splat in general outline of a fiddle. Modern term.

FIELD BED: Four-post bed with a framed and domed canopy, often in ogee curves.

FILGRAINED, FILIGREED: "Filgrained is a dressing box or basket or whatever else is made of silver works in wyre [wire]." Ladies' Dictionary, 1694.

FILIGREE: Fine wirework, of silver, plaster-coated, enameled, et cetera.

FILLET: A thin band, a strip of molding; a facet.

FINIALS: Toppieces (épis) in form of flame, urn, vase, spire, ball, bird, flower, leaf, bud, et cetera.

FIREBOARD: Board cut to fit fireplace opening and used as a stopper during summer. Often covered with fancy paper, or painted in some design or pattern. Sometimes embellished with scenes, portraits, genre subjects, or flower pieces.

FIREBOARD PRINTS: Prints in various designs made to serve as decorative elements for fireboards, the boards used to block openings of fireplaces when not in use. These prints are about 24 × 24 inches.

FIRE BOTTLE: Small bottle in which phosphorus was kept, covered with water. A sliver of wood dipped in the phosphorus, rubbed on dry surface, became a sort of friction match.

FIREBOX: Metal box with one compartment to hold wood sticks tipped with chlorate of potash and another holding a vial of sulphuric acid. Matches ignited when touched to acid.

FIRE FORK: A shovel. —IRON: Steel piece of flint and steel. —PAN: Shovel or fire carrier. —PIKE: Fire fork. —POINT: A poker. —STONE: Flint stone.

FIRE MARKS: Actually early fire insurance company markers of cast iron, apparently peculiar to Philadelphia, 1750–1825.

FIRE MILL: A small mechanical mill for home use in which a rough steel wheel engages flint and directs sparks into a tin drawer of tinder.

FIRE-SCREEN DESK: Shallow drop-front desk box set between two uprights and serving both as a fire screen and a desk. Late eighteenth-century conceit. Of little practical value.

FIRESIDE FIGURES: Scarce and even rare, once used to decorate the cheeks of a chimney, the corbels or side piers. Many forms, even to effigies of kings and queens, but usually pages, guards, et cetera. Loderwijk Bamper, glass manufacturer of New York, had two pairs of these in large size; one set was a pair of grenadiers and one set displayed Loderwijk and his good Frau. Made of wood, painted, or covered with needlepoint or gros point.

FISH-SCALE WORK: Fish scales, dried, used in embroidery work.

FLABELLUM: Circular folding fan of accordionlike pleating.

FLAG BOTTOM: Rush bottom. FLAGGED CHAIR: Rush-seated chair.

FLAG FAN: Fan in which the blade of leaf is mounted to one side of the handle as a flag on a pole.

FLAME FINIAL: See Finials.

FLASH, FLASHING: Overcoloring applied to glass, fixed by firing. Flashing of this kind wears off in time.

FLAT JOINT: When the leaf of a table joining table top has neither tongue and groove nor table joint, it is said to be flat-jointed.

FLEA-BITTEN: Dark speckled color. FLEA-ZOO: Small fur collars. Term "floozie" said to derive from this word for small collars worn by women but particularly by street wantons.

FLECKSTONE: Small stone used in spinning.

FLINTWARE: Any pottery with a flint glaze.

FLIP: Drinking glass in form of a large tumbler.

FLOCK PATTERN: Ground or scraped felt, or fuzz, blown upon wet adhesive applied as a design to paper and cloth. Flock sticking to adhesive-coated surface formed a raised pattern.

FLOORCLOTH: See page 128.

FLORENTINE: Rich Christmas custard pie.

FLOWERED FURNITURE: Lacquered William and Mary and Queen Anne furniture embellished with gilded flowers, and scenes in the Chinese manner.

FLOWERED TABBY: Flowered silk.

FLOWER HORN: Horn-shaped vessel to hang upon wall to hold flowers. Also on base to serve as vase. Mid-eighteenth century.

FLUMMERY: Hulled oatmeal boiled until thick and gelatinous, served with sugar and whipped or clotted cream.

FLUTED MOLDING, FLUTING: Opposite of reeding; in reeding it is the rounded sections (as a pile of reeds) which stand out. In fluting the rounded section is gouged in and a serrated surface or section is the result. A fluted column in section looks like a cogwheel. Fluting was applied to round columns, plain and curved surfaces.

FOINS: Skunk furs.

FOLDED RIM, FOLDED FOOT (LIPPED RIM, LIPPED FOOT): The rim or the foot of a vessel folded over to provide a smooth rounded edge as well as double thickness at places where most scars or chips occur. Usually found in glass and metal pieces.

FOLIO: A paper size. Used generally to designate sizes of prints or pictures as: SMALL FOLIO: 11 × 14 to 11 × 17 inches; MEDIUM FOLIO: 14 × 18 to 15 × 20 inches; LARGE FOLIO: 19 × 24 to 23 × 27 inches. See also Paper Sizes.

FOOLSCAP: Sheet of paper size 12½ × 16 usually folded once to 8 × 12½ or twice to 6¼ × 8. Generally watermarked with a foolscap—hence the name.

FOOT BANKE: A metal container for hot coals; a foot warmer.

FOOTPACE: A dais; a stair landing; a raised hearth; a railed walk on a rooftop. Later also called CAPTAIN'S WALK.

FOOT STOVE: Wood-framed metal box to hold hot coals; carried to churches, ballrooms, theaters, et cetera, for warmth.

FORCER: A chest or coffer.

FORELOW: Aslant, askew, catterwampus, catty-cornered, cockeyed.

FORM: Frame upon which boards were laid to make a stool or table; a long stool; a bench without back.

FORMER: A gouge.

FORMPIECE: Muntin of window frame.

FORMULUS: Cut-outs used to compose decorative works of art. Known also as POONAHS, THEOREMS, and STENCILS. Used mostly in early nineteenth century to about 1860 in home and shop decorating of all sorts.

FORRE: Handkerchief bordering.

FOX-HEAD CUPS: Small beakers or jiggers footed with a fox head, the snout and ears forming the footing.

FRACTUR: See Script Hangings.

FRAME TABLE: A permanent table of four legs with frame and stretchers and top permanently affixed, as compared to trestle table or form table, made up when wanted for use.

FRANCIS WARE: Japanned tinware made and decorated by Henry and Thomas Francis, Philadelphia, 1832–45.

FRANKLIN STOVE: See page 149.

FREE-BLOWN: Glass blown only with the aid of blowpipe and pontil without recourse to use of pattern molds, and other devices.

FRENCH PROVINCIAL: Misnomer for French Provençal furniture, which is not at all "provincial," but rather is highly sophisticated and having high style influence; much copied by cabinetmakers of Paris.

FRESCO: A kind of painting done on wet plaster; color goes into the plaster and penetrates to a minute depth. Much wall painting in America called fresco is not fresco at all.

FRETWORK, FRETTED: Borders or sections made up of ornaments cut with a fret saw. A painted border simulating fretwork.

FREY FURNITURE: Made 1790–1810 by Jacob Frey, of Milton, Pennsylvania, in the Valley of the Susquehanna. Crude country-style Chippendale.

FRICKLE: Fruit basket.

FRIENDSHIP QUILT: Quilt made of blocks or squares borrowed from or made by the quilter's friends. 1840–60.

FRIESLAND CLOCK: Ornate filigreed clock cases housing eight-day weight-driven movements made in The Netherlands seventeenth century and earlier.

FRIEZE: A border; more properly the midsection on an entablature. A border placed anywhere on wall between ceiling and floor.

FRIGGER: Any piece of glass made after hours by workmen. Not offhand, as they are at times called, but made as what the workmen themselves called a government job, meaning the boss's materials used freely at no cost. Also an experimental piece of glass. Apprentices' efforts. Amateurish attempt. FRIGGING: Literally, doodling with tools and materials, in potteries, glass houses, foundries, forges, et cetera.

FRIZZ: Wool baize with one side napped.

FROG MUGS: Ale, beer, and cider mugs with a painted or molded form in the bottom.

FROMARD, FROW: Lath-splitting tool.

FROST RUG PATTERNS: See section on Hooked Rugs, page 131.

FRUIT COOLER: Urn-shaped vessel of deep body for holding ice or cold water, with dish or bowl over this to hold fruit for cooling.

FRUGGAN: Iron to stir ashes in oven.

FRUMENTY: Hulled wheat, boiled in milk and seasoned.

FUMING BOX: Pastille burner.

FUNK: Tinder, touchwood.

FUSTIAN: Velveteen, corduroy, and related pile fabrics, lesser than velvets.

FUSTICK: Yellow olive color deriving from a dyewood.

FYKE: A funnel-shaped fish net used to catch chad, or shad; on the Swedes' Brandewijn (Brandywine) River, the Delaware, and the Susquehanna in Pennsylvania. Perhaps of Swedish origin.

FYOLL: Woodenware; a cup. Also a cook pot of iron.

GABIE: Large-holed sieve or collander.

GAD: Measuring rod ten feet long.

GAD NAIL: A long nail.

GADROON: Properly GODROON. A form or ornamentation using the formalized ruffle and olive fruit. Name is from French "godron," plait. Deep rounded fluting as on glass or pottery, on edges of objects.

GAIL, GAIL CLEAR, GAIL DISH: Woodenware; a large tub. A brewing tub.

GALAGE: Galloche, a clog or patten; a "goloshoe" or golosh.

GALLERIED: Any surface surrounded wholly or in part with a low railing or fencing of rails and balusters. The gallery may be fretted, pierced, built up, arcaded (a series of arches), or have other forms. Trays are said to be galleried when they have a rim at right angles to surface, or flaring outward at acute angles (sixty degrees or more). Tables, trays, desk tops, stand tops, and the tops of some chests of drawers are galleried.

GALLEY BAULK: Fixed beam in old chimneys to hold pots: usually of green wood. Iron was preferred and, when movable on a pivot, became known as the crane.

GALLIPOT: Vase form pots with narrow necks from the old Holland Dutch "gleypot," a pot for ointments and unguents; for gley; greases.

GALLOON: A kind of lace and a name for lacemaking.

GALLS: Wood tumors yielding dyestuffs. Oak galls yield a violet and a black, used much in early inkmaking.

GALLUCHAT, GALUCHAT: Leather made of sharkskin.

GALLY TILES: Snell tiles.

GAME PLATES: Special plates for service of game with painted pictures of wild fowl. Eighteenth century.

GANTREE: A stand for barrels and kegs.

GAPESTICK: Woodenware; a large wooden spoon; so large that to use it in eating you had to gape to get it in your mouth.

GARD-MANGER: A meat safe; a meat cupboard. Often with sides and front panels of pierced tin.

GARDEROBE: Clothes cupboard; a wardrobe. A clothes kas.

GARNISH, GARNISHING: Any decorative assembly of pieces; especially a set of twelve plates, beakers, saucers, cups, bowls, et cetera; old name for a set of china. "A garnish of Lowestoft" means a set representing service for twelve places. GARNITURE: Any service or display pieces in sets.

GARN WINDLE, GARNWYN: A yarn reel; often mounted on a narrow stand with turned, canted legs and having a wheel made up of spokes the ends of which terminate in crosspieces, turned and spool-ended.

GARRETED: Stone splinters driven into masonry joints.

GARRISON HOUSE: A residence also designated as a fort; usually a frontier house to which other settlers were wont to go in times of danger.

GARRONS, GARRON NAILS: Large spikes.

GAS CANDLES: Illuminating gas was introduced as a home convenience about 1815–20. American gas plants were set up in the 1820s. The first fixtures to burn the new illuminant were after existing lamp and candlestick forms.

GATE-LEG DESK: Seventeenth- and early eighteenth-century desk box with slopefall front, mounted on frame having a pair of gated legs to the fore; these, when pulled out, supported the slope-fall desk lid. Jacobean and William and Mary.

GAUBERT: An iron rack used in fireplace as a support for pans and pots.

GAUDY DUTCH: See page 124.

GAUDY IRONSTONE: F. Morley and Sons, successors to Mason's Ironstone Pottery, 1851, decorated ironstone ware in large colorful patterns similar to so-called Gaudy Dutch ware.

GAUDY WELSH: The more appropriate name for what is called Gaudy Dutch; this name is used in England.

GEBURTSCHEIN: Birth certificate or memorial, usually hand-drawn and -lettered, but sometimes made on printed forms filled in by hand and hand-colored. Pennsylvania, Ohio, Indiana, Iowa, Delaware, New Jersey, New York, and New England and the Shenandoah Valley south to Winchester, Virginia. Not a distinctive Pennsylvania German practice as generally claimed. Said actually to be of Scandinavian origin. Much used in Flanders, The Netherlands, the French provinces, and Switzerland.

GENRE: A style of picture; one which tells a story. See page 144.

GESSO: Painted plaster ornamentation; raised work in plaster, pargetry work.

GEWGAG: The jewjay, geegaw, or mouth harp, corrupted to jew's-harp.

GIBBY STICK: Woodenware; a hooked stick (also in iron).

GIBCROKE: A pot hook, or jack, used in fireplace.

GILLYFLOWER: The clove pink; flowers used in spicing salads of raw greens and in cookery.

GILLY POT: A small pot.

GILLYVINE PEN: Plumbago stick punched through the pith of gillyflower stems.

GILT LATTEN: Gilded brass.

GIMCRACK: The works of a watch or clock. Any busy little machinery, as a small turnspit.

GIMLIN: Woodenware; a salting tub.

GIMMEW: Woodenware; a hinge or joint.

GIN: A snare, a trap, any tricky machine; hence cotton gin; machine for cotton seeding.

GIPSE: Woodenware; a mortar.

GIRONDOLE: A branched candlestick.

GIRONDOLE MIRROR: A mirror with round, convex glass, framed and with candle brackets; any mirror panel with candle brackets. Name "girondole" is not as old as the objects to which it is applied as the term came into use during the Girond, or Girondin, period of the French Revolution.

GIRT, GIRTLED, GIRTED, GIRTH: Broad tapes arranged as a lattice over a frame, as bedframe, day-bed frame, inside of a chest or box lid. Used to support mattresses, to hold objects placed under it secure, and to pin other objects to it.

GISPEN, GYPSEN, GESPIN: A leathern pot; a blackjack; a leather beaker.

GLASS BEDS: Stourbridge and other English glassmakers blew decorative cylindrical columns of glass which were used, in section, to make up bedposts and -rails by stringing them on metal rods.

GLASS KNOBS: Pressed, cut, swirled, silvered, and blown-glass knobs used on furniture from about 1810 to 1860.

GLASS SHADE: A bell of glass to place over clocks, waxworks, objets d'art, et cetera.

GLASS STAND: A rack for holding glassware, tumblers, et cetera. Seventeenth century.

GLATTON: Flannel made by the Welsh weavers of Pennsylvania in the eighteenth century.

GLEYPOT: An earthen jar for ointments; an apothecary's jar; corrupted to "gallipot."

GLIDDERED: Glazed with a tough varnish.

GLIMSTOCK: A candlestick.

GLOBE WRITING TABLE: A conceit of early nineteenth century; a terrestrial globe of large size on stand, so constructed that the upper section rotates into the lower, exposing a writing surface and various compartments for writing materials.

GLOBOSE: Globular in form.

GLORIA: The melodeon of the eighteenth century. Colloquialism.

GLORY HOLE: The reheating chamber of a glass furnace; a broom and brush closet.

GLOST: In pottery, an oven or kiln in which the biscuit coated with glaze is fired; the fixed glaze before decoration or transfer printing. Glost-fired ware is always refired.

GLUM POT: Gleypot; gallipot.

GOBELIN: Tapestry made at the works founded 1667 as the Manufacture Royale des Meubles de la Couronne, the concern which took over the Cooman tapestry works, operated by the Gobelins. This Flemish family were wool dyers in 1443.

GOBSTICK: Woodenware, a spoon. GOB: a spoonful. GOBS: Spoonfuls.

GODDARD: A tankard, sometimes of woodenware.

GODDARD, JOHN: See block-front furniture section, page 17.

GOFFER, GOFFERING IRON: Crimping or fluting iron; to crimp or flute.

GOLOSSIANS: Goloshoes; goloshes; bad-weather pattens.

GONDOLA CHAIR: Victorian upholstered chairs of ornate pattern and important appearance; the upholstery in shell, quilting, and tufting. Redolent of eighteenth-century French furniture. Name said to derive from a gondola seat.

GOOSE BASKET: A neck and wing basket to secure a goose for plucking. Often confused with eel basket (eel trap) which it somewhat resembles.

GOSSIP POT: A two-handled pot.

GOSTELOW: Philadelphia cabinetmaker of Swedish ancestry (1744-95), who made exceptionally fine furniture and is second only to Savery as a general craftsman.

GOTCHBELLY: Large round-bellied pitcher or spouted jug.

GOTHIC-BACK: Chippendale and other chairs in which the back splat is pierced and shaped in Gothic design. Far removed from pure Gothic in form. Also mid-nineteenth-century chairs with more Gothiclike backs, redolent of church officials' chairs.

GOTHIC TABLE: Victorian table with two- or three-leg end sections arranged as a tier or colonnade of Gothic-style arches.

GOUT CHAIR: Day beds made in two sections—a large chair and a long stool.

GOVERNMENT JOB: Workmen's pieces made on their own or the master's time, of the master's materials and facilities.

GOWER: Woodenware; a great platter for a mess of pottage, as a boiled dinner.

GRAAL: A large basin for serving meat; sometimes of woodenware or pottery but also of pewter and silver.

GRANDCHILD, GRANDDAUGHTER, GRANDFATHER, GRANDMOTHER CLOCKS: Small and large tall-case clocks; clock casing housing weights and pendulum, movement and dial.

GRATE APRON: A fireboard; an apron of paperwork to cover a laid fire in summer.

GRECIAN SOFAS: Federal sofas reflecting Greek Revival influence.

GREENLING: Refined name for the codfish.

GREYRUSSET: Coarse gray cloth.

GRIFFIN: Mythological winged creature with body of a lioness and head of eagle.

GRIPE, GROPE, GRIP: A three-tined fork.

GRISAILLE: Painted in various tones and shades of gray. *En grisaille*, in gray. Grizzled; graying.

GROGRAINE: Coarse, stiff taffeta.

GROOVED DRAWER: Early tables, cabinets, and chests, when fitted with drawers, show drawer sides with deep grooves fitting in tongues of wood fixed in the drawer orifice. Generally connotes seventeenth-century workmanship or tradition.

GROUT: Liquid mortar.

GROWME: A woolen stretcher.

GRUEZ, JOHN: Cabinetmaker of New York City who succeeded H. Lannuier, the Frenchman of that city, in cabinetmaking, c. 1820.

GUILLOCHE: Decoration consisting of a series of interlaced or overlapping circles.

GULLY MOUTH: Small pitcher.

GUM STICK: A teething stick for babies; known in silver, bone, ivory, jade, coral, or other "safe" material.

GUNPOWDER PUNCH: This was the hell-fire club members' drink. Hell-fire clubs were popular gentlemen's clubs after the Revolution, particularly in Virginia. The gentry were atheists, materialists, hunters, gamesters, hard and high livers. They dissolved a measure of gunpowder in wine and drank it for tipple. Also to lace ale and small beer. Hell-fire clubs are now considered to have been more a pose than anything else. They seem to have gone out of fashion by 1800.

GYMP: Passementerie; narrow ornamental tape used for trimming garments and as a finishing border in upholstery. Fringed gymp; stayned gymp, et cetera.

GYMP HEAD: Dimity and fringe used to make a bed canopy.

HAGGADAYS: Woodenware; door latches and fasteners wrought from wood.

HAGSTONE: Witch doctor's stone; a stone bored and suspended from bedpost to prevent nightmares.

HAIR BOTTOM: A chair bottomed, or seated, with horsehair fabric; probably also a chair covered with mohair fabrics, et cetera.

HAIR PENCILS: Brushes of sable, badger, camel, and cat hair, fitted in quills. Crow quills provided the smallest pencils. They are less than one sixteenth of an inch thick. Swan quills are largest; up to three eighths of an inch thick.

HALF TESTER: Early-type folding bed; bedstead hinged to a testered headboard; when folded up entire stead was covered by the tester. Sheraton and Adam influence, Federal style, late eighteenth century and up to 1840.

HALLMARK: Literally the mark of the guildhall; a college of heraldry for artisans, especially silversmiths and goldsmiths, stationers, printers, and pewterers.

HAND COOLER: Ovals of glass shaped to fit palm; made in the manner of fancy paperweights; a vogue of Victorian days.

H AND HL HINGES: The more common form of wrought-iron and brass hinges of the eighteenth century; the H hinge composed of two vertical straps joined by the hinge in form of letter H; the HL being similar but having an extra strap section projecting from a lower section of the H at right angle. It should be noted that H and HL hinges are reproduced today in both iron and brass and that appearance of such hinges on a piece of furniture is no guarantee of age or authenticity.

HANGING CUPBOARD: Any cupboard of shelves or closets, or both, made to hang upon the wall and without a base for support. Seventeenth and eighteenth centuries, New England, New York, and Pennsylvania, nineteenth century Ohio. A type of pioneer furniture. Also made in highly sophisticated forms from mid-eighteenth century to end of Federal period.

HANGING WARDROBE: Any clothes closet in which clothes could be hung. The wardrobe was not hung; it was fitted inside with wooden pegs upon which to hang the garments.

HAPHARLOT: A coarse coverlet.

HARD PASTE: Term given to any hard-bodied porcelain. If a rattail file is applied to porcelain the file will penetrate the soft-paste variety and will be turned by the hard paste. This is not a test for amateurs to use. Study the books recommended on page 178.

HARD PEWTER: Alloy of antimony and copper. Whiter and harder than regular tin-lead-antimony pewter.

HARPSICHORD: This is the ancestor of the grand piano; not a spinet. Chief difference is in number of strings and method of impact on strings. Harpsichord had three to four strings for each note, and they were plucked by a quill. Spinet had striking action and one string for each note. Dutch: STAARSTUCK. French: CLAVECIN À QUEUE.

HARRATINE CHAIR: Early name for easy chair, upholstered in harratine, a fine fabric of lasting quality.

HARVARD CHAIR: Three-legged chair of stick construction, pioneer in quality and dating 1640–1700.

HASTENER: Tin reflector to heat roasting meat on the side away from fire.

HAYSTACK MEASURES: Jug-shaped, of pewter, brass, and rarely silver, with wide belly, narrow neck, and funnel mouth. All have handles. Made from less than pint size to several gallons.

HEALINGS: Bedclothes.

HEARN: Coarse linen.

HEART AND CROWN: A form of cresting used on chairs; the crest having the outline of a crown or tiara while the wood under it is pierced with heart shape. Cresting seldom looks like a crown but the name (probably twentieth century) is nonetheless used to designate the pattern.

HEART BACK: A form used by Hepplewhite in which the heart shape is used in design of chair back.

HEARTH GARNITURE: Sets of andirons; fire tools and fire screen, scuttles and hods.

HEDDLES: Small pegs on a loom to hold loops through which warp is strung.

HEMICYCLE: A semicircle, a half circle.

HEMIGLOBULAR: Half a globe in shape, as certain hot water urns, teapots, sugar basins, and ewers.

HERALDIC POSITIONS: Animal erect on one paw looking to left, is Rampant. Same position, looking down, is Gardant. Same position, head turned to right, is Regardant. On two paws, looking left, is Salient. Four paws on ground, looking out, is Statant Gardant. Three paws on ground, looking left, is Passant. Squatting with stiff forelegs is Sejant. Down on all fours, is Couchant. Down on all fours, head in paws, is Dormant.

HERB MORTAR: Woodenware; a mortar in which to pulverize dried herbs and spices.

HERCULANEUM CHAIRS: Fancy chairs in ancient Roman antique style advocated by Sheraton, Adam, and others.

HERCULANEUM WARE: Made at pottery of this name, Liverpool, 1790–1860.

HERRINGBONE: A form on inlay; narrow bands with pattern laid diagonally as a herringbone.

HEXAFOIL: Any circumference so divided as to form six foils or leaves; six-petaled; six serrations around edge; six semicircular projections on rim, et cetera.

HEX SQUARE, HEXFOLIATE: Six-sided.

HIGHBOY: Late nineteenth-century name for high chests and high chests on frames.

HIGH CHEST (HIGHBOY) STEPS, CHEST STEPS: A run of three steps in the form of three tiers of boxes permitting use from left, right, and front; usually kept under a high chest to provide access to top drawers but sometimes placed atop a flat-topped high chest and used as ledges on which to display china and pottery. Late seventeenth and early eighteenth centuries.

HODDEN GRAY: Woven from the natural white and black wool of sheep.

HOGARTH CHAIR: William Hogarth, famed English artist and moralist (1697–1764), who called the cyma curve the line of beauty, and who helped so to popularize this line in chair legs of Queen Anne and Georgian periods that his name is given to a fine armchair of the periods.

HOLLANDS: A fine low-country linen, later filled with oil and wood flour to make it opaque and used in window shades; hollands shades.

HOMAN BRITANNIA: Homan, of Cincinnati, 1840s to 1850s, made Britannia wares and marked them Homan and Company, Cincinnati. Asaph Flagg was a partner.

HOODED WASHSTAND: Washstands with splashboards and a shelf which serves as a hood to prevent splashing of water on wall behind stand.

HOOFED FOOT: Any foot of chair, table, or cabinet piece having feet in imitation of a horse, pony, or deer. Usually the hoof is uncloven; solid.

HOOP: Woodenware; a tankard of staves with three hoops. Each hoop marked a drink. "Don't give a whoop" believed to derive from this vessel's use in drinking.

HOOP BACK: A type of Windsor chair; a Hepplewhite chair with a hooped back rail but with decorative splat.

HOPNISS: Roots of *Glycine apios*, resembling potatoes, used by Swedes on Delaware about 1660.

HORNBEAM: Hardwood of birch or beech variety.

HORNPANE: A pane of thin horn used instead of glass in windows, lamps, and lanterns.

HORN SALTS: Saltcellars made of animal horn in sections about three inches high. Wood or horn bottoms were pegged in. Frequently scratch-carved.

HORSEBELLS: Arches of wrought iron fixed over horse collars and fitted with bells (two to four but usually in threes) suspended from the arch. Such bells are true bells, having clappers.

HORSE FIRE SCREEN: Fire screen suspended between two high poles joined at their base.

HORSEHAIR: Almost everlasting upholstery fabric made in various colors in eighteenth century. Victorian black horsehair marks the nadir of the art.

HORSESHOE CHAIR: Eighteenth-century upholstered chairs with back rail in form of horseshoe.

HORSESHOE WINDSOR: A Windsor armchair that is essentially a loop back without the loop; hence the arm rail displays a sort of horseshoe shape.

HOUND HANDLES: Pitcher and ewer handles in form of a coursing hound; the vessels are usually also embellished with figures of game and game birds.

HOUSE SAGEN: Literally "house sayings" and meaning mottoes, precepts, blessings, et cetera, done by hand in a form of black letter or Gothic type (miscalled Old English). Originally used by Swedes,

Swiss, and Huguenots of Pennsylvania and by Huguenots in New York and New England, finally in late eighteenth century made by German immigrants in Pennsylvania. The use of these delightful homemade pieces seems to have persisted until at least 1860. Today avidly collected. Many are now found in Kentucky, Ohio, Indiana, and even as far west as Iowa.

H STRETCHER: An arrangement of underbracing of chairs, tables, and cabinet pieces in which a pair of stretchers connect front and rear legs and another stretcher joins these as the crossbar of the letter H.

HUCCHES: Lidded chests; hutches.

HUDSON RIVER PORTFOLIO: A series of landscape aquatints of Hudson River scenery, published in five parts of four prints each by Megary, of New York, after drawings by W. G. Wall. Some few plates engraved by J. Rubens Smith. Balance by John Hill. Twenty-four views were proposed, but only twenty published. Some numbers of first issue run above twenty, but only twenty prints were made. Engraved surface measures 13¾ × 21 inches. Hand-colored. First issue 1818. Most valuable view is New York from Governors Island.

HUMPED BOW BACK: A scarce type of Windsor chair in which the regular bow of back has an extra bow or hump bent into it as a cresting; found in chairs and settees. Rare.

HUNT BOARD: A sophisticated piece of furniture similar to high sideboard, upon which food and drink was laid out for self-service at hunt breakfasts. Southern Pennsylvania, Maryland, Virginia and Carolina. Early nineteenth century. Usually in Hepplewhite or Federal period designs. Many varieties.

HUNTING CHAIR: Library chairs with horseshoe-shaped back arm rails.

HUNTING CUP: Carved ivory and horn beakers with or without base or feet, to hold a draught of ale or wine taken in the saddle.

HUNTING PITCHER: Beverage pitcher with hunting scenes modeled or painted or printed on sides and with a sporting handle; often a hound handle.

HUNT TABLE: A semicircular table ensemble made up of two tables, the fixed tops of which are the shape of a twelfth segment of a circle, each having two leaves also shaped as a segment. Thus with leaves up, and the two tables joined, the table is a half circle when set up; sometimes complete, and sometimes cut out at the center, as though to fit around a large column. These tables are now often used as dining tables in front of a window. Southern United States and England. 1790–1820.

HURRICANE SNUFFERS: A rare type of snuffer made for use in snuffing candles in hurricane shades. The usual scissors terminates in a circular box, below which descends a metal tube to length of six to twelve inches. At end of tube, another boxlike assembly houses the mechanism of snuffing box and shielded blade which project from its side. Thus a candle could be snuffed without removing the large glass shade. Silver and Sheffield plate; also iron and brass. Rare.

IMARI: Japanese wares made in direct imitation of the Chinese original of the K'ang Hsi period; the latter is the prototype of Gaudy Dutch.

IMBOWED: Fashioned into loops.

IMPERIAL OTTOMAN: Circular or oval sofa equipped with many cushions. Period is about 1810.

INCISED CARVING: When the pattern is cut in or below the surface it is incised.

INCROYABLE CHAIRS: Sheraton and Directoire style chairs with deep seat, narrow in front, and having upholstered top rail on the back. Sat in "backward" or facing to rear, resting arms on back rail. Also called CONVERSATION CHAIR and LOUNGING CHAIR, 1792–1812.

INGRAVED CHEST: Believed to have meant inlaid, though it may have meant carved.

INKHORNISM: Studied expressions not clear to others, used by writers and scholars.

INKLE: Linen tape, braid, or lace. Also crewelwork.

INK STICK: India ink, so called, but of Chinese make, imported in sticks and ground with water on a slab to produce the best and finest inks. The slab had a well for collecting the prepared ink.

INTARSIA: Inlay of bone, wood, shell, or metal. Marquetry. Inlay. A word much favored by those addicted to inkhornisms. "Inlaid" tells the story.

INTERLACED HEART: A chair-back design composed of heart-shaped forms interlaced with an oval. Hepplewhite style.

INTERLACED SPLAT: Either simple or ornately carved chairbacks in which the curving elements form an interlaced design. Various forms. Chippendale and Georgian.

INVECTED: Indented. Cut into, serrated, scalloped.

IONICS: Candlesticks of silver or brass in form of classic Ionic column. 1760–1810.

IRISH BUTTER: Often considered an eighteenth-century joke but not so. Neither is it term for salted goose grease. The finest salted butter obtainable (1750–70) was imported in firkins from Ireland.

IRISH WINDSORS: Stick chairs, the sticks spool or sausage turned, having a rush seat. Irish, 1760–1820. Made of elm and oak. Imported in great numbers by antique dealers after 1900.

IRONING TABLE: Overlong stretcher table of cottage style, made by the Shakers for use as a dining table and an ironing board.

ISINGLASS: Gelatine obtained from fishes; a foodstuff; used in the making of gelatines, galantines, et cetera, in the eighteenth century. Not mica.

IVORYTYPE: A richly hand-colored photographic portrait, protected with plate glass. Made between 1840 and 1860. No longer common.

JACK: A quartern; one quarter of a pint.

JACKSON BRASS: Jonathan Jackson, brazier, maker of basins, candlesticks, door knockers, skillets, stirrups, spurs, et cetera, prior to 1736. New England.

JACK TAR JUG: A Toby-type vessel featuring the figure of a sailor. 1810–30.

JACOBEAN: Another name for Carolean. Refers to period of James I, Charles I, the restoration of Charles II, and the short reign of James II. Roughly 1605–85.

JACONET: Fine cotton fabric from India, 1750–1850.

JAGGING IRON: A pastry-making tool.

JALOUSIES: Wood shutters with movable, adjustable slats as in venetian blinds.

JAMB HOOKS: Metal hooks, screws, or spikes driven in jambs of fireplace to hold or secure fire tools.

JENNEN & BETTRIDGE: English makers of japanned wares, 1815 to 1860.

JEWELED TOLE: Fine decorated tinware, flecked with colored beads.

JIGGER: Earthenware cheese toaster.

JIGSAW MIRROR: Pierced and fretted frame mirrors.

JILLMILLS: Fine gauze or netting used as mosquito and fly screening, eighteenth century.

JOHNSON, JONATHAN: Chairmaker of Lynn, Massachusetts, 1720–40.

JOINED CHEST: Chest made by a joiner; a chest dovetailed; mortised; fitted. All parts joined. Best kind of construction. Term used in the seventeenth century.

JOINT STOOL, JOINED STOOL: Stool with turned legs, stretchers, and rails, all joined or fitted together.

JONATHAN: Four-footed iron stand fitted also with hooks above, for toasting before the fire or by suspension from crane or bar.

JORDAN: A chamber pot.

JOURNAL RACK: Rack or stand with fretted, slatted, or solid compartments, spread fanwise to hold periodicals, journals, newspapers. Late eighteenth and first half nineteenth centuries.

JOYNED, JOINED: Any work done by a joyner, or joiner. Fitted by key, dovetail, mortise, et cetera.

JULEP CUP: A short beaker, generally of silver, extensively used by the gentry in making and serving mint juleps: bourbon whisky poured over cracked ice and crushed mint. Rapid decomposition of the ice in alcohol caused outside of cup to gather moisture and then freeze, or frost.

KAIL POT: A cabbage-cooking pot.

KALEMDAM: A pen case.

KAS: A wardrobe chest of huge, or at least generous, proportions; tall and stately. Usually with ball or bun feet. Dutch in style. A native Amsterdam Dutch piece. Brought to New York and Pennsylvania by the Dutch.

KATNISS: Native root of the *Sagittaria*, an arrow-leaved swamp plant, used by the Swedes on the Delaware.

KEALER, KEELER: Woodenware; a cooling tub.

KEEP: A meat safe.

KEEPING ROOM: Parlor-living room of the seventeenth century.

KELT: Natural gray cloth made from natural black and white wool.

KERMESSE BED: A temporary cot; a shakedown.

KETTLE BODY, KETTLE-BOTTOMED, BOMBÉ: Cabinet furniture characterized by a belled-out swelling of the body, especially chests of draws and desks.

KEYHOLE PIERCING: Metal pierced with oval or keyhole-shaped holes, as the gallery of a tray or the gallery work on cabinet furniture.

KIBBLE: Woodenware; the bucket of a draw well.

KIBOSH: Blowing of cement or plaster on sculptured or wooden forms; hence the old phrase "to put the kibosh on," meaning to change the shape and form.

KIDDERMINSTER: Coarse linen and woolen fabric. Later a form of floor carpeting.

KIDNEY TABLE (TABLE À ROGNON): Name derives from the curved oval kidney shape of top.

KILDERKIN: A measure of sixteen to eighteen gallons.

KILLIKINICK: Dried inner bark of the red willow and dried annual twigs of the upland sumac, mixed half and half and used as incense, burned or roasted, or to add spice to smoking tobacco. Eighteenth century.

KIT KAT SIZE: A portrait size 28 × 36 inches. So called because this was the size portrait used in decorating the Kit Kat Club. Early eighteenth-century London.

KNEADING TABLE: Placing a bread-board on a dough trough made a kneading table.

KNEE CARVING: The knee of a chair or table leg, highboy or lowboy leg of the bandy, or cabriole type, carved in various forms and in various décor. Queen Anne, Georgian, Chippendale. Also on mid-Victorian.

KNEEHOLE DESKS: Desks with an aperture for knees of the sitter; usually flat-top desks having piers or pedestals in pairs, separated for the kneehole.

KNOCKER LATCH: Door latch of brass or iron serving also as a door knocker. Twisting the hammer of the knocker operated the latch. Eighteenth century.

KNOBS, KNOB PULLS, KNOB BRASSES: Brass knobs extending forward from a plate, used as drawer pulls and cupboard handles from around 1790 to 1840. Many different classical, decorative, floral, and portrait-head patterns, eagles, et cetera, are known. Sometimes named for the style or the portrait, as flowered knobs, Washington knobs, eagle knobs, et cetera.

KNOB, KNOPPED: In glass parlance, a knob; knobbed stem = knopped stem.

KRATER, KRATER VASE: Ancient wide-mouthed jars; wider at mouth than at any part of the interior. Sometimes spouted. Krater vases of eighteenth century are after Greek and Roman forms. They are usually bell-mouthed, rising from a squat bulbous section which is in turn on a stem rising above a pedestal base. Pottery, china, and porcelain.

LACE: The making of lace has engaged the attention of women for countless ages. Collecting lace has been a minor vogue for centuries. *Seven Centuries of Lace*, by J. H. Pollen, is a good reference book to consult.

LACE BOX: Finery box. Sometimes called bride's box.

LACE-EDGE TRAY: Fancy tin trays with a flat edging added to rim, the edging pierced, or painted in lace-like pattern. Popular after the Revolution. Paul Revere and other silversmiths are said to have made such trays and thus entered into competition with tinsmiths.

LACKABOYS: Thin-soled shoes.

LADDER BACK: Any chair back characterized by upright extensions of back legs, and fitted with from three to six crosspieces as rungs in a ladder. Known in plain, bowed, and shaped forms of pioneer and seventeenth-century type, and also in highly sophisticated, carved, and shaped Chippendale.

LADIES' TWIST: A dainty roll of flavored tobacco favored by ladies who chewed it as the most genteel manner of using tobacco, 1760–1830.

LADY BIRD CAGE: Female figure, generally of period 1650–1720, with carved wood head, torso fashioned of close strap and wire work, wire-work arms, and a voluminous skirt of more open wire work serving as a bird cage. Not a cage for "Ladybirds" but a bird cage in the form of a lady.

LADY JANE: Demijohn; a translation of Dame Jeanne, the name of the container in France.

LAFAYETTE SALTS: Boat-shaped salts or salt dishes of glass, impressed with name "Sandwich" and, on bottom, B&S Glass Co" (Boston and Sandwich Glass Company).

LAMPAS PANEL: Panel of damask, usually in two colors. Used in wall décor, upholstery, et cetera.

LAMP FLUIDS: Camphen, or camphene (rectified spirits of turpentine with alcohol). Porters' fluid (a patent fluid). Lard oil, whale oil, kerosene or coal oil, liquid suet.

LAMP TEAPOT: Teapot in form of ancient Roman lamp.

LANGDON TAPERS: Candles made by John Langdon of Boston, c. 1770.

LANGE LEISEN, LANGE LEIZEN, LANGE LEIJSEN, LONG ELIZA, ET CETERA: Dutch name for the Chinese porcelains characterized by the "long" male and female figures; the attentuated figures of formal Chinese expression in art.

LANNUIER: French cabinetmaker (Honoré Lannuier) of New York, 1805–20. Did some superlatively fine work in the Directoire style. As good if not better than Phyfe.

LANTERN CASE: A bell of glass; a metal- or wood-cased glass box for display of objects, as in a lantern. Usually dust-proof.

LANTERN CLOCK, (BIRD-CAGE, PILLAR-AND-BUTTON, SHEEP'S-HEAD, BUTTON-AND-PILLAR CLOCKS): A square-shaped brass clock assembly with round dial extending beyond sides of case proper, finials on either side of front at top, and with a fretted or pierced cresting at top center, with similar "ears" at sides. The whole surmounted with upward and incurving bands from each corner, terminating in a central finial, under which is placed the alarm or bell. Operated by weights. Having one or two hands (depending on date) and designed to be placed on a wall bracket or hooded stand. Sixteenth, seventeenth, and eighteenth centuries. Now exceedingly rare in original condition. Most examples are much repaired; many outright "antique" fakes abound. Never purchase without expert opinion and advice.

LANTHORN: A horn-cased lamp, the horn peeled thin and having translucency almost to point of clear transparency.

LAQUEAR, LAQUER: Originally, to make a ceiling.

LASTING: Two- or three-thread double-warp fabrics, plain, twilled, and figured.

LATCH PAN: Dripping pan.

LATTEN: An alloy resembling brass. Essentially brass. Sometimes gilded, and then called gilt latten. Also once used to designate tin-plated sheet iron.

LATTICINIO: Form of glass paperweight decoration, formed by the crossing of curved lines. See section on paperweights, page 107.

LAUREATED: Crowned with laurel; with chaplet of laurel. Any decorative element showing a profile so treated is said to be "laureated."

LAVABO: A washstand consisting of bowl and fountain supported upon a wooden or metal stand.

LAY'D WORK: Inlay, as in cabinetmaking. A form of embroidery.

LEADED DIAMOND: Lead muntins (cames) set diamond pattern in wood frames for use as casement windows. Set with glass (clear, bull's-eye, yellow, and violet), with sheets of thin horn, or varitinted mica. Used in America mainly in the seventeenth century.

LEAD GLASS: Glass made of forty to sixty parts lead (galena) to one hundred parts clean sand. CRYSTAL GLASS, FLINT GLASS. Not soda glass.

LEAD MIRRORS: Early mirrors made by pouring melted lead on heated sheets of glass.

LEAD SAUCER: Pulverized graphite or plumbago ground in gum water and dried in thick deposits on saucers. Moistened by breathing upon it and removed with a dauber or pounce, this was used in making "theorem" pictures, so-called "mezzotint" painting, et cetera, in which the plumbago was applied to the surface to be painted, through a stencil. Not a saucer made of lead.

LEADWORK: Wrought- and cast-lead ornamentation and decoration, chiefly statues, busts, cisterns, wellheads, garden figures, sundials, and architectural and funerary elements, were used in America in the formal gardens of Virginia and Maryland very early in the eighteenth century. Most likely they were all imported. *English Leadwork, Its Art and History,* by Lawrence Weaver, is a splendid reference book with 441 illustrations.

LEATHERWORK: Tooled- and wrought-leather objects such as handbags, small cases, boxes, envelopes, pouches, portfolios, et cetera, are known in superbly tooled and cutwork examples. Reference is made to *The Decoration of Leather,* by Georges De Recy. It is certain that many expert saddlers and bookbinders in America made good decorated leatherwork. Little or no attention has been paid to this subject as yet, but a few wise collectors are gathering it very quietly.

LEGS: Many and various names abound to designate types of legs of furniture; bandy, turned, trumpet, ball, fretted, splayed, cerule, concave, round, reeded, cluster, winged lion, et cetera. Most are self-explanatory.

LEHR: A glass furnace.

LEUWIN, LEWIN: Tablecloth.

LEY CASK: Wooden cask used for leaching lye (ley) from wood ashes.

LIBRARY-STEP CHAIR: A chair of Chippendale style, leather-upholstered, with a series of steps arranged under the seat which, tipped up or to one side, enabled unfolding of the steps to serve as a ladder to reach books on high shelves.

LIDDED LIP: Any lipped or spouted vessel having a cover which extends over the lip or spout.

LIGHTHOUSE CLOCK: Lighthouse-shaped cabinet section housing the weights and pendulum of a lantern or bird-cage-type clock, mounted atop the section. The lighthouse casing of these clocks is much later than the clocks. But rare.

LIGHTHOUSE COFFEEPOT: Name derives from tapering, high, cylindrical shape.

Silver, pewter, tin. Seventeenth, eighteenth, and nineteenth centuries.

LIGHTSTAND: Small, four-legged table used to hold camphene lamps, kerosene, and whale-oil lamps and similar "patent" lamps. Date from second decade of nineteenth century, marking the beginning of the end of the tri-footed, vase-columned candlestands. Lightstands are in what we have called the Federal period style.

LIGNUM VITAE: Hardest of woods; will "turn" a saw or ax blade. Often used for drinking cups, paperweights, chocolate cups, et cetera. A rare wood.

LILY PAD: A form of glass decoration in which a coating of molten glass over an already formed vessel is tooled into looped sections called lily pads.

LIME SEAT, LINDEN SEAT: Chair seats made of twisted fibers of the inner bark of the linden.

LIME WOOD: Usually linden wood; not the wood of the lime, a citrus fruit. Inner bark of linden used also to make "lime rope."

LINEAR CARVING: Groove carving; flat carving; the kind of carving in line which was used on early New England chests.

LINENFOLD CARVING: Carving to simulate classic or formalized linen folding, or folds. Used in wall panels, chest panels, and cabinetwork. Early English.

LINEN PRESS: Wooden form, or press, with a wood screw engaging upper of two boards between which linen was pressed.

LINSET: A spinning stool; small stool for the spinner to use at the wheel.

LINSEY-WOOLSEY, LYSLE-WULSE: Originally poor woolen stuffs, eked out with flax in the weaving.

LIST: A frame. Pictures in lists; framed pictures.

LIVERY CUPBOARD: A cupboard of early type (seventeenth century) akin to press cupboard. See page 6.

LOBSTOCK: Chinese candles with cotton wick wrapped around a sliver of bamboo.

LOCO-FOCO: From locus, place; and focus, hearth. Name given (1832) to a new strike-anywhere match. At a Tammany Convention (1835) the regulars turned out the gas. The "equal-rights" or "reform" faction were ready with loco-focos and candles. Hence this name was given to a political reform party. Locofoco party.

LOCOMOTIVE CHAIR: Invalid's chair with three wheels, the forewheel geared to a hand lever operated by sitter and so propelling the chair on smooth sidewalks and paths.

LOGGERHEAD: A heavy head of iron on a rod, and set in a turned handle. The head heated in hot coals was used to make hot drinks by plunging into the mug or beaker.

LOLLIPOT, LOLLIPOP: Any common sweetmeat or confection.

LONG CLOCK: Any tall-case or grand-father-type clock.

LONG LADY: A tall candle.

LOOKING-GLASS CLOCK: (1) Clock set in upper panel of a mirror. (2) Clock with its lower door section (the tablet) made of mirror glass instead of painted or stenciled.

LOO TABLE: Gaming table; a card table for playing the game of loo, or fip-loo.

LORIMER, LORIMERY: A maker of spurs and metalwork of saddlery; the gear so made.

LOSSET: Woodenware; a dish or trencher.

LOUIS PHILIPPE: A revival, during 1830–50, of the styles of Louis XV. Reflected in the United States in chairs of black walnut, often mistaken for Victorian, and some cabinets of the same period.

LOUIS QUATORZE, QUINZE, SEIZE, TREIZE: Refers, respectively, to the styles of France during reigns of (1) Louis XIV, (2) Louis XV, (3) Louis XVI, (4) Henri IV or Louis XIII.

LOVERS' CHAIR: A chair wide enough for two people; known in Queen Anne and Chippendale. Also called SPORTING CHAIR and DRUNKARD'S CHAIR.

LOWBOY: Low case or stand; similar to lower half of a highboy. See furniture sections, pages 11 to 20.

LOW CASE OF DRAWERS: Designating in eighteenth century what is today called a bureau. Not a lowboy.

LOWPOST BED: Any stubby-posted bed having posts below the heights required for canopy or tester.

LUCIFERS: Sulphured splints tipped with potash and antimony. These splints were flexible shavings, not sticks, and to ignite them they were drawn through folded sheets of sandpaper. 1830–40.

LUG HANDLES: Bosses or knobs projecting from sides of earthenware, china, or metal vessels, or woodenware, around which cords or thongs were passed to form a handle for lugging.

LUKES: Velvet cloth.

LUSTRES: Glass chandeliers, hung low to give maximum light. Also pendants of glass around a candlestick, suspended from bobeches.

LUTE: Crockery cement. Gum arabic, chamber lye, and flour, cooked for fifteen minutes to a jelly. Used to repair crockery, eighteenth century.

LUTE: A stringed instrument similar to the guitar. Lutestring, name for fine fabric, is believed to derive from this instrument.

LYE LEACH, LYE DROPPER, LYE LATCH: Small box with perforated bottom for straining water through wood ashes to get a small quantity of lye.

LYRE BACK: Chairs with backs formed as lyres, ancient Grecian harps.

LYRE CLOCK: Clock cases in form of lyre; a variety of banjo clock. Fine.

MAID, BAKE MAID: Iron frame of the backstone; bakestone.

MALEFACTOR'S CAGE (HOOSEGOW): A cage of iron bars, open to view from all sides, and very cramped. Petty malefactors were confined in such cages and exposed to public view. Eighteenth century.

MANSION HOUSE DWARFS: Staffordshire figures of merry little men in Toby style.

MANTEL MIRRORS: Any mirror designed for use on a chimney breast, over a mantel. Usually three times as wide as high, compartmented in three sections, the center section being largest. Some known without compartmenting. Rare in Queen Anne, Chippendale, and Hepplewhite periods (when *of* the period; that is, contemporary and not reproductions) but common in late Federal and Empire styles, which are usually heavy-framed, carved, rosetted, and gilded. Made by

hundreds of looking-glass manufactories between 1810 and 1850. See section on mirrors, page 63.

MANTEL TREE: Properly the tree, or beam, over the fireplace opening, but later applied to the mantelpiece, mantel shelf, or overmantel.

MANTEL TREE SETS: "Sets" of garniture for the mantel; delftware, porcelain, Staffordshire, pewter, and silver plate. Vases, covered and open; beakers, jars, pots, et cetera, matched in pairs and sets of three to five pieces.

MAQUETTE: A room in miniature; a play toy for grownups and children, usually furnished with miniature furniture, rugs, wall coverings, and garniture, the whole in a vitrine, or glass, case.

MARBLE TABLES, MARBLE-TOPPED TABLES: Not to be confused with slate-top tables. The true marble table or marble-topped table was both rich and rare in seventeenth and eighteenth centuries, but almost common in the Victorian Era of nineteenth century (1850–70 especially).

MARBLEIZE: To simulate the appearance of marble by painting and veining on wood, iron, plaster, paper, et cetera. Iron mantels were often marbleized. Marbleized paper was used for wall panels.

MARCHPANE, MARZIPAN, MARCHIPAN: Confection of almond meal, egg whites, sugar, et cetera, molded in various forms, plaques and cakes, and often colored with vegetable dyes. A 1616 recipe reads: "Take meal of pine-nuts, filberts, pistachios, almonds and rosed sugar, bray it with egg whites, mould, and dry it, or toast it lightly."

MARCHPANE, MARZIPAN MOLDS: Wood, metal, slate, and pottery molds for pressing marchpane into decorative forms. The décor is cut deeply in the mold and on the finished product, appears in high relief. Known in sizes from 2 × 2 to 14 × 20 inches and larger. Used generally from 1500–1860. Still used in modern form, as this candy is still made in form of fruits, vegetables, et cetera, cast in plaster or sulphur molds. Many Early American molds are religious, historic, memorial, and special, as for a fire-fighting or military company. Early molds are avidly collected as fine examples of woodenware, iron, et cetera. No collection as yet seems to be owned by any American candy company. No books on subject and very few articles have appeared on marchpane or marzipan molds.

MARLBOROUGH CHAIRS: Name given to the Chippendale square-legged armchairs.

MARLBOROUGH LEGS: Square legs without taper, ending in an enlargement in the form of an elongated block, or plinth. Plain and decorated legs and blocks are known.

MARQUETRY, PARQUETRY: Ornamental work in wood on wood; inlay work. Wood mosaic. Geometrical, floral, scenic, in varicolored wood, on table tops, chair panels, chest fronts, et cetera.

MARQUISE: A love seat.

MARRIED-OFF: Any antique piece, or piece offered as original antique, which has been created by the merging of elements from several old pieces. Matching vagrant lowboy sections with chest sections to make highboys, reassembling chests and desks on frames, reassembling chairs, et cetera. Such faking may not be recent, or even intentional deceit, but, when known to be a practice, the pieces are so called.

MARTHA WASHINGTON ARMCHAIRS: Bare-armed Adam, Hepplewhite, and Sheraton chairs with upholstered seats and backs are so called. The vogue lasted well into the 1800s. An American term.

MARTHA WASHINGTON SEWING TABLE: A nineteenth-century term for what is apparently a very early Federal furniture development. A sewing table on four legs (Sheraton style) with outstanding seven-sided pockets or catchalls, having flap lids. The dating of this piece would seem to be after 1790 and perhaps as late as 1800. Doubtful if Martha Washington ever had one, although she may have been pictured by nineteenth-century artists posed aside of one.

MARZIPAN: See Marchpane.

MARZIPAN MOLDS: See Marchpane Molds.

MASCARON: Decorative element in form of a mask.

MASELIN: A cup made of alloyed metal called maslin.

MASER, MAZER: Woodenware; a bowl or goblet of mazer (maple) wood.

MASTER CHAIRS: Exceptionally fine ex- amples, usually having extra decoration or exaggerated characteristics of the type or style, as a Master Roundabout, a Master Windsor, et cetera.

MATCH-LIGHT BOX: Bottle containing sulphuric acid on a pad of asbestos, into which wood splints tipped with chlorate of potash were dipped. The combining of the two chemicals ignited the splint. 1814-25.

MATCH SAFES: With the advent of friction and strike-anywhere matches, many china and metal containers, with ridged or roughened surfaces on inside of lid, were made. Many English china ones, with lovely figurines, groups, eagles, et cetera, were imported by American dealers. Metal "safes" to carry matches in pocket were made of silver, brass, iron, pewter, and tin. Also horn, bone, and gutta-percha. The china, figurine-topped match safes are collectors' items of general interest. Some few collectors are interested in the metal pocket-match safes. These, when embossed or engraved with historic scenes, portraits and medallions, are quite valuable, especially in silver and brass. Fine ones are known with Wedgwood cameo inserts. Made mostly after 1830.

MAUND: A container. Any woodbox for storing things. Salt maund; salt box.

MAZARINE, MAZERINE: A porringer.

MAZARINS, MAZERS: Masers; maplewood bowls and mugs, sometimes with silver rims. See Maser.

McINTIRE FURNITURE: Samuel McIntire, of Salem, Massachusetts, designer, master builder, and carver. According to recognized authorities his specialty in furniture was sofas. No marked pieces made by him are known but certain pieces are attributed to him because of carving similar to that used by him in houses.

MEAT WARE: Believe it or not, this means "vegetables." In the early days meat was food other than "flesh"; hence, "he hath eaten of meat and flesh," or "we did have flesh for noon-meat."

MELON FOOT: A rare-type ball foot with the ball carved or grooved to simulate the ridging and segmentation of a melon. Usually on chests and cabinets.

MELON SHAPE: Descriptive of the pitcher shape evolved at Liverpool, England, prior to 1750. Most Liverpool transfer-printed pitchers with emblems and scenes of American interest are melon-shaped. They are known in miniatures only two and one-half inches high and in advertising or promotion piece sizes twenty inches high. The general run of these pitchers is from nine to fifteen inches high.

MERESE: The button or pad of glass between bowl and stem, or parts of stem.

MERIDEN BRITANNIA: Hard pewter known as Britannia was made by the Meriden (Connecticut) Britannia Company prior to 1860. They made a full line, sold through jewelers and merchants generally.

MERLIN CHAIR: Self-propelled chair with cranks on top of arms conveying power to gears which moved wheels on front legs.

MERMAID BOTTLE: A glass flask shaped and frilled in the form of a seahorse. Eighteenth and nineteenth centuries. Also made in pottery, at Bennington, Vermont.

MESSING: Two eating from one plate.

METAL POLISHERS: Many were used in past three centuries. Most used were: Tripoli, a finely pulverized silica; rotten stone; chalk; whiting; tin putty (oxide of tin), and Dutch rushes. These were stems of *Equisetum hyemale,* the outer bark of which has minute grains of flint embedded in it as a natural process of growth.

METAMORPHIC LIBRARY CHAIR: The library chair with folding four-step ladder under seat.

MEZZOGRAPH: A daguerreotype on paper; a form of photograph introduced 1852.

MEZZO-RILIEVO: Middle relief carving or molding; raised work higher and more pronounced than bas-relief.

MILK BENCH: A cupboard and shelf arrangement for the dairy, milkhouse, or kitchen shed. Used to hold crocks, milk pans, et cetera.

MILK PAINT: Fresh curds of milk, smoothed and mixed with slaked lime, linseed oil, and color. Used for interior painting. A good paint. Better than most interior paints used today.

MILK WOOD, WILLOWWARE: White willow wood, considered best for woodenware used in dairy. Especially milk pails and milk bowls.

MILKYDOW, ASCLEDOW, EISELDOWN: Down

from pods of the milkweed; soft and silky. Stripped of seeds and used as stuffing for pillows and padding in quilts. Down from one pod just enough to tuft one square inch of quilting.

MILLER FURNITURE: Greek revival furniture made by George Miller of New York, after designs by Hope. He used gold stenciling. 1820–30.

MILLIKENS: Stencils made by John Milliken of Lawrence, Massachusetts, who made stencils for home craftsmen and had a mail-order business, 1850–60.

MIRROR KNOBS: Battersea enamel, porcelain, glass, brass, paperweight glass, and other materials forming decorative heads fixed on long screws, used to support the bottom rail or frame of a mirror. This permitted the mirror to be tilted to permit reflection at oblique angle. 1760–1850.

MISCHIANZA: The grand ball given 1778 by British officers to Sir William Howe during the British occupation of Philadelphia. The most lavish affair of the Revolution. A special interior decorating job was done for this British and Tory blowout. Special chairs, mirrors, lights, et cetera, were made for it. Hence Mischianza mirrors, chairs, et cetera. Mirrors were either marked "for" the ball, or were marked in commemoration by those who fell heir to them.

MIXING TABLE: A small sideboard or butler's cabinet with end compartments for liquor and wine bottles, and a mixing table which, in some examples, is fitted with a sliding tambour cover. Believed used mostly in South during Federal period.

MOCK TAPESTRY: Cloth painted in imitation of tapestry.

MOHAIR: Angora wool fabric from the angora goat; not the angora rabbit.

MOLDED, MOULDED: In cabinetwork means shaped with tools on the bench, rather than turned, spokeshaved, et cetera.

MONEY BUCKLES: Shoe buckles of coin silver.

MONTAGUE CHAIRS: Made at Montague, Mass., by Richardson and Dike, about 1850. Fancy chairs of decadent style, and Boston rockers.

MONTEET: Wineglass cooler.

MONTEITH: Punch bowl with broad, deep serrations along edge, designed to hold wine glasses by stem and base. Silver and Sheffield plate.

MONTEITH TWO-LIPPED BOWL: Glass bowls, cut-decorated, usually of Waterford, Cork, or Stourbridge make, having two lips which serve as holders for wine glasses as the bowl, filled with ice, chilled them. MONTEET.

MONTGOLFIER: Iron stove of Franklin style but made to fit in fireplace and reduce size of opening in order to correct faulty draft. Late eighteenth and early nineteenth centuries.

MONUMENTAL CANDLESTICKS: High-footed columnar candlesticks of seventeenth century. Silver, brass, and gilded brass.

MOON: A globe-shaped frame of iron or brass, fitted with panes of horn or mica to enclose a torch or flare.

MOON QUARTER BOARD: See Crescent Sideboard.

MOON'S-AGE CLOCK: Any clock over the dial of which a disk rotates and carries picture of moon. Globes at either side provide screens to display the moon in phases. The disk revolves once in twenty-eight days. Seldom accurate, but approximately so.

MOREEN: A fabric related to silks and damask; an upholstery and curtain fabric, made "watered" (moiré) or plain.

MORRIS: William Morris (1834–96), English artist and craftsman, leader of movement for new, simple designs. Originator of the Morris chair. Also Morris wallpapers, et cetera.

MORTAR AND PESTLE: Bell-mouthed, mortar-shaped metal vessel used for pulverizing and powdering, with the aid of a pestle of similar metal, or stone, bone, or wood. Bronze and iron and brass in large sizes; also stone. Small sizes known in silver.

MORTLAKE TAPESTRY: English. Loomed at Mortlake after 1619. Rubens and Van Dyck made designs for this tapestry works. Fifty Flemish weavers were employed. Through them, and their associate artists, the Flemish styles (scrolls, et cetera) were implanted on the Carolean (Jacobite) furniture. Works ceased about 1665.

MOUNTS: Any brasses, handles, knobs, drawer pulls, handles, scutcheons, et cetera, used in cabinetwork and on chairs.

MOURNING LOCKETS: Gold and silver lockets containing keepsakes of departed loved ones. Locks of hair, miniature portraits, miniatures of tombs, nail parings, et cetera. Eighteenth and nineteenth centuries.

MOWER'S RING: A pottery bottle in form of a ring large enough to be pulled over arm and slung on shoulder. Carried in the fields as a water bottle. Nineteenth century.

MUFFINEER: A tall shaker with pierced top used to sugar muffins; also as a salt and spice shaker. Silver, pewter, Sheffield plate.

MUGGER: A dealer in crockery; a jug maker; a mug maker. A gypsy.

MUNTINS: Dividing bars in window frames, door frames, et cetera, in which glass is mounted.

MUSHROOM KNOBS: Flat knobs on posts of early chairs.

MUSIC COVERS: 1820–80. Music sheets carried covers which in many cases are illustrated with views, scenes, events, people, et cetera. Early ones are engraved. After 1830 almost all are lithographed. Several thousand, all different, are believed to have been issued.

MUSICAL GLASSES: Bowl-like glasses mounted in felted wood frames, as a chromatic scale. Rubbed with wetted fingers, they emit tones of sweet quality. Some played by lightly tapping with drumsticks or bits of rawhide. Seventeenth and eighteenth centuries.

MUSTARDED COFFEE: Early American practice of adding mustard to ground coffee before boiling to fortify and enliven the brew. This resulted in development of a meat sauce of drippings, mustard, and cooked coffee.

NAIL: A measure; two and a quarter inches.

NANKEEN: Chamois or fawn-colored cotton fabric, closely woven and strong. Color is natural, not dyed. Woven in China and India. A popular breeches material.

NANKIN: A good grade exported porcelain from Nanking, China. Also a matting of woven straw in various Chinese patterns.

NAPPERY, NAPERY: Cloth, particularly table linens. Said (1) to derive from Latin *mappa*, a cloth; (2) from Icelandic *Knappa*, the back of the neck, or button; and (3) from *nape, naper,* the name once given linen neckcloths.

NATTE: A tablecloth.

NAVAL MIRRORS: Misnomer for tabernacle mirrors with ships or naval scenes painted in the upper panels. Naval victories of 1812 are displayed on such mirrors. They are for home, not naval, use.

NECESSAIRE: A toilet case; a vanity box; a grooming kit.

NEF: Ship-shaped cabinet for keeping the salt, the hand towel, and the rose water for use of personages at table. Also a clock in the shape or form of a ship.

NELLY BLY: Novelties, particularly small lamps and gadgets, named for the woman who beat Jules Verne's eighty-day schedule around the world.

NEROLI: Orange oil.

NIDDY-NODDY: Hand reel for hanking yarns, shaped like a double-ended anchor. Made of wood.

NIGHT CLOCK, CANDLE CLOCK: Clock with moving dial on which numerals are cut in open silhouette instead of painted. Dial revolved and brought the hour to a slot. The lighted candle within the clock shone through the opening and thus told the time at night. Rare.

NIGHT CROW: A night jar; a chamber pot.

NOCTURNAL: Device for time telling by the stars. A sort of circular slide rule with a sighting bar. Angle established by adjustment to sight the bar on a star marked the time (approximately) on the scale.

NOGGINS: Woodenware and pewter mugs with handles.

NOSING: Projecting rounded or molded section of a stair tread.

NURSING CHAIR: Any small, comfortable, low chair used by nursing mothers. A very old type of chair; in sixteenth century very ornate.

NUTMEG LAMP: Trade name of Gausler, Hoffman, and Company, 1875, for a small night lamp.

NUTMEG SPOON: Eighteenth-century gadget; silver spoon with a nutmeg-grating section on underside of spoon handle.

NUTTO WOOD, NUTTEN WOOD: Hickory.

OAST: A hop-drying kiln.

OBLES, OBLE IRON: Thin ceremonial wafers; the iron in which they are pressed, formed, and baked.

OBSQUARE: Oblong.

OBVERSE: The right side of any medal coin or medallion. The recto, or right-hand page.

OCCASIONAL TABLE: Any small table, particularly the pedestal type, but properly any small table of good taste and style.

OCIVAL: Objective of Ogive; an arch, pointed or vaulted.

OCO DENTAL SNUFF: Offered as a dentrifrice but really a chewing snuff for women. First offered under this trade name about 1858.

OCTAFOIL: A foil is a segment of a circle, roughly 120 degrees. Any round table with eight scallops is octafoil. Quatrefoil, trefoil, sextafoil would be four, three or six scallops. Bifoil would be a pointed ellipse.

ODOUR CASE: Perfume box for keeping handkerchiefs, et cetera.

OFFHAND: Term applied to work ordered and agreed upon but out of ordinary routine, especially of a glass furnace or pottery. Today making bull's-eye glass is offhand work. Workmen, doing things for themselves, were not engaging in offhand work. This they called a "government job."

OGEE: Any molding or element using the cyma curve with its convex portion above and its concave below, as the italic *s*.

OGEE FOOT: A bracket foot of squat cyma curve, achieved by the mitering of an ogee molding for the outer edge of foot and a stepped-back cutting, usually flowing into the skirting of the piece, on inner sides.

OIL-BOILED CALICO: Name given chintz in some sections of country.

OIL-GILDED: Gold leaf or foil applied over the tacky oil varnish known as gold size.

OIL STAND: Oil fountain of japanned tinware, fitted with a small tap and used to fill lamps. A household oil can. Advertised in 1833.

OJAS: Unglazed pottery water jars which absorbed and evaporated absorbed water by contact with outside air over entire outer surface, hence cooling water within jar. Early water coolers.

OLIVER'S SKULL: Virginia cavaliers' term for chamber pot. "Oliver" meaning Cromwell.

OMBRE TABLES: Three-cornered tables for playing the three-party (cutthroat) game of cards, ombre.

ONION FOOT: Variant of ball foot, of flattened onion shape. Used on chests and cabinets.

OPEN BACK: Chair backs with turned or curved ladderlike pieces set between posts.

ORCEL: A small vase.

ORFRAYS: Gold-embroidered cloth. John Hancock had a scarlet coat of orfrays.

ORIENTAL RUGS: As has been noted in the section on floorcloths, the Oriental rug as we know it today was first introduced to America about 1750. Prior to that the "rugs" were table, mantel, window-sill, and bedcovers. The Oriental floor coverings of commerce, and those preferred by collectors, are best studied by referring to the great American book on the subject *Oriental Rugs and Carpets* by Arthur U. Dilley.

ORION WARE: Faience, or tin-glazed ware (akin to delft), made at pottery of Madam Helen Gouffier at Orion, 1525–50, and later. Very rare.

ORMULU: Brass.

ORRERY: Instrument showing orbits of planets of our solar system, with moons, operated by crank or clockwork which imparted speeded-up motions of our system.

ORRERY STAND: A table to hold an orrery, usually fitted with a vitrine, or dome-like frame of muntins holding panes of glass which stood over the orrery machine.

OSCHIVE: Bone-handled knife.

OSTADES: Netherlands woolens.

OSTRANDER BRITANNIA: Made by Charles Ostrander, 1840–50. New York.

OTTOMAN COUCH: A large couch with "return ends"; this return being an angular extension of the couch at either or both ends. A sort of double cozy-corner couch.

OUDENAARDE: Flemish or Dutch (Belgian) tapestry woven in sixteenth and seventeenth centuries.

OUTSHOT: Overhanging upper story of a house.

OVAL BRASSES (1785–1825): Drawer pulls, handles, et cetera, were mounted on ovals of brass, stamped and engraved in various designs and patterns. The handles, when bail, or bail-drop, conformed to the oval and were affixed to small bosses at each side of oval.

OVALS: So popular was the oval picture frame 1835–75 that its general name became "oval." Made plain and with little or much carving.

OVERLAY: A thin layer of glass, usually of color; or opaque, applied over other glass. Any application over another surface.

OVERMANTEL: Paneling or other formal treatment of chimney breast over a mantel.

OVER-UPHOLSTERED: Term now used to designate chair seats in which upholstery is over the seat and nailed down around it, as opposed to upholstered slip seats which, while upholstered, can be removed from chair. Term has no relation to "overstuffed" or overdone.

OVOGLOBULAR: Oval forms almost globular; an oval with a waistline.

OYSTERING: Oyster veneering; cross sections of hardwood burls cut on the bias to produce forms like oyster shells. Used as a veneer, usually laid on in matching, opposite panels.

OYSTER WALNUT: The burl in walnut having oyster shapes and forms in it and obvious when cut on bias. A fine veneer pattern.

PAAS: Pash, or pascal; Easter. PAAS PATTERNS: Paper sheets with dyed designs for coloring and decorating Easter eggs. PAAS FLOWER: Paschal, pasqual flower. PAAS ROTA: A paper disk with movable slide to determine Easter Sunday, a movable feast governed by the moon. PASS-MOON, PAAS-MOON: The Easter moon.

PACKSTAFF: Peddler's long staff. Hence "plain as a packstaff."

PADUASOI: Heavy silk of Padua, Italy.

PAINTED FLOOR CLOTHS: See section on floor coverings, page 128.

PAINTED PARSONS: Signboards; signposts. Americanism growing out of saying, "Like parsons, they point the way but do not take it." Signposts are now collected.

PAINTED PEWTER: In The Netherlands and Flanders pewter was japanned and decorated, 1750–1800. Some of it came to America.

PAKTONG: White brass. Extensively used in fine fireplace equipment.

PALAMPORE, PALIMPURE: Hand-painted and resist-dyed cottons, chintzes, and calicos, as made before the era of block printing. Original tree-of-life pattern was so made. Used here as quilt covers, bedspreads, and scarves, before 1750. Scarce.

PALLADE: A rich cloth often used to cover a corpse.

PALMER CANDLES: Double-wicked candles with the wicks coiled. Required a special candlestick of lamplike shape. Palmer's magnum candles had three and four wicks, burned eight hours, and gave as much light as an Argand burner. See section on lighting, page 109.

PANATRY: Pantry; from the bread (pan) room.

PAN CUPBOARD: Low cabinet with wide stiles and one door. Shaker-made. A cabinet for pots and pans.

PANE PARCHMENT: Parchment skin soaked in strong lye until transparent. Stretched on frames until dry, it was cut into panes and used in windows instead of glass.

PANEL PAPERS: Wall hangings in gilt, velvet, imitation wood, and marble, et cetera, sold in panels or pieces about 2½ × 8½ feet to 3 × 9 feet in 1820–50. Wallpaper.

PANKIN, PANNIKIN, PANCROCK: An earthenware pan.

PANNER, PENNER: A pen case.

PANSHON: Pan with beveled or insloping sides.

PANTILE: Roofing tiles in a kind of S shape, laid ridgelike and overlapping.

PANTINS: Articulated paper dolls. Gestured and jumped when a thread or a slide was pulled. See section on paper dolls, page 166.

PAPER SIZES: Many terms were used to designate paper sizes. The following names were most common, the size of each given in inches: Double Imperial 32 × 44. Super Royal 27 × 42. Medium Royal 24 × 38. Royal and Half 25 × 29. Imperial and Half 25 × 32. Super Royal 20 × 28. Royal 19 × 24. Square Demy 17 × 17. Foolscap 12½ × 16. Letter 10 × 16. Packet Note 9 × 11. Ladies' Bath 7½ × 11. Octavo 7 × 9. Note 6 × 8. Billet 6 × 8. Packet Post 11½ × 18. Packet Post Extra 11½ × 18½. Bath Note 8½ × 14. Double Elephant 26 × 40. Atlas 26 × 33. Columbier 23 × 33¼. Elephant 22¼ × 27¾. Imperial 22 × 30. Super Royal 20 × 28. Royal 19 × 24. Medium Royal 18 × 23. Extra Folio 19 × 23. Double Cap 17 × 28. Check Folio 17 × 24. Folio Post 17 × 22. Law Blank 13 × 16. Imperial 23 × 31. Census 18 × 26. Crown 15 × 19. Flat Cap 14 × 17, 13 × 16, 12 × 15. Antiquarian 31 × 52. Emperor 47 × 68. (These sizes were in use in sixteenth, seventeenth, eighteenth and early nineteenth centuries.)

PAPER FIREBOARDS, STOVE BOARDS: Frames of a size to fit hearth opening, covered with heavy paper, muslin, hollands, or canvas, and decorated with paper borders and cutouts in imitation of Wedgwood, Sèvres, Du Barry, and other china, Indian prints, Della Robbia tiles, et cetera. Used 1840–80.

PAPIER-MÂCHÉ: Paper macerated and reduced to a wet pulp, mixed with glue, and used as a plastic in molded décor, toys, trays, et cetera. Even furniture was pressed from it.

PAPILLONS: Wallpapers. Named for Jean-Baptiste Papillon (1698–1768), block cutter and fancy paper printer. Maker of fine wall hangings.

PAPYROTOMIA: Hubbard, the American Silhouette cutter's fancy term for his art. 1825.

PARAPLUYE, PARAPLUIE: An umbrella.

PARCEL, PARCELL: Partly; as parcel gilt, partly gilt, or gilded.

PARFURNISHED: Entirely furnished. Completely fitted.

PARGET: Roughcast plaster. PARGETTER: A rough mason. PARGETTED DECORATION: Molded plaster.

PARIS CANDLE: A large wax candle.

PARISON: A globule of blown glass metal, the first step in blowing any piece of glass. Any dip into the pot of molten glass to form an original or augmented gathering.

PARISON CARPET: Made first in 1747 at Paddington, London. Patronized by Duke of Cumberland. These carpets were imported by America after 1750. They were floor carpets. Parison had the first carpet mill in England.

PARLIAMENT HINGE: A two-leaf hinge, each leaf carrying one segment of the joint.

PARREL: Chimney piece.

PASSEMENTERIE: Trimmings, particularly laces, beads, fringe, frogs, guimps, et cetera.

PASTE PAPERS: Not gummed papers, but papers decorated with color application on a coating of paste or size. A sort of fresco work on paper. Made in eighteenth and nineteenth centuries in America.

PASTILLES AROMATIQUES: Briquettes of combustible material (as punk) impregnated with perfumes, emitted when burned. Recipe for making is found in *Ladies' Fancy Work*, issued in 1876. But used from 1750 or earlier. PASTILLE BURNERS: Little cottages in which to burn these briquettes.

PATCH BOXES: Small dainty boxes of gold, silver, pewter, tin, horn, Wedgwood, and enamel, to hold patches, or beauty spots. Often jeweled, and with small vials of perfume. Also the cavity in the stock of an American rifle-barreled gun to hold the patches of oiled cloth in which balls or bullets were wrapped before ramming down the barrel on the firing charge.

PATERA: Ornamentation in the form of round or oval flat dishes, decorated or plain. A form used in Adam, Hope, and Greek Revival styles. Also by Hepplewhite and Sheraton.

PÂTE-SUR-PÂTE: Paste on paste; paste decoration applied to paste body of porcelain. Paste; the pasty porcelain clay before firing, and "in paste" after firing but before decoration.

PATNA: A chintz of India, from Patna.

PATRIOTIC COVERS: Stamp-collecting term for the envelopes embellished with a wide variety of patriotic emblems, scenes, et cetera. Used mostly during War between the States. Several thousand varieties noted. There are Confederate patriotic covers as well as Union.

PATTENS: Lifts, or elevators, for shoes. Light metal frames on low stilts. Open clogs.

PATTERN PAPERS: Flowered and decorated papers printed in colors from wood blocks. Made from sixteenth century. Often copied for embroidery designs, decoration and pen writing.

PAW FOOT: Stylized carved paw used on cabinetwork, or in metals applied to the legs of chairs and tables.

PAWN, RUFFLED: A ruffled valance.

PEACHBLOW GLASS: In imitation of peachblow porcelain, made by Cambridge Glass Company, and Hobbs, Rockunier of Wheeling. Former is colored through. Latter is white-lined. Late American. After 1886.

PEARLED RUG: Tufted rag rug made by winding the rags on two-tined parallel spreader of iron, laid on base material, and stitched by hand or on sewing machine. Late 1880s.

PEARLINS: Coarse bone lace.

PEDESTAL DESK: Flat-topped desk made up of two pedestals set apart to form a kneehole. Top is often leather-covered, and the finest of these desks are made up in sections for ease in transporting. Mostly of English make.

PEDESTAL GATE-LEG: Table with heavily turned single supports at either end of a fixed top, terminating in footed pedestal. Gates on either side support leaves.

PEDIMENT: Triangular section above doors, porticos, et cetera.

PEEL: Pillow or bolster. Also a pillow as used in lacemaking. PEEL BERE is another term for PILLOW BERE, PILLOW BEARIS, et cetera; pillowcase.

PEEL: Bread peel; a flat paddle of wood with long handle used to deposit and remove bread from deep ovens and to handle in the baking.

PEGGING: Extra heavy crocheting.

PEGGYPOKER: Small pokers with short right-angular bend at end.

PELISSE: A soft twilled woolen cloth. A garment of same.

PELLOW BERIS, PILLOW BERE: Pillow covers or cases. "A felour and tester styned with floris, a coverlyte and ii pillow bearis and pelows" is a typical early inventory entry. Term persisted as late as 1870 when "plowbers" was back-country name for pillow shams.

PEMBROKE TABLE: Any Hepplewhite, Adam, Sheraton, or Federal drop-leaf breakfast table is a Pembroke table. Term is often thought to be exclusive of application to X-stretchered small table with short drop leaves. Earlier breakfast tables are not called Pembroke, as term was not in use until about 1770.

PENCIL-POST BED: Four-post beds of Queen Anne and Georgian periods, having very slender octagonal posts.

PENDANT: Sometimes used same as "pennant," the long official flag of early naval office. Drooping; dropping, hanging, as pendant crystals, pendant prisms hanging from bobeches, shade rings, et cetera. Pendants of glass cut or pressed. Shapes are coffin, star, spear, drop, pear, leaf, chain, and bead. Finest are cut. Also carved and turned ornaments on cabinet-work, turnings affixed to lower cabinet sections of Queen Anne high- and low-boys.

PENNSYLVANIA DUTCH: Apparently a New York term first applied to the Dutch who settled the Hoarkill Valley of what was later Pennsylvania. Now applied, and entirely in error, to the German immigrants to Penn's colony. Present-day enthusiasts and pro-Pennsylvania-German groups explain that the term means Pennsylvania Deutsch. This has been a movement and miseducation program since 1876. There is true Pennsylvania Dutch ware, architecture, and furniture, but it isn't German.

PENNSYLVANIA SLAT BACK: The finest slat-back chair, with shaped curved slats, deep turned ball and wheel stretchers between front legs, and with from four to seven slats in back. City cabinetmakers and country cabinetmakers made it. Some even made it with Queen Anne

legs. Is of *Dutch* origin, with probably some Swedish influence. 1660–1725 is first period; 1725–1800 is second. Very fine ones made in both periods.

PENRHYN MARBLE: Welsh name given to imitation marble; it is painted slate.

PERDU, PERDUE: Hidden, as profile perdu, facing away from the observer.

PERPETUAL OVEN: Sheet-iron oven connected in series to flue from any fire in common and constant use. Hence the oven was always ready for baking. Offered about 1790. Advertised in 1800.

PERPETUANA: Long-lasting wool fabric. EVERLASTING CLOTH was another name.

PERRY: Fermented, foamy drink made from pears. Not a cider. It was not kept in barrels or kegs but in stone or glass bottles in which great pressure was generated by the beverage. Very much like champagne and considered better by early connoisseurs. PERRY GLASSES: Made for serving this drink. It was not served in long drafts as cider, but as a wine. Popular from 1660–1850. Now very rarely made.

PETIT CONSOLE: Small or miniature console. PETIT COMMODE: A small commode. PETIT: Anything of small size.

PETTICOAT VALANCE: Full gathered valance used on bed (four-poster) and across the mantelshelf (in New York and Pennsylvania, by the Dutch).

PEWTER: Alloy of tin, antimony, and lead. Plate metal is mostly tin. Triple metal is lead and tin with some copper. Ley metal is mostly lead, with some tin. PHILADELPHIA CHAIR: The Windsor chair, introduced about 1725, was first known by this name.

PHILADELPHIA DRESSING TABLE: After the Queen Anne idea, but made in a combined Adam, Hepplewhite, Sheraton (Federal) design into what looks like a small sideboard. Very effective and delightful. 1790–1825.

PHILADELPHIA HANGINGS: Wallpaper made in the Quaker City, the earliest center of this craft in America. Said to have been made as early as 1740.

PHILOM, PHILOMATH: Lover of mathematics; compiler of almanacs.

PHOEBE LAMPS: Similar to Betty lamps but often with two wicks. First ones of iron, later of sheet metal, tinned, and copper. Have an extra dish to catch oil drip.

PHOENIX: Mythical bird which nested in fire. Used decoratively as a motif and effigy for pediments, mirrors, et cetera.

PHYFE: New York cabinetmaker. See page 38.

PICTURE SAMPLER: Any sampler with an embroidery picture on it.

PIECRUST TRAY: Chippendale tray characterized by a fluted, shaped border imitating a decorative piecrust.

PIERCED-BACK CHAIRS: Originally designating carved and pierced chairs of Carolean period, of Flemish design, which, in turn, originated in China. Seventeenth century. Made in New England, New York, Pennsylvania, and Virginia.

PIERCED CARVING: Any carving which pierces the wood as a part of the pattern or design.

PIER GLASS, PIER TABLE: A pier is the architectural term for solid spaces of wall between windows, more or less regularly spaced. Pier glasses, mirrors, tables, et cetera, are so named because they are designed to stand against the piers.

PIETRA DURA: A precious marble used in inlay work.

PIGTAIL: A small candle or taper affixed angularly, through its body, on the pricket of a pricket candlestick.

PILCHPIN: A large pin.

PILGRIM FORM: Name given to bottles of flask shape with ears to accommodate a tying cord for carrying. Used by pilgrims to carry water or wine with them.

PILLAR AND SCROLL: Side pillars, free standing, surmounted by a scrolled member. Clock form designed by Eli Terry.

PILLBOX FOOT: Foot terminating in a disk with beading around it, found but rarely on some Queen Anne pieces. Name was applied about 1880, when there was a reawakened interest in American antiques.

PILLOW BEERS: See Pellow Beris. Inventory of Captain Tyng, of Boston, 1653, had the Pellow Beris spelled as here: Pillow Beers.

PINEAPPLE TEAPOT: China or pottery teapot of pineapple shape, eyed as the fruit and colored to simulate it as in nature.

PINK WOOD: That part of yew wood that is naturally pink and pale rose in color.

PINS: These present-day items of common use were scarce and expensive in colonial days. In 1776 they sold for seven shillings a dozen. Household and dress pins were called, according to sizes, lillikins, lace, short-white, mourning, middlings, and corkings. After the machine to make them was invented (1830) they became cheap. Once they were handmade from wire on a pin anvil.

PIPE CLAY: Fine white clay used in pottery and pipe making, sold also in cakes for whitening breeches, military accouterments, bands, et cetera, and for making white crayons.

PIPES: Long reeding in furniture; cut or painted. PIPE TONGS: Small tongs to lift live coals from fire to light a tobacco pipe.

PISTOL GRIP, PISTOL-HANDLED: Knives and forks of late seventeenth- and early eighteenth-century pattern, the handles of which are shaped like the grip, or handle, of early pistols.

PLANISH: To beat a metal smooth and bright, as pewter, silver, and iron.

PLATE BACK: A type of Queen Anne chair, also early Georgian, with a solid splat in the back, shaped to contour of human form.

PLATE TOP: Round table top having four to nine circular platelike depressions gouged in surface around periphery, to hold plates. Often the round top has a scalloped edge serrated according to the number of depressions in surface.

PLATE TRENCHER: Woodenware; a trencher laid under a pot or pan to keep the cloth clean.

PLUNKET: Coarse woolen cloth.

PLYMOUTH ROCKS (GLASS): Made at Providence, Rhode Island, by the Ink Stand Company, 1876. These "rocks," dated 1620, are souvenirs. A centennial novelty.

PODGER: A pewter plate.

POINT DEVICE: With exactness. Nice to excess.

POINT D'HONGRIE: A form of embroidery in zigzag or waved bands of colors, shading from dark to light.

POINT LACE: Tagged lace. To truss a point was to cross and tie the tags, or points.

POKAL: Large covered goblet of glass, silver, pewter, et cetera, usually with elaborate chasing, cutting, repoussé, and engraving.

POLE BED: Low-post bed standing lengthwise against a wall. From the wall, midway between head and foot, there is a pole over bed upon which drapery is affixed. 1780–1850.

POLE LATHE: Turner's lathe, operated by a heavy cord running from a foot treadle looped over lathe spindle, and affixed to a hickory pole acting as a spring. The turner needed only to depress treadle; this increased tension on pole, which pulled upward and kept lathe spinning until next treadle push.

POLE SCREEN: A pole on a footed pedestal having a shaped shield, or screen, from 2 × 2 to 3 × 3 feet in size, adjustable to varying heights on the pole.

POLE-SCREEN CANDLESTAND: When the pole-screen shield element is fitted with a shelf to hold a candlestick, the assembly is called by this name.

POLYGONS: Regular, balanced geometrical forms of pleasing proportions as pentagon (five-sided), hexagon (six-sided), septagon (seven-sided), octagon (eight-sided), nonagon (nine-sided), decagon (ten-sided), undecagon (eleven-sided), dodecagon (twelve-sided).

POMANDER BALLS: Whole oranges (or lemons) stuck full of whole cloves until completely covered, rolled in orris root and cinnamon, cured for three to four weeks in parchment, then shaken loose of all powder, and hung in closets as perfumers. Also carried in perforated metal cases (POMANDER CASES).

POMPADOUR PARASOL: Small parasol head carried on a long stick, jointed to permit adjustment of the sunshade at various rakish angles. Late eighteenth and early nineteenth centuries.

POND-LILY PITCHERS: Made at Bennington, Vermont. Pottery in blue and white and all white Parian ware, in a pond-lily design. Apparently an American pattern; not copied from any other designs. Bennington made charter oak, Paul and

Virginia design pitchers following the pond lily, which appeared about 1846.

POND RUG PATTERNS: D. Pond and Company, Biddeford, Maine, made stenciled burlap patterns for hooked rugs. See page 132.

PONTIPOOL WARE: Japanned tinware (see Painted Tin, Japanned Ware, and Tole, page 85), advertised as "Pontipool" in 1768. Imported, or made in imitation of the tinwares of Pontipool, England.

POONAH: A stencil used in theorem or poonah painting. Usually cut of horn paper, tracing paper, or plain paper oiled with linseed oil.

PORRINGER: Shallow, circular dish of metal (silver or pewter, sometimes of wood) with one or two shaped ears, solid or pierced in designs: pouring-ears; pour-ers. In England called bleeding bowls. See sections on pewter and silver.

PORTE-MANTEAUX: Costumers; clothes trees. Not trunks.

PORT-FIRE: Portable fire; phosphoric matches in small sealed glass tubes. Breaking the tube ignited the match. 1792–1810.

PORT-PANE: Bread cloth, often embroidered in cross-stitch. Shaped like early samplers; long and narrow. Pennsylvania door panels may have been port-panes or bread cloths.

POSNET: Small skillet.

POSSET: Hot milk, with wine and spice, sugared. A going-to-bed drink.

POSSET-PAN: The pan used in heating posset.

POSSET POT, POSSET CUP: Pot or cup similar to a tyg, but with cover, and somewhat shallower. Tulip-decorated red ware. Many shipped to America in seventeenth and early eighteenth centuries.

POTBELLY STOVES: Barrel-shaped stoves made in sizes from sixteen inches to fifty inches in diameter; produced about 1845.

POT BRUSH: Polishing brush.

POT BUTTONS: American term for brass buttons stamped from sections cut from brass pots and buckets.

POT DOGS: Fire irons to support cooking pot over coals.

POTHOOKS: Trammels, brakes, crokes, gallow balks—all devices for holding, securing, or staying pots at varying heights over fire.

POTICHE: A temple jar; Chinese.

POTICHOMANIA: A popular art of mid-nineteenth century. Glass vases in imitation of Chinese potiches were decorated from the inside by gluing on, face outward, a variety of colored pictures, elements, et cetera, to form a chinoiserie design. When dry, the inner surface was coated with a thin layer of liquid plaster of Paris, which, when set, gave the entire job a porcelain effect. The plastering was coated with wax. Many potichomania vases have been cleaned of all this décor and sold as clear glass vases of Early American design. Some have even been sold as Stiegel. In spite of the fact that most of these vases are hand-blown and have large pontil marks, they are hardly a hundred years old, dating from at best 1845 and mostly from the 1850s.

POTPOURRI: Collections of flower petals kept in a jar with cover. Recipes called for violets, jasmine, lavender, clove-gilly-flowers, rosemary, marjoram, balm of Gilead, damask rose, rose geranium, orris, gum benjamin, storax, musk, cloves, orange flower, lemon thyme and mint, chopped up and laid in thin layers of salt. Also name of the jar for keeping such materials.

POTSTONE: The *lapis ollaris* of the ancients. Stone from which pots and other cooking vessels could be carved, turned, and worked. Early Swedes on Delaware noted native Indians using this stone in preference to the pottery vessels which they could not fire properly to last.

POUNCED: Originally, and in eighteenth century, meaning perforated. A lid pounced meant a lid perforated.

POWDER BOWLS: Glass, china, or metal bowls; footed, stemmed, and flat-based, designed as face-powder containers, often equipped with powder puff.

POWDER BUCKETS: Pairs of wooden or leathern buckets used in toting powder from magazine of a man-of-war to the gun decks.

PRENE: An iron pan.

PRESS BED: Folding bed, fitting into a press or cupboard.

PRESS CUPBOARD: See page 6.

PRICKET CANDLESTICK;—PLUG;—SOCKET: These terms derive from the candlestick made without socket but having a spike or pricket upon which to impale the candle. Known in small sizes to huge ecclesiastical forms, over six feet tall. Said to have originated in China. Candles for pricket sticks were called fats. Pricket plug was a plug for inserting in a socketed stick to make it a pricket stick. Pricket socket was a candle-socketed section having a deep hole in lower half for fitting over a pricket and converting the pricket stick into a socket candlestick.

PRICKLE: Basketry of willow, or wicker.

PRIG: A brass skillet.

PRINCE OF WALES BACK: Hepplewhite and Adam chairs having backs displaying three feathers as a pattern or design.

PRINTED BURLAP: Cheap burlap, printed in carpet designs on both sides. Victorian.

PRISON COVERLETS: Woven coverlets of wool, wool and linen, and linen and cotton, in the patterns popular 1820–80, never having name of weaver or other designation in the panels or corners usually so utilized. These are prison-woven, or workhouse-woven, coverlets, made by convicts and prisoners, under the direction of a master weaver, and sold by the county commissioners to produce revenue. Thousands sold through shops between dates noted. Any unmarked coverlet was, at one time, called prison coverlet by housewives in the know.

PROFILE PERDU: A profile portrait in which the head or face is not full profile, but turned away, partially, from the observer; partly concealed.

PROMETHEANS: Rolls of paper with fire-caps at end. Unrolled, and the end hit with a hammer, the paper ignited and became a match. The secret was a glass bead containing sulphuric acid, embedded in chlorate of potash. When crushed the acid-chlorate compound ignited.

PROVENANCE: Point, time, or place of origin; the "whenceabouts" of a thing or idea; the "whence" from which it comes.

PRUNT: A blob of glass made into a decorative element by application of molds, or as a badge bearing names, initials, advertising labels, et cetera. Used in making glass labels on bottles.

PSYCHE: A sofa, also known as a kangaroo; dating from about 1840. The basic design is Directoire, made heavy, and in Empire style. Upholstered.

PULK: A squat, dumpy stool.

PULSIFER CARPETS: Painted floorcloths made by N. Pulsifer, of Salem, first half of the nineteenth century. He called them "painted carpets." Made in sizes up to 18 × 36 feet.

PUMPERNICKEL: A black peasant bread, so named after 1805, and deriving not from Germany, as a name, but from the French *bon pour Nichol* uttered by a French officer upon being offered the peasant bread of Germany. "Good for [my horse] Nichol", was his comment.

PUNCHED TIN: Not punctured tin, but tinware fashioned from sheets previously punched or hammered in molds to achieve a design; usually bold designs were punched but finer repoussé designs are also known.

PUNCH FONT, WINE FONT: A glass vessel in the shape of a huge wineglass on a domed foot, with an opening blown into bottom of wine bowl into which a tap, or faucet, was fitted for drawing wine. Believed to be Irish.

PUNCTURED TIN: Tinware punctured or pierced clear through, made into graters, lanterns, and other objects.

PUPITRE DESK: Scholar's desk. A countinghouse desk. A big desk.

PURPAIN: A napkin.

PUTTO: Nude, cherubic figure of a boy; a figurine.

PUTZ: A display of images of religious significance, as a crèche. Usually set up at Christmas, and less frequently at Easter and Whitsunday. Christmas putz would display the Nativity, shepherds, sheep, cattle, men, women, village, star of Bethlehem, et cetera. A Moravian custom that is far older than Germanic Lutheranism. The Germans adapted or appropriated the idea from the Czechs.

PUZZLE TEAPOT: See Cadogan Teapot.

PYKED CANDLESTICK: Pricket candlestick.

PYLE: A pillow.

PYRIFORM: Pear-shaped.

PYROPHORUS: Three parts alum and one part wheat flour, calcined in a vial to a black powder. Kept dry and stoppered. This powder, when shaken out on dry lint, "made fire." Another of the many inventions and efforts to make fire kindling easy.

QUAICH: Two-eared drinking mug of wood, pottery, glass, brass, pewter, or silver.

QUARRIER: A small block of wax with wick in center; a square, stubby candle.

QUARRY, QUARREL: A square pane of glass.

QUARTETTO TABLES: Sets of tables, usually four, each one smaller in size, all nesting in and under largest one and so arranged as to permit pulling any table out. Probably a Sheraton design.

QUATREFOIL: Four-part ornamentation of Gothic origin.

QUEEN ANNE SCALE: Very fine balance scale with copper or silver scoop, used by spice dealers and confectioners. Nineteenth century.

QUEEN ANNE STYLE: See page 12.

QUEEN MARY: Consort of William of Orange; a great collector of china and textiles of oriental (Chinese) and Dutch make. The people followed the Queen's taste and it is a moot question as to whether or not it was this Queen's love for china that begat the term "queen's ware" or Queen Charlotte.

QUEEN'S METAL: An alloy of nine parts tin, one bismuth, one antimony, one lead. Fine pewter.

QUEEN'S WARE: Originally yellow-ware, but named queen's because the reigning Queen Charlotte was so fond of it. 1769.

QUERN: A miniature burr mill, consisting of two stones, the upper moved by grasping a rod affixed to a bracket above and engaging a hole in top stone. A home mill for grinding wheat, corn, and other grains.

QUESTED, QUESTERN: Baked goods which stuck together in oven were said to be quested. Quest, or questern, meant the side or sides of the oven.

QUICK VARNISH: Egg white, brandy, and onion juice, laid over fresh paint to keep insects and flies away. When paint dried it was washed off.

QUILLED: Glass bands, pinched into wavy forms; a kind of glass decoration.

QUILL HOLDER, QUILL CASE: Hollow cylinder of metal, often of japanned tin and decorated, but known in pewter, brass, and silver, having a narrow slot running almost from end to end and with a long cylindrical cap. Used to encase a quill pen to carry in pocket or writing case. Kalemdam.

QUILL PENCILS: Hair pencils; brushes, known in sizes from large to small as big swan, middle swan, little swan, extra small swan, goose, duck, pigeon, and crow.

QUILT: Padded skirting, from the old French *cuilte* and the Latin *culita*. Any double fabric with padding between, stitched through in a pattern; imitation counterpane. Students of bed quilts are referred to *Old Patchwork Quilts and the Women Who Made Them* by Ruth E. Finley, and *The Romance of Patchwork Quilt in America* by C. Hall and R. Kretsinger.

QUINTUPLE DISH: Any dish or vessel composed of a central section surfounded by four other sections, all joined.

QUIRK: A rhomb-shaped pane of glass.

QUISHON: Cushion.

QUITESOL, QUIETSOL: A sunshade; a parasol.

QUONIAM: A drinking cup.

RABBET: Correct form of this term is "rebated"; meaning notching or forming ends of boards and other joints to make a close bond.

RABBIT'S EAR: Windsor-type chair of late style having a splat or top rail set between outflaring stiles which look like the long, tapering ears of a rabbit.

RABIT: Woodenware; a drinking vessel.

RACKING CROOK: A pothook.

RAFFLES: Subdivisions of a leaf as used in furniture decoration.

RAG GOLD: Tinder gilt.

RAMEKIN: Originally a cheesecake baked in a pottery dish.

RAMPANT, COUNTERRAMPANT: In heraldry when animal forms are depicted erect, standing with one foot on ground, others elevated, and head to left, they are rampant. Counterrampant is same figure facing to right; this usually occurs only when figures are used decoratively in pairs.

RAM'S FOOT: Cloven foot, as used in furniture and in some silver spoon handles.

RANTER: A large beer mug.

RANTREE, ROANTREE, ROANOAK: The mountain ash.

RATEEN: Coarse woolen cloth.

RAT FOOT: Type foot found on some legs of pedestal and tripod tables. The "claws" are tenuous and clutch a pad instead of a ball.

RATTAIL: When the handle of a spoon joins the bowl as a tapering extension running almost to front of bowl, it is called a rattail handle.

RATTAIL HINGE: Much more desirable than H and HL hinge, this type hinge has a main leaf hidden in a mortise in the door, usually fastened with two pins. Thus only the joint of the hinge is exposed and the spindle or axle of this joint extends downward and ends in a curvate manner with a finial. The curve varies with the whim of the fitter, usually to conform to width of stile.

RAVEDORE: A tapestry.

RAVENSCROFT GLASS: Ravenscroft, glassmaker of England, is credited with the invention of lead glass about 1674. He produced soda glass of high quality before making lead, or flint, glass. Sometimes his mark, a raven's head, is impressed upon a prunt of glass on the piece. Quite rare.

RAVEN'S DUCK: White canvas mentioned early in nineteenth century.

RAYNES: A fine linen sheeting made at Rennes, France, sixteenth, seventeenth, and eighteenth centuries.

REAMER, REAM MUG, RIMMER: A cream pot.

REBATED: Joining of wood sections by tongue and groove on or near edges and ends of planks.

RÉCAMIER SOFA: Symmetrically scrolled sofa with high ends, of Directoire style.

RECTO: The right-hand page. The right side; the obverse; see Verso and Reverse.

REEDED: Opposite of fluted; the effect is a series of rounded elements looking like reeds.

REFECTORY PORRINGER: Solid-eared porringer usually with insignia of some religious organization or order, as a monastery or a nunnery.

REGENCY: A style promoted if not invented by the interior decorators; the term, roughly, is the equivalent of our Federal period between 1790–1825.

RELICT: A widow.

RENFREW SPRIG: American derisive term for the three-feather emblem of Prince of Wales.

RENT TABLE: A large revolving drum-type table with many drawers, presumably one for each tenant paying rent to some lord and master of lands. English in origin; doubtful if ever used in America save in offices of solicitors.

REPOUSSÉ: Light punching into sheet metal against a soft wood backing, effecting a raised design without piercing the metal.

RESSAUNT: The ogee molding.

RESTRIKE: Any late impression made from an engraved or lithographed plate; sometimes printed on old paper and sold as originals. Expert advice needed; much experience required to tell the faked restrike.

RETICELLA: Linen cutwork; linen figures cut out and worked in a lace square; used from fifteenth century. Best work done in sixteenth and seventeenth centuries.

RETICULATED: In the form of, or simulating, network; pierced and foliated.

REVERSE: Left or minor side of a coin or medal; the verso or left-hand page.

RIBBAND BACK: Chair back with a design in form of interlaced ribbons.

RICHMOND BED WARMERS: Copper pans made by H. D. Richmond, Boston, c. 1830. Made to hold hot water rather than hot coals.

RIDELS, RIDDLES: Bed curtains.

RIDGEWOOD CASES: Metallic cases decorated with military scenes, American eagle, et cetera, made to hold a pipe bowl, stem, tobacco, and matches. Used by army and navy men in Civil War.

RIGAREE: Narrow ribs of glass applied in parallel lines and tooled. Glass décor.

RIGHT TINWARE: Pure block tinware, not plated, advertised in America as early as 1760. Much advertised after 1786. Use of term "right" is traditional. In Early English "right" meant true.

RILEY WARE: A kind of Gaudy Dutch made by the potter Riley, of England.

RING BRASS: Round brass mounts with handles of ring shape. Noted on furniture of 1785–1825.

RISING DESK TABLE: Deep-skirted table with an arrangement of three leaves, manipulation of which causes a desk box to rise upward from its nest in deep skirting. Of French origin. Imported by wealthy Americans. Some few have survived. Eighteenth century.

RISING TABLE: What looks like a three-topped round-pedestal table; actually a series of round tops, of graduated size, with pedestals nesting in each other and rising to form a dumb-waiter or Lazy Susan. Early nineteenth century.

RIVED: Split, not sawed; the wood of a tree trunk from ground to first branches was used for riving; hence riven panels; riven timbers; free from knots.

ROBBLE: Woodenware; a dough paddle, often chip carved.

ROCAILLE: A kind of work using flowing lines, shells, curlicues, leaves, et cetera, as motifs.

ROCKING-SHIP CLOCK: Clock dial surmounted with a cut-out painting of a ship which rocks as the pendulum swings.

ROCOCO: Literally "rock and shell," or *rocaille et coquille*. A kind of décor in which these natural forms are used as motifs.

ROLL HANGINGS: Wallpaper, originally printed in sheets, when pasted together in 24-sheet-long sections and rolled, were called roll hangings instead of sheet hangings.

ROLLIPOKE: Coarse hempen cloth.

ROOT WALNUT: Root wood of walnut trees having a burllike marking.

ROPE BED: Any bed having a series of pins along side rails or entire frame, over which rope was laced to hold the bed sack or mattress.

ROPE BOTTOM: Rope used to make a laced chair seat similar to rush seating.

ROSETTES: Circular bosses, having as décor a series of concentric rings, plain or waved in the heraldic manner of displaying a rose full blown.

ROSTER: A gridiron.

ROTARY STOVE: A small stove with a large rotating top turned by a crank. Any part of the rotating top could be brought over the fire. 1840.

ROUGH-AND-READY TOBY, TAYLOR TOBY: A face pitcher; a crudely modeled effigy of General Taylor in form of a pitcher. Believed to be American. Scarce.

ROUNDABOUT CHAIR: See page 61.

ROUNDED RAIL: When top rail and stiles of a chair back meet in a rounded joint it is called a rounded rail.

RUE BED STOVE: Pottery foot warmer made by the Rue Pottery at Matawan, New Jersey, mid-nineteenth century.

RUG: Up to 1750 "rug" meant any coarse, heavy wool fabric, plain or patterned, for use as a bedcover, not a floor covering. Between 1750 and 1800 it is best to be sure a floor covering is meant before assuming this to be the case. Only when called a floor rug by name can we be sure. After 1800 "rug," generally, meant carpeting for the floor.

RUG CHEST-ON-FRAME: A huge oblong chest-on-frame, chest having a box lid; frame sometimes with drawers. Known from Jacobean to Chippendale and even later; also in pioneer and cottage forms. This item of furniture was a bedclothing box or chest.

RUINATED: In ruins; "dilapidated" was reserved for its proper use; applied only to stone and stone structures. "Ruinated" meant damnified, spoiled, broken, deteriorated.

RUMFORD CASE: Box or case made to look like a book, used for storing tracts, pamphlets, et cetera. Used on bookshelves in upright position, as books. Late eighteenth and early nineteenth centuries. Invented by Count Rumford, or Roumfort.

RUMPEL: The jaws harp, or jew's-harp.

RUNGE: Woodenware; an oval-shaped two-handled tub.

RUNNELS, RUNNELED: Small runways appearing on platters of silver, pewter, wood planks used in roasting, et cetera. Small troughs on or under a grill or gridiron which catch meat juices.

RUSH-BOTTOMED: A chair seat of twisted and woven rushes or flags.

RUSHLIGHT, RUSHLIGHT HOLDER: Green stems of rushes, peeled except for a spine strip, down to the pith, dried, and soaked in fat. Burned as a light. Holder was a base with a pincerlike grip which kept burning rush in desired position.

RUSTIC PICTURES: Almost too terrible to tell about, these monstrosities were made by women as fancywork, or art, between 1850 and 1880. You paint or draw a picture, preferably a scene, and then begin to build up with mosses, twigs, bits of sponge, shell, stone, et cetera; small blocks of wood, putty, and other substances were also used. The result is a three-dimensional picture in a deep frame. *Ladies' Fancy Work* by Mrs. C. S. Jones and Henry Williams, published 1876, tells how to make them.

RYVES PAPERS: "The first paper hangings manufactured on this continent" is the way Edward Ryves advertised his trade as paper stainer, and his product, Philadelphia, April 10, 1776.

SACK BED: Bands of canvas, or an entire form of canvas, laced or tied to the frame of a bed to hold the bed sack or mattress. Used as late as 1800. Many day beds are also sack-bottomed.

SACRISTY CHEST: Technically any church chest for storing vestments of priests, altar cloths, et cetera, but generally applied to the Flemish, Dutch, French, Italian, and Spanish church chests of fine construction, carved, and with linenfold panels.

SAD: Anything "saed" or sad is "heavy." Hence sad ware, or sad iron—heavy ware, a heavy smoothing iron.

SADDLE BOTTLES: Gourd-shaped bottles with round bottoms, carried in slings. Actually bottles of this shape were made by thousands and not for saddle use; they were stood in beds of sand in wine cellars, or hung on walls.

SADDLE-CHEEK CHAIR: Any wing chair was so called in eighteenth century.

ST. ANDREW STRETCHER: The saltire or X stretcher.

ST. CYR EMBROIDERY: Done at the school founded by Mme. de Maintenon, mistress of the King of France.

ST. MEMIN: Jean, B. F., French artist and engraver who made many "physionotrace" portraits in America. Also famed for his view of the first voyage of Fulton's steamboat, the *Clermont*.

SALAMANDER MARBLE: Cast iron, enameled to simulate marble for mantels, table tops, et cetera. 1840-60.

SALEM CHAIRS: A type of chair of the Chippendale era, the back of which is eared and has a very beautiful open and cut scrolled splat.

SALEM FURNITURE: Under the guidance of Elijah and Jacob Sanderson, the cabinetmakers of Salem, Massachusetts, formed a kind of cartel for making and shipping furniture to coastal cities and for export to West Indies and South America. The cabinetmakers involved, according to C. M. Stow and other authorities, were Adams, Pulcifer, Appleton, Austin, Hook, Luther, Burbank, and Swan. 1780-1815. Salem furniture was of the finest quality and is now very highly regarded by connoisseurs of Americana.

SALLET STAND, BOWLED TABLE: A stand, or pedestal, bearing a top akin to a dish top but actually a shallow bowl. Very rare. Late seventeenth and early eighteenth centuries. Used to serve "sallet," or salad, at table.

SALT: Name now given any saltcellar made of any material.

SALTIRE, SALTIER, CHI: Any X-shaped element in the form of St. Andrew's cross is said to be saltire, or "chi," formed, after the Greek X. Often very ornate, curvate, carved, domed, et cetera, as stretchers joining table legs in Pembroke tables and Chippendale chairs.

SAMITE: A rich silk.

SAMMEN (NOT SALMON) BRICKS: Soft bricks; partly burned or underdone bricks. Often prized for use in polishing metals.

SAMPLES-IN-LITTLE: Much miniature furniture, pottery, and glass today prized as miniatures were really salesmen's samples. By carrying miniatures the selling agents were able to display quite a line of goods.

SANDERS: Sandalwood.

SANDWICH GLASS: See page 100.

SANDWICH TRAY: Reference is to tray with flat border, elevated above base of tray by a riser one half to one inch high.

SANG DE BŒUF: Oxblood; a color.

SANTA CLAUS: From the Dutch San Niklaus, pronounced san-nik-claus. Use of term in America dates from about 1640. First picture of genial old saint of children at Christmas appeared about 1820, substantially as we know the figure today. Also BELZNICKLE, FATHER CHRISTMAS, CHRIS KRINGLE.

SARCANET: A thin silk fabric.

SAUCEPAN, SAUCER: A bulbous-shaped covered vessel with turned wood handle affixed to the bowl. Used generally in preparing sauces; 1680-1840.

SAUNDERS: Natural hardwood with a rose-musk odor. Much prized in cabinetmaking in eighteenth and nineteenth centuries.

SAVE ALL: Small pan to hold a candle end; small boss with pricket upon which to affix a candle end for burning to very end.

SAVERY, WILLIAM: Philadelphia cabinetmaker, 1722-87, credited with making some of the finest furniture of Philadelphia.

SAWBUCK TABLE: A table top supported on X-shaped members at either end, joined by a long stretcher. A type probably introduced by Swedes.

SAW MARKS: All straight saws, whether of 1600 or 1900 type, make the same kind of cut marks on timber. The circular saw, invented about 1815, makes rounded or curved marks. Hence any "old" furniture, the timbers of which show rounded or curvate saw marks, are known to be faked. No furniture of the seventeenth and eighteenth centuries was made of wood cut with a circular saw.

SAY: A fine-textured cloth similar to serge, sometimes partly silk. Sixteenth to eighteenth centuries.

SCADLE: A stand for sacks of grain, et cetera.

SCAGLIOLA: A composition imitation of marble invented by H. S. Farley, of New York, 1840.

SCALE CASE: A case fitted with numerous wooden or ivory rulers, used by architects and designers. The usual set consists of rules arranged from one eighth inch to one and one half inches to the foot. Eighteenth century.

SCAMEL: A stool.

SCENOGRAPHY: The art of drawing in perspective.

SCENT APPLE: Ball-shaped case of filigreed silver, brass, gold, et cetera, filled with a strong scent. Known from thirteenth to eighteenth centuries.

SCHIMMEL: See page 170.

SCHOOL SHEET: Subjects of educational interest printed around the sides of a sheet, the center of which is left blank for students' calligraphic exercises. Now, when found in quantities (and they were made by the million), they are used as mirror mats and sold as antiques. Mostly English, 1780–1840.

SCIAGRAPH: A drawing of a building made to exhibit the interior.

SCOB: Early school desk; a desk box with flat lid; probably, says Dr. Lyon, a schoolboy's reversal of bocs (box) to scob.

SCONCE: Properly an ornamental wall bracket to hold a candle or candle branches.

SCOTCH MULL: A snuffbox made of a ram's horn.

SCRATCH CARVING: Intentional scratching, shallow or deep, to form a design or pattern on a piece of furniture.

SCREW NAIL: Any early wood screw. These were without point and had to be set in bored holes.

SCRICK SHOE: An ice skate; originally made from bone, and then from wood with an iron runner. Dutch and Swedes introduced the scrick shoe to America.

SCRIPT HANGINGS: As early as 1650 fine pen-and-brush-worked hangings of paper were made in New England, New Amsterdam, and New Sweden. Because of a great deal of promotion such work has been miscalled "fractur" work by German immigrants to Pennsylvania. To call script hangings fractur is fatuous. Script hangings were made in America at least a hundred years before the first dated fractur was done by Germans and, in the latter case, it may be significant that the early Germanic fractur is in almost direct imitation of Penn's English-written deeds.

SCRIPTORY, SCRITTORE, SCRUTOIRE, SECRETAIRE, SCRIPTURE, ET CETERA: All are variants of 'scrutoire, or secretary.

SCRIVENER's DESK: A tall-legged desk with gradual slope to writing surface, as used by scriveners, or professional writers, and engrossers.

SCRODDLE WARE, AGATEWARE, LAVA WARE: Pottery of variegated colors, deriving from use of varicolored clays, arranged in layers and sliced crosswise before spinning on potter's wheel or molding into forms.

SCROLL AND PEDIMENT: A pair of scrolls ending in rosettes or other volute terminals, centering to right and left toward a pedestal upon which rests a finial. Scroll top.

SCROLL FOOT: Found on Carolean chairs, of two basic types, the English and Flemish. Main point of difference is that in English scroll the scroll turns under and to back of foot while in Flemish the reverse is true.

SCROWLED CHAIR: High-backed wainscot chair, the back of which is finished with a carved and scrolled top rail.

SCRUMBLED: Softening of outline in painting, achieved with a dry brush.

SCRUTOIRE: The slope-fall bureau desk. Described in dictionaries as early as 1696. Phillips' *New World of Words* defines it: "a sort of large cabinet with several boxes and a place for pen, ink and paper, the door of which, opening downward and resting upon frames that are to be drawn out and put back, serves as a table to write upon."

SEAHORSE BOTTLE: See Mermaid Bottle.

SEAUX: Woodenware; a small tub. Also of pottery or stone.

SECOND ROCOCO: 1830–60 period; the furniture commonly called early Victorian. Of Austrian and French influence.

SECRETAIRE ABBATANT: Cabinet-shaped piece of furniture with an upright panel that falls to provide writing surface.

SECRET DRAWER: A section, usually in a desk, cabinet, or chest, that is hidden behind drawers and closets, and requires certain manipulation to gain access to it. Student is referred to Chapter I, *Collecting Antiques in America* by T. H. Ormsbee.

SEDAN CHAIR: A covered chair on bars designed for carriage by four men.

SEGMENTED: Made up of joined segments or sections; parts distinguishable, joined into a whole.

SEILER: A ropemaker.

SEMPITERNUM: An "everlasting cloth" often fringed and used for table and cupboard covers.

SEPHARDIC: Of the colony of Hebrews who settled at Newport, Rhode Island, in the eighteenth century.

SERASS: Brilliant lead glass; fine crystal. Flint glass.

SERVING TABLE: Properly a small side "board" or side table, the ancestor of the sideboard as we know it today. Used from seventeenth century, but always a table until Adam, Hepplewhite, and Sheraton made it a cabinet piece.

SETWORK: Inlay.

SEWING BIRD: A metal bird with swinging beak, mounted on a clamp or vise. Fastened to a table top by the clamp, the beak of the bird held fabrics for ease in sewing.

SEYMOUR: Boston cabinetmaker (1790–1820) who made Federal furniture of Sheraton influence every bit as fine as Duncan Phyfe.

SHAKER HERB BOXES, SHAKER SPICE BOXES: Boxes of spices and herbs prepared by the United Society, New Lebanon, New York (Shakers); the boxes of stamped tin, with paper labels.

SHALLOON: Textile woven at Châlons, France. A loose twilled dress fabric.

SHAMMY: Chamois leather; a textile, soft and fine.

SHANKS' MARE: Travel on your own two legs.

SHARP RIFLE: American prototype of the breech-loading rifle.

SHAVING HORSE: A bench fitted with a wooden vise to hold a split shingle for shaving.

SHAVING MUGS: After 1830 several American shaving-soap makers began issuing their products in fancy china boxes and finally in mugs. Since the mug met with much favor the shaving-mug habit spread, and finally almost every man had a private mug at the barber's and another at home. These mugs, with innumerable different and colorful emblems and with names or initials of one-time owners, are now collected. Most of them date 1850–1900 and even later.

SHAVING STONE: A ladies' aid made of raw pumice treated to ease the drag. Raw pumice is almost glasslike, with innumerable cutting edges. Once used by men who had no razors. A depilatory almost as old as history.

SHEEP'S-HEAD CLOCK: The lantern or bird-cage clock, for table or wall.

SHEFFIELD RIGHT, SOLID, OR TRUE: Solid silver made at Sheffield and marked with an anchor after 1773, when Sheffield was granted an assay office.

SHELL BACK: A chair back fluted and carved as a shell and mounted between back posts that are extensions of legs. One of the few early Victorian styles of virtue.

SHELL BOXES: Late Victorian conceit; wood or paper boxes coated with plaster or cement and imbedded with shells. Made as late as 1896.

SHENANDOAH POTTERY: Almost deserving of a section of its own, this pottery was produced at Winchester, Virginia, Strasburg, Virginia, Waynesboro, Pennsylvania, all in the Shenandoah Valley. There were also potteries at Hagerstown, Maryland, Hickory, Jugtown, and Thurmont, Virginia. Most of the ware was made after 1830 and some of it was still being made in 1900. Potters were Bell (John, Upton, Edward, and others), Eberly, Keister, and Baecher. It is earthenware, glazed and decorated. The range is from flowerpots to picture frames, from candlesticks to animal figurines, from bird boxes to monumental jugs and pots. The student and collector is referred to *The Shenandoah Pottery* by A. H. Rice and John Baer Stoudt. This volume tells the story of the pottery and the potters, most of whom were descendants of Pennsylvania families who had immigrated from Switzerland, The Netherlands, and the Palatinate regions of Germany. There is French, Flemish, Walloon, Swiss, and Holland influence in this pottery, both in form and in decoration. Some of the potters employed by the masters were recent immigrants and, undoubtedly, these brought to America some late nineteenth-century European patterns. The only unfortunate circumstance in connection with these wares is that they are often assumed to be much older, and scarcer, than is actually the case. A great quantity of this ware was made between 1850 and 1900, and sold to the kind of people who have the habit of keeping what they buy and passing it on to their children. Shenandoah wares were cheap wares for the people and they are what might be called a form of pioneer pottery.

SHERATON: See page 30.

SHERIVAREE: A ribald serenade to a wedded couple. Calathumpian music. Sherivaree was practiced to such an extent in the early nineteenth century in St. Augustine that a contemporary writer made major comment on it in an early book on Florida. Still practiced in small towns, villages, and mountain country.

SHIELD BACK: A chair back design by Hepplewhite which may have derived from Robert Adams' designs.

S HINGE: A hinge in which each "leaf" is a pair of opposing Ss. When mounted they give the effect of two S scrolls.

SHIN PIECE: Derisive term coined by Randolph of Roanoke applied to Trumbull's painting of the Declaration of Independence, engraved by Durand, 1820.

SHIP GRINDER, BOAT GRINDER, SPICE BOAT: Names used for the Sow and Pig Mill, which see.

SHOOKS, SHUCKS: Barrel staves, bent and chimed (chamfered to hold ends), but before assembly by the cooper, or hooper.

SHORT FORM: A jointed stool.

SHOVEL SPOON: Miniature shovel, usually of silver, for lifting salt from cellar. Seventeenth, eighteenth, and nineteenth centuries. Many varieties.

SIDEBOARD CUPBOARD: Another name for court cupboard.

SIDEBOARD TABLE: Oversize and extra high legged table used as serving board, seventeenth and eighteenth centuries, developed into a cabinet piece by Adam and Hepplewhite.

SIDE BOYS, SYTTEBORDES: Long tables placed at sides of rooms, along walls. Early eating habits included dining at a table so placed.

SIDE CHAIR: Applies to all chairs without arms, but without much reason. There is some evidence that in the sixteenth century the term meant a chair with sides, that is, with cheeks, or arms.

SIDE HINGE: An early strap hinge with vertical straps on both door and stile. An early H hinge.

SIDE LANTERN: Actually an enclosed sconce; a wall bracket with lantern enclosure for candle. 1700–1800.

SIDE TABLE: Any table without leaves, or any table with drop or fold-up leaves, which, when not in use, stood against wall. May be oblong, serpentine-fronted, bow-fronted, or half-moon. Often in pairs with an oblong to match. 1690–1860.

SIFTER SUGAR SPOON: Large spoon with a pierced bowl; a small ladle with pierced bowl. Used to lift sugar from basin or caddy and sift it over food.

SIGH CLOUT: A straining cloth.

SIGNPOST BAROMETER: Folding barometer of which one arm swings out like a signpost. Eighteenth century.

SILESIAN STEM: A variant of Sandwich-glass stem styling, in form of a straight column. It has a knopping after the styles of the seventeenth and eighteenth centuries. Not apparently of Silesian origin.

SILHOUETTE: Etienne de Silhouette, Contrôleur Général de France, 1757, instituted so many petty economies that anything cheap was called à la Silhouette. Name given almost at once to cheap profiles of paper made by any method, cut, traced, or painted.

SILHOUETTE CHAIR: An armchair to the arms of which were affixed large frames in which thin paper was stretched. The sitter's profile or likeness was focused on this paper as a shadow when a candle was placed on opposite arm. Any chair fitted with tracing frame on arms; any specially constructed chair for use of silhouette artist. Date mostly from 1770–1835.

SILK GRASS: The milkweed; down of the pod used for wicking. Since sixteenth century this weed has been considered as rich in promise. No use save wicking and quilt stuffing had been made of it until the war year 1942. It is known to contain latex in its sap, and the down is almost like silk. It can be spun and woven.

SILVERED BRASS OR COPPER: Silver filings were dissolved in niter (nitric acid) precipitated in salt water and the resulting silver curd, mixed with salt of tartar, common salt, and whiting, was rubbed on copper or brass. This put a deposit or microscopic plating of silver on the base metal. It wore off in use but was found admirable for clock and watch dials. Seventeenth and eighteenth centuries.

SILVER LAY, SILVER INLAY: Silver or tin leaf melted and amalgamated with mercury, ground into a curd, or putty, and worked into undercut carving on wood. When hard, this was burnished and became silver inlay on wood. Eighteenth century.

SILVER RESIST: Platinum luster; see page 177.

SILVER TABLE: A fine side table for the display of silver.

SINISTER: Heraldic term for the "proper" left side of anything; hence the right side of a shield as you view it; thus the "bar sinister" always appears on the right side of any coat of arms as it is viewed because that side is the proper left side; its own left side.

SIX MARKS: Six characters used on Chinese wares of Yung Cheng period, 1723–35. Dutch were particularly fond of this ware and called it Lange Lijsen of the six marks.

SIXTEEN-POST BED: Seventeenth-century four-post bed, the foot posts of which were embellished with a cluster of five posts surrounding each.

SKELETON BREAK: A carriage body with single seat and exposed running gear. Nineteenth-century smart-set vehicle.

SKELTERY: Toy theater material; tableaux of paper cutouts arranged in a toy theater with curtains, scenery, et cetera. Named for Skelt of London who made them. West, Lloyd, Park, Webb, Redington and Pollock also made them; nineteenth century, 1825–75. Children's toys.

Very sophisticated models also prepared by artists for the secret enjoyment of grownups. Some very "hush-hush" models are known. Robert Louis Stevenson mentions skeltery. Sold by many American fancy stores, 1840–70.

SKIRRET: A Chinese root vegetable, about the size of a small carrot, popular in the seventeenth century, and cultivated in New England and Virginia. SKIRRET POT: Name for the pot in which any roots were cooked. Name died out beginning of eighteenth century.

SKIRT, APRON, FRIEZE: In cabinetwork, a valance; the framing of a table, et cetera.

SKITTLE BALL: Skittles is a game played on alleys, as tenpins, but with a ball flattened on two sides. Hence any bulbous vessel, not quite round, is called "skittle ball," especially any vessel that looks as though it had been squashed a bit at top and bottom, somewhat like an Edam cheese. A very engaging shape in silver teapots, pitchers, sauceboats, et cetera.

SKYNN COUCH: Any leather-covered couch, day bed, or sofa.

SLAAP BANK, SLAAP BANK OP ROLLEN: New York and Pennsylvania Dutch term for a bed in a shuttered alcove, a similar bed on rollers for ease in moving about a room. Seventeenth century.

SLAT-BACK CHAIR: Really deserving a special section, the slat-back chair, from the pioneer and cottage type to the most sophisticated ones of Chippendale style, is found everywhere in America and in so many forms that at least a thousand could be pictured without exhausting the subject. The various books recommended in most of the sections on furniture will be found ample to supply the students' requirements for information. Made from seventeenth century, we find that Savery of Philadelphia made slat backs with Queen Anne legs, rush seats, and formed slats. They were made by the thousands in hickory chair shops, often with seats of hickory withes (flat ribbons of hickory, soaked in water until pliant, and then woven, or interlaced, over seat rails to form a seat), between 1825 and 1890.

SLATE TABLES: Slate-topped tables, with frames of cedar, teak, and other oriental wood. Of Chinese origin. But also known in oak, walnut, maple, and from styles as early as Elizabethan, with tops made up of sections of slate. The original stainless top; also used in meat cutting. Very scarce. Oriental ones date from 1680–1750, with some few brought in 1790–1825.

SLATE TOP: Any cabinet piece with a slate top (sometimes called flag top). Very rare. Known from seventeenth century and not common then. The piece or pieces of slate or flagging are ground smooth and set into a depression in the regular wood top of the piece.

SLEEPING BANK: A cot; a trundle bed.

SLIPPER CHAIR: Any short-legged chair with seat close to floor for ease of ladies in putting on slippers or shoes. Also used in nursing infants.

SLIPPER FOOT: Outcurving chair foot somewhat like a slipper in shape.

SLIP SEAT: Any chair, stool, or bench seat which can be lifted out of frame; seat may be rush- or hickory-bottomed, upholstered, roped, or leather-covered. The seat removable means slip seat.

SLIP WARE: Earthenware decorated with thinned clay of different color, called slip. See page 124.

SLOPE FRONT: Same as slant top.

SLUB: A candle molded by hand by squeezing warm, soft tallow tightly around a wick.

SMALLWOOD: Probably America's first antique dealers were Smallwood and Morton, of Roxbury, Massachusetts, who had an antique shop in 1850. They also made modern furniture of the period.

SMALTING: Deep blue glass, ground fine, strewn on tacky paint to make it weatherproof. A technique of painting used from seventeenth century down to today. Considered a very elegant form of painting in seventeenth century.

SMOKE BELL: Deep or flattened bell shaped of glass hung over lamps to catch carbons and prevent smoking of ceiling. Eighteenth and nineteenth centuries. Many sizes, shapes, and forms. Some engraved and cut. Usually with a hole, a hook, or some other protuberance to which a cord or wire could be affixed for suspension.

SNAKE FOOT: Akin to the rat foot in contour but without claws.

SNOW BIRDS: Wrought- or cast-iron bird shapes on long iron rods affixed at angle; these were set in roofs, in rows, to prevent the slipping and cascading of snow over the roof front. Many forms known, from eagles to robins. Also called SNOW ROBBINS. Used very generally in nineteenth century, especially 1830–90. An item not yet generally collected but a most engaging subject for collectors' attention.

SNOW WEIGHTS: Paperweights filled with alcohol and some flakelike whiting. When shaken they provide a miniature snowstorm until the sediment of flakes again settles. Usually a cottage, a boy and girl with umbrella, or some scene is in the globe. French; nineteenth century. Sold in fancy stores.

SNUFFBOXES: Almost deserving a section in this Primer, snuffboxes are now collected by an ever-growing group of specialists, in addition to having any number of occasional buyers among the entire collecting fraternity. Snuffboxes made in America range from gold to papier-mâché. Some of the gold ones are worth no more than certain of the papier-mâché ones, because the latter are of rare historic interest, with picture views, sometimes on both top and bottom, of great naval and land victories of the War of 1812. (As the cynic might well remark, the great land victory is singular; there was but one, New Orleans.) Silver, gold, and pewter snuffboxes date mostly from the eighteenth century, and particularly after the "no-smoking" ban of James II in England had popularized the gentle art of snuff taking. Any metal snuffbox, of making prior to 1860, and the papier-mâché snuffboxes of 1812–45 are valued antiques today. *The Story of Snuff and Snuff Boxes,* by M. M. Curtis, tells a good part of the story.

SNUFFERS: Scissors-shaped device with box or receptacle, used to trim candlewick while candle burned. Not an extinguisher. Mostly eighteenth century, but used into mid-nineteenth century.

SNYTEL: A snuffer.

SOAP PRESS: It is not generally known that the so-called French milled soap was made here in the eighteenth century, even in homes. Boiled soap was grated fine and the flakes piled high in a soap press. This fixture is a bench press with turn screw. The grated soap was pressed tightly in this, as a great cake, and cut apart.

SOAPSTONE GRIDDLE: Literally a large oval dish or pan of soapstone used in making griddle cakes.

SOCLE: A plain, square, unmolded base supporting a statue; any base supporting a wall or a section of cabinetwork.

SODDEN IRON: An iron for grinding or mincing.

SOFA TABLE: Table designed for use by side of, behind, or in front of a sofa, for taking tea, reading matter, lamps, et cetera. Adam seems to have made first ones, although low-legged tables with splayed legs were used for this purpose as early as 1700. Made in many forms of Federal period. SOFA WRITING TABLE: A form of sofa table with leaves folding over to form a sloping writing surface. Made about 1810.

SOFFIT: Underside of an arch, lintel, cornice, et cetera; any finish of the underside. SOFFITED.

SOFT PASTE: Dull, chalky body of porcelain, as contrasted with Hard Paste, which see.

SOHO LAMP: Crosse & Blackwell, grocers and suppliers, 1830, made this lamp to burn a special candle which slipped free in the base and could be raised by turn of a small thumbscrew. Fitted with globe and shade. Many base designs.

SOLAR CLOCK: A sundial.

SOLER: Upper story; an upstairs room.

SOMNOLE: A night table.

SOVEREIGN HEAD: Touch mark (1784–1890) on gold and silver, indicating tax paid.

SOW AND PIG MILL: Boat-shaped metal trough in which a large iron wheel with axle was rolled back and forth. Used on floor; the boat, filled with spices, et cetera, was ground by rolling large wheel back and forth. The operator, barefooted, sat on a chair and placed a foot on each arm of axle, pushing back and forth. Chinese in origin but much used in America in early nineteenth century.

Many forms are known. BOAT MILL, SHIP MILL are other names.

SOY CRUETS: Cruets for soy sauce, advertised in New York, 1772. Soy sauce was known here long before the invention of chop suey.

SPADE FOOT: Typical of Adam and Hepplewhite furniture, the spade foot is a terminal that is simply an enlargement of the leg; it may be straight-sided or tapered.

SPANIEL JUGS: Pitchers molded in form of spaniels, erect, in begging attitude. A kind of Toby, but scarcer. 1760–1820.

SPANISH FOOT: A simplified form of scroll foot, outflaring and with a little carving.

SPARKING CHAIR: Lovers' chair; a chair large enough for two.

SPARKING LAMP: Small lamp; single-wick whale-oil lamp; a lamp preferred by lovers. Courting lamp. Any lamp giving a dim light.

SPATULATE: Oblong, with attenuated or narrowed base; spatula- or sword-shaped.

SPICE CABINET: Any box of small drawers, often fitted with pairs of doors, in which to keep a variety of spices and herbs. Known in crude and highly sophisticated forms. Finally made in tin.

SPICE DREDGERS: Silver, pewter, tin, and brass shaker-top boxes for dispensing cinnamon, pepper, and other spices on food and baked goods.

SPICE MILLS, SPICE MORTARS: The former for grinding spices (pepper, et cetera); the latter for pounding them to powder.

SPIDER-LEG TABLE: Gate-leg-type tables with very thin legs.

SPILL POT: A container of any material from silver to paper, used to hold spills—rolled-up coils of paper with pinched ends which, lighted at hearth, were used as matches.

SPINDLE-BACK ROUNDABOUT: Corner chair with stick back of Windsor quality and style.

SPINET: Keyboard musical instrument, the originals of which played by action of quills, "spina," on the strings.

SPIRIT KEGS: Keg-shaped containers for rum, whisky, gin, irish, et cetera, usually of Staffordshire pottery or stoneware, some elegantly decorated with sporting scenes. A gentleman's item of property for storage of ardent spirits. Eighteenth century.

SPIT IRONS: A pair of footed irons to hold a turnspit. The feet of spit irons rested on hearth, the heads on breast beam of fireplace.

SPIT STOOL: The low chair or stool for use at hearthside by person turning the roasting spit.

SPITZEN: Hungarian for flagon.

SPLASHBOARDED STAND: Night stands or washstands with three sides around top, cut in pleasing shape, and further covered at rear with a hood; designed to prevent splashing wall when using washbowl.

SPLIT BACK, SPLIT BANISTER: A back made of banisters, split in half. Flat side of split banister forms the back of chair and each shows the contour of turning.

SPLIT BRASSES: An American invention in brass casting; two halves of a candlestick column, andiron, or other object were cast and then joined by brazing with silver solder. Thus the piece could be cast "hollow" and made lighter. Also using much less metal. The white line of brazing is infallible hallmark of genuine American brass.

SPODE: Josiah Spode (1733–97) founded the pottery which still bears his name. Made salt-glaze stoneware, red and jasper ware, Historic Staffordshire, delftware, earthenware, busts, figures, figurines, porcelain, et cetera. Various marks. See *Spode and His Successors* by Arthur Hayden.

SPOOL BANJO: Spool turning used as rests for brass side boys of a banjo clock. Rare.

SPOOL TURNING: Ball, sausage and actual turning to simulate a series of spools. See page 50.

SPOONED BACK: Any chair back, regardless of outline, that is contoured in the curve of a spoon to fit the contours of the sitter's back. Eighteenth century.

SPOONER: Spoonholder.

SPOON WARMER: Silly but nonetheless much-used elegancy of the nineteenth century; shell-shaped vessels of Britannia, Sheffield, et cetera, to hold hot water in which spoons were immersed at table to take off the chill.

SPOUT CUPS, PAP CUPS, FEEDING CUPS: Spouted cups or pots, often with cover, which is sometimes pierced to insert a stirring spoon as early chocolate pots. Used in feeding infants. Sixteenth to nineteenth centuries.

SPRIGGED WARE, SPRIG: Made 1820–50; a chinaware with embossed décor in form of sprigs of flowers, and colored. From 1900–15 any ware décored with sprays of flowers was called sprig, even Chinese export porcelain, or Lowestoft.

SPRING ROCKER: A late-type rocking chair. Rockers were immediately under seat of chair and engaged a flat runner that was over base of chair. Held together with heavy coil springs in cast-iron housing. These rockers were put forth as noncreepers, a bad feature of many rockers in which each rock of the chair moved it a fraction of an inch over the floor. But the spring rockers often developed squeaks worse than the creep of other rockers.

SPRING SEAT: Two explanations must be offered for this term: (1) upholstered over coil springs; (2) fitted with leaf springs that are in turn covered by upholstery fabric. Term used about 1850.

SPUD: A peeling iron; hence "spud" for "potato."

SPUE BOX: Spittoon; cuspidor.

SPUNKS: Sulphur-tipped slivers of wood; the first wood matches.

SPURRED CANDLESTICK: Tubular bedside candlestick with the socket having a movable bottom, actuated by a spur and moving upward in a slot. Seventeenth, eighteenth, and nineteenth centuries.

SQUAB: Small stuffed stool. A stuffed cushion. A large stool fitted with pillows.

SQUATTING-DAME IRONS: Obscene andirons in form of squatting naked woman. Eighteenth and early nineteenth centuries.

SQUEAK TOYS: Papier-mâché and composition figures of fowl, birds, animals, et cetera, mounted on a bellows which, when depressed, emits a squeak in imitation of the cry or call of the figure. Made from eighteenth century down to 1900.

SQUIRREL - CAGE CHAIR: Writing - arm Windsors with revolving seats were so called.

STAGGERED-BACK WINDSOR: A rare form of bow back in which the spindles are not continuous but one set extends from seat to rail and then another set, spaced between these, starts at rail and continues to bow.

STANDFAST CANDLESTICKS: Screw candlesticks, anchored firmly where needed.

STANDING BOOKSHELF: Tier of three to five shelves set between posts, having a back and feet; standing on floor and not suspended on wall.

STANDING DESK: A desk-on-frame.

STANDISH: A standing dish of metal (pewter or silver). Also a writing-material assembly, often of silver, with inkwell, wafer box, sandbox, et cetera.

STANZA SAMPLER: A fine cross-stitch sampler with pious or amatory verses.

STARCH BELLOWS: Woodenware; an insufflator for dusting starch or flour over food.

STARS (IN FLAG OR SHIELD) AS A GUIDE TO DATING AN ANTIQUE: Thirteen stars date a piece as 1776–90; fourteen, 1791; fifteen, 1792; sixteen, 1796; seventeen, 1803; eighteen, 1812; nineteen, 1816; twenty, 1817; twenty-one, 1818; twenty-two, 1819; twenty-three, 1820; twenty-four, 1821; twenty-five, 1836; and so on. Any good geography or the World Almanac will give further data.

STATE CHAIRS: Chiefly of fifteenth and sixteenth centuries, of Renaissance and Flemish style. Important and stately, made for lords and high officials.

STEAMBOAT KETTLE: A hatmaker's felting kettle of copper or brass built into or on a firebox with flue and used to size (glue-impregnate) bats of raw felted material from which hats were formed. Often thought to be an unusual form of household kettle but not so.

STEEPLE SALTS, STANDING SALTS: Elizabethan-style saltcellars of standing type with steeple-shaped covers. Now quite scarce. Said to have been used in New England and Virginia. Most likely in latter colony.

STENCIL: A cutout pattern for use in making decorative designs on any sur-

face. An ancient method, Chinese or Indian in origin. Other names: PATRONEN, MOULE, POCHOIR, ESTENCILIER (to cover with stars), THEOREM, POONAH.

STEPPED WINDSOR: Late type, with some fancy chair influence, having a shaped back rail with three to four spindles extending upward to a smaller back rail.

STEPPING STOOL: Shaker furniture; a stool with three to five steps on it.

STERLING: Seventeenth-century new money standard (specie) of England, and having six times the value of old tenor. Thus one pound sterling (new tenor) was equal to six pounds old tenor.

STEVENS SILK PICTURES: Thomas Stevens, of Coventry, England, using a Jacquard loom, made innumerable pictures on ribbon, marked "woven in silk by Thomas Stevens." Thousands of these were sold at New York Crystal Palace exhibition in 1850s, Columbian Exposition, 1893, and Centennial, 1876. Sold also by fancy stores.

STICK CHAIR: See page 52.

STIEGEL GLASS: See page 91.

STILE: Upright standing sections of any kind; the stiles of a door, the stiles of a chair, a chest, et cetera.

STILE-GATED TABLE: Pedestal-type table with a wide gate fixed on a pivot midway between its ends. When swung, this gate extended outward from both sides of table and supported two leaves.

STITCHED SEAT: Upholstery carried down over sides of seat rails and fixed with fancy nails and fringe, or with brads over tape.

STONE TOP: Any marble or slate top was so called.

STOOFT: A stool.

STOOP, STOEP: Entrance to a porch, with or without steps, often covered with a canopy or hood; sometimes galleried and made into a vestibule.

STORK LAMP: Holland lamp composed of a reservoir for fluid, a hang-up handle, long, covered drip spout, and also a conical base. It looks like a stork.

STOUP: A basin or font.

STOURBRIDGE GLASS: A fine English glass of eighteenth and nineteenth centuries.

STOVE HOLLOW WARE: Cast-iron kettles, pans, et cetera, often with recessed bottoms to fit down through stove holes. Any iron hollow ware for use on a stove. 1800–1900.

STOVES: See sections on pages 149–52.

STRAINER: Painting term. The stretcher frame on which canvas is mounted.

STRAINING RAIL: A stretcher, particularly a stretcher set low and joining legs of tables, benches, and chairs.

STRAP HINGE: Said to be entirely American in design; made up of leaves that are heavy horizontal straps, longer on the door than on the stile.

STRAWBERRY DISH: Shallow bowl with pierced bottom for airing and draining berries. Eighteenth and nineteenth centuries.

STRAW CHAIRS: A straw-seated chair.

STRIATED: Striped with narrow streaks or bands.

STRING BOX: Any holder for a ball of twine, with hole somewhere for withdrawing the twine as needed. Silver, pewter, iron, tin, wood, et cetera. 1800–75. Still made in cast iron and used in many country stores and small shops.

STUB FOOT: A block foot, shaped or square, usually on chests.

STUCCO PAPERS: Embossed papers used to line ceilings in imitation of raised plaster work.

STUCK SHANK: The stem of a glass or other vessel, made separately and welded to bowl with hot glass. APPLIED STEM.

STUMP FOOT: Any leg extending to floor without special footing is said to be stump-footed.

SUCKET FORK: Two-tined fork, sometimes with spurs, and a handle which terminates in a spoon bowl. Dual-purpose tableware of seventeenth century. Scarce.

SUFFOLK LATCH: A handle fitting the palm or fingers, affixed to decorative plate in form of tulip, ball, spear, fish, et cetera, with a thumb press on handle to operate the latch. Made 1640–1840.

SUGAR CLEAVER: Loaf-sugar cutter; cone-sugar cutter. It is shaped like a cleaver. Sometimes the shear-shaped sugar cutters are called cleavers.

SUGAR CONE: The early sugar of commerce; a great cone through which passed a heavy cord for hanging from ceiling. Weight, three to thirty pounds; pieces and bits were broken from the cone and used as desired. Sometimes small pieces were held in mouth and coffee or tea sipped "through" it. Barley, grape, and other sugars were coned.

SUGAR LOAF: Blocks or cones of sugar.

SUGAR MOLD: Glazed pottery molds in which sugar syrup was poured to crystallize.

SUGAR NIPPERS: Sugar shears. Sometimes of silver. 1700–1825.

SULPHIDE CAMEOS: Small clay molded busts, imbedded in molten glass (stems, paperweights, et cetera) and there, by action of glass, looking like silver. Eighteenth to twentieth centuries.

SUMMER BEDS: Twin beds designed by Sheraton. Idea suggested by an officer of a duke's household. Made as a one-bed assembly with a narrow aisle between the two couches, but joined overhead with arch and canopy.

SUN CHIMNEYS: A blown-glass lamp chimney looking very much like a miniature hurricane shade but used with the wide end down, over spring clips on the lamp or candleholder. Made 1830–90.

SUNFLOWER PATTERN: A motif of Gaudy Dutch, so called, of the later period.

SUNFLOWER CHEST: Chest of New England (Connecticut) carved with sunflowers and tulips. Seventeenth century.

SUPPER DISH: A hollow dish with several depressions that are deep wells containing three or four food dishes. Dish proper, filled with hot water, kept food hot for service. Sheffield plate and solid silver. Also in copper, china, and pottery. Also called SUPPER SERVICE.

SUPREME: A tall sherbet glass. Hence the service of "supreme of fruit," "supreme of ice cream," et cetera. Early nineteenth century.

SWAN FINIALS: Blobs of glass swirled into the effigy of a swan; often these look more like ducks than swans.

SWANSKIN: Thick, closely woven wool cloth for clothing of seamen and laborers.

SWEDES' GLASS: Made in what is now Pennsylvania, 1638–40. Little is known of this early glass furnace said to have been erected by the Swedes.

SWEDES IN AMERICA: It is not generally known that, in addition to the great Swedish effort at colonization in what is now Pennsylvania, many Swedes also settled in The Netherlands in the sixteenth and seventeenth centuries and are largely responsible for the impressment of Swedish decorative forms on certain minor art of The Netherlands. One of the major techniques brought to The Netherlands by the Swedes was the art of carving in geometrical forms—circles, stars, opposed hearts, et cetera. This is evident in many spoon racks, clocks, and other wooden items of furniture, both in New York and Pennsylvania. It is almost traditional in early Netherlands minor art. Certain Swedes enlisted in the Dutch West Indies Company, settled in New Amsterdam, and assumed Dutch names.

SWEEP TOP: A bed canopy similar to the curve and sweep of a field bed but richly embellished and ornamented.

SWISS BARN: The great storied and forebayed barns of Pennsylvania are not German but Swiss in type and were built originally by the Amish and Swiss Mennonites who settled there 1690–1730. These peoples were originally from The Netherlands and fled that land under the Spanish domination. They followed Menno Simonus, the Dutch reformer.

SWORD CLOCK: A toothed sword, fixed upright, serving as a track down which a cased clock movement travels from top to bottom, the clock movement and case serving as the "weight" to cause clock mechanism to run, via a wheel engaging the teeth of the sword. When hitting bottom the clock was again raised to top. Eighteenth and nineteenth centuries. Scarce.

SWORD STICK: A rapierlike blade sheathed in a cane; fifteenth to nineteenth centuries.

SYLLABUB: (1) The glass bowl commonly called baptismal bowl consisted of a blown bowl and plate to stand it upon, and was used in the making of syllabub, a frothy drink somewhat like Tom and Jerry. (2) The drink so served. (3) The bulbous glass in which it was served.

TABBY: Coarse watered taffeta.

TABERNACLE MIRROR: The Federal mirror of upright, oblong shape with side columns reeded or shaped, corner rosettes, and a tablet or section at top on which is painted or stenciled a scene, view, or allegorical picture or symbol. Sometimes the panel is in black and gold leaf. Made by the hundreds of thousands by looking-glass makers and factories, 1800–1860. Sold in every city, village, and town and vended by peddlers. Sold also by steamboat and canalboat stores. Offered at prices ranging from one dollar upward to a hundred dollars. An American mirror. *Not* Sheraton, as has often been alleged.

TABLE À ROGNON: French term for kidney-shaped table.

TABLE BOARD: A board laid upon trestles or framing; said to be of Cornish origin, set up as required and then disassembled. Fifteenth to seventeenth centuries. Trestle table. Swedes also used this type of table board, and several examples survive in Pennsylvania.

TABLE CASE OF DRAWERS: A highboy form; a chest of drawers on a table.

TABLE CLOCK: A clock with its dial on top, and used on tables to look down upon to tell time. Early sixteenth to eighteenth centuries.

TABLE DE CHEVET: A table for use beside a chair or at side wall.

TABLE DORMANT, TABLE DORMAND: The table board. Fourteenth- and fifteenth-century name.

TABLE JOINT: See page 3.

TABLE SCRUTOIRE: A desk box for table use, hinged in two sections to open and form a complete little secretary with sloping writing surface. Nineteenth century.

TABLE SUZIE: A table Lazy Suzan composed of circular shelves rotating on a central shaft on a broad base, for self-service of condiments and sauces. 1800–50.

TABOURET: Low four-legged stools or stands for display of fernery, pottery, and other objects.

TAILORS' GOOSE: A large sadiron with a gooseneck handle.

TALBOTYPE: A photograph made direct on paper in a camera and then developed. Early form, c. 1850.

GLOSSARY AND INDEX

TALCS: Expensive toy or conceit for adults of mid-seventeenth century, consisting of a miniature portrait on copper or silver with a series of thin, transparent sheets of talc (mica) upon which elements of a costume were painted. Certain layers of talc thus built up a completely costumed picture, changing a damsel to a cavalier, et cetera. Known also as costume miniatures.

TALL CLOCK: Grandfather's clock.

TAMBOUR: (1) Series of narrow strips, rounded or beveled, mounted side by side on heavy linen, to make a rolling panel or door. (2) A form of fancy needlework done on a tambour frame. (3) A set of embroidery rings.

TAMMY, DURANT, CALIMANICO: Glazed, twilled fabric much used for petticoats.

TANKARD: Originally a large wooden vessel to carry liquids in service; a small tank. After the sixteenth century a large drinking vessel for individual use, having handle and lid; known in wood, pewter, silver, et cetera.

TANTALUS: A holder for bottles and decanters with a frame locking over the top and preventing use unless one has the key.

TAPE LOOM: A small hand loom for weaving tape and other narrow fabrics.

TAPER STICK: A candlestick.

TAPPIT: Crested, or crowned.

TAUFSCHEIN: Baptismal certificate done by hand entirely or in part. Popular among Germanic immigrants of religious turn.

TAWHO: Root of the wake-robin, baked and eaten as food. Poisonous when raw.

TAZZA: A large ornamental cup; a footed salver somewhat like a late nineteenth-century footed cake plate or stand.

TEA (AMERICAN SUBSTITUTES): Hyperion, of raspberry leaves; liberty, of four-leaved loosestrife, strawberry and currant leaves; also leaves of camomile, sage, ribwort, and thoroughwort.

TEABOARD: Any tea table.

TEAKWOOD FURNITURE: Native East Indian and Chinese furniture of teak imported in some quantities 1800–40. Some teak boards were made into furniture at Boston, Salem, New York, and Baltimore.

TEA POISE: Covered stand on pedestal, containing several canisters of tea.

TEAPOT WASHINGTON: Full-length portraits of Washington in which the general strikes an attitude with left hand on hip, left arm crooked and right arm extended, the body somewhat dumpy; his left arm is the handle, his right the spout, his body the pot.

TEAPOY: (From Tea Poise); a tea table of oblong shape, made as late as 1894 in spool-turned style.

TEAR: Bubble of air imprisoned in glass.

TEARDROP HANDLES, PEAR-DROP HANDLES: Tear- or pear-shaped handles hinged to plates and affixed to cabinet furniture with wire pins. William and Mary period.

TEAT SPOON: Spoon with bowl partly covered and with a teat or suckle at spoon end. Used in feeding infants and for administering drugs to the sick.

TEAZEL: Thistlelike burr used in teazling linen, raising nap in finishing.

TELEGRAPH FANS: Flat and folding fans with letters of alphabet and a pointer. User could thus send messages to one close by without making conversation. Late eighteenth century.

TELESCOPIC CANDLESTICKS: Silver and Sheffield-plate candlesticks made telescopic so the candle could be maintained at same level in burning; late eighteenth century.

TEMPERA: Water paints mixed with milk curds, egg whites, glue, et cetera, as a binder. Used in painting scenery, large water colors, walls, and wall paper.

TEMSE: A sieve.

TESSELLATED: Stones or tiles of various colors laid in patterns; from the material called "tessera."

TESTER: The canopy framework over post beds.

TEXTILOGRAPHS: Jacquard-loomed ribbon pictures, used for bookmarks, Christmas cards, mottoes, Mother Goose characters, maxims, Alice in Wonderland, et cetera, 1865–80.

THEOREM: A stencil, also a painting made through stencils.

THISTLEDOWN: Fine down from thistle pods used as quilt padding; unbelievable job of gathering and removal of down;

six to twelve pods yield enough down for one square inch of quilting, 140,000 pods for a piece 1 × 10 yards! Warm as toast and light as a feather; rare as a garment of thistledown, the "garment" being a quilting.

THOUSAND-EYE SCONCE: Tin or iron sconce, the reflector made up of a mosaic of mirror glass.

THREADING: Applied threads of glass to glass as a form of décor.

THREE-LEGGED CHAIR: Rare turned chair of three turned legs and a multiplicity of other turnery making up side rails and back frame. Made from fifteenth to seventeenth centuries.

THREE-TIER COMB BACK: A rare type of Windsor chair, the arm rail counting as first comb, surmounted by a straight piece connected with spindles and also by sloping sidepieces to rail, and surmounted by comb supported on at least seven spindles.

THRESTULE, THRESSTOOL: Three-legged seat of early fifteenth century. Used until late sixteenth and even early seventeenth century. From this term we derive "trestle."

THROWN CHAIR: Any turned chair; "thrown" meaning turned.

TICK-TACK-TOE FRAMES: Mid-nineteenth-century picture frames in which frame molding is not mitered at corners but cross each other at right angles and extend beyond the juncture by several inches.

TIGER JUG: Bulbous, potbellied drinking jug of pottery, finished to simulate tiger skin; early sixteenth century.

TILTING CHAIR: A Shaker invention. American habit of tilting a chair backward while seated in it caused many minor upsets and accidents. Shakers made chairs which permitted tilting as much as 40 degrees by simple device of turning a ball-shaped cup in chair-leg ends and placing this over a ball-shaped element on a base, fastening the ball to its socket in chair leg with heavy cord or leather thong. 1820–50. Rare.

TILT-TOP, TIP-TOP TABLE: Usually candlestands but at times larger, the tops tilting upright by virtue of hinge and special hardware to fasten top firmly when not tilted. Very large tilt-tops

were made about 1830–50. Some are four and one half feet in diameter. Tilt-top tables when tilted made useful screens, and the tops, especially those having decorative shape, make a lovely silhouette against a wall. Eighteenth and nineteenth centuries.

TINDER: Tow; charred linen, scraped linen; any quick-igniting material used to start fires.

TINDERBOX: Flint, steel, and tinder in a box for fire making.

TINDER GILT: Gold dissolved in muriatic and nitric acid. Rags were dipped in the solution, dried, and burned on hearth. This "tinder" bearing gold was rubbed on metal to be gilded, with a cork block dipped in salt. Thus were clock faces and other ornamental pieces coated with pure gold. Seventeenth and eighteenth centuries.

TING: A footed caldron.

TINSEL PICTURES: Decorative objects made from cut tinsel papers and pictures, mounted and pasted.

TINSELED PRINTS: Cheap prints decorated with tinsel, fragments of lace, et cetera. About 1800–50.

TOASTING FORK: Long-handled two-tined fork, or wire form on handle to hold bread slices.

TOBY: American: Made from English patterns by D. and J. Henderson, Jersey City Pottery, nineteenth century.

TOBY JUG: Drinking jugs in effigy of Toby Philpot, a legendary bon vivant.

TOBY TEAPOT: Toby Jug character made into a teapot; in some his wooden leg is spout.

TOILE, TOILES DE JOUY: Color-printed chintz printed at the works of Oberkampf at Jouy, c. 1760. Made also at Mulhouse, Orange, Lyons, Rouen, Nantes, Agen, and other cities. Introduced in seventeenth century by Portuguese traders. Eastern in origin.

TOILET GLASS, TOILET STAND, DRESSING GLASS, ET CETERA: Small cases with drawers having uprights between which are mounted a tilting mirror in frame. In styles from William and Mary to Victorian.

TOILETTE DRESSING CASQUE: A Regency- and Federal-period conceit, many drawers with mirrors on folding stands; as many as five mirrors in some ensembles.

TOLE: The term means to attract with bait, to allure, to decoy. It is applied to fancy painted tinwares, probably because they look like what they ain't.

TOMBACK: Alloy of sixteen parts copper, one tin, and one zinc.

TONGUE-AND-GROOVE JOINT: See Section One, page 3.

TOOTH ORNAMENTATION: "Dog's tooth," "shark's tooth," and the French "Violette" are used to describe ornamentation of a row of dentils or a row of teeth.

TOPPAN FURNITURE: Made by Abner Toppan, Newbury, Massachusetts, working from about 1785 to 1825 or later.

TORCHERE: Tall, trifooted or round based pedestal candlestand.

TORUS: A large convex molding.

TOURNAI: Tapestry from French city of that name which, after fifteenth century, rivaled Arras as tapestry center.

TOURNEAUX TRINKETS: M. Le Tourneaux, silversmith, of New York, 1797, made cheap gold and silver trinkets and ornaments especially for use in Indian trade.

TRAFALGAR CHAIR: Fancy chair of Sheraton influence, comparable to our Cleopatra's Barge chairs. An early type on which the Hitchcock chair is based.

TRAFALGAR VASES: Classic, ovoid urns made in glass, pottery, and silver in memory of the great naval victory at Trafalgar. There is Adam influence in their styling.

TRAMMELS: See Pothooks. Adjustable pairs of holders in metal or wood, with ratchets that permit adjusting to any length.

TRANSFER ENGRAVINGS ON GLASS: Aquatints, mezzotints, and line engravings transferred to glass by process of varnishing glass, laying print face down, and then, when varnish dried, soaking off paper from glass and leaving only the film of varnish with the engraved surface on it. This was then colored. Clock panels and tablets, mirror mounts, et cetera, were so decorated.

TRANSITIONAL: Any piece that represents a changing from one style to another with some of the elements of both.

TRANSPARENCIES: (1) Starched window-panes, painted with scenes and emblems and illuminated from behind with candles. (2) Paper work with many scenic effects produced by cutouts of colored paper. Full directions for these are in *The Art of Amusing* by Frank Bellew, (New York, 1866).

TRANSPARENT RUSTICS: Pictures made 1850–70 in which the houses and buildings have windows cut out, verdure cut to form and silhouetted against sky. Light from behind did the rest. An early form of the "shoe-box" lantern of the 1900s.

TRANSPARENT WINDOW SHADES: Shades of oiled hollands linen painted with transparent colors in scenic, emblematic, and patriotic designs. These shades, when drawn in daytime, provided a transparency picture within the room and at night provided one outdoors. Advertised by many specialists and fancy stores, 1830–50. Used also in large sizes by stores and shops.

TREMOR: A headpiece; a hood for cupboard. Fifteenth- to eighteenth-century term.

TRENAIL, TREENAIL, TRUNNEL: Woodenware; large spikes of hardwood used in building; IRON: A large spike. "A treenail can fasten tree to tree."

TRENCHER: Woodenware; platters, from the French *tranche*, to slice. Slices of bread were the first trenchers.

TRENCHER SALTS: Woodenware; a wood saltcellar; also the depression in a wood trencher side to serve as saltcellar; known also in silver, gold, glass, china, et cetera.

TRESTLE FOOT: The footing of a trestle table, the supports of which meet the floor at an angle, was often fitted with a shallow block.

TRESTLE TABLE: Long, narrow table on supports joined by stretchers. Such tables were used from one side only. American examples date from first half seventeenth century; English usage known as early as fourteenth century.

TRIANGLE TABLE: Three-legged table with triangular top having three triangular leaves. Main top is pivoted in center and turns, bringing leaves over corners of frame which holds them. Known also with rounded leaves making the triangular table a round table when turned and leaves are up.

TRICOTEUSE TABLE: Circular- or square-topped table on pedestal having a yarn basket affixed to it. Probably from "tricotene," a yarn.

TRIC-TRAC TABLE: Oblong gaming table, top recessed to hold a game board; trictrac is similar in many ways to backgammon.

TRIFOOT, TRIPOD CREAMERS, SAUCERS, PITCHERS: When the bulbous-formed style of Queen Anne hollowware is footed it is usually on three feet, outflaring from a knee joint which is often decorated.

TRILOBATE TABLE: The triangle table in its early form, of Dutch origin.

TRIO STOVE: A nightmare stove of the 1850s looking like a huge bassoon, the bell of the horn being the fire chamber and the rest of it a circulator for the hot gases.

TRIPLE-BACK WINDSOR: A comb section on three to five spindles surmounting a bow back.

TRIPOD CANDLESTICK: William and Mary and Queen Anne silver candlestick, a shallow tray on three feet, having a candleholder in center. Rare.

TRIPOD TABLES: Three-legged tables usually with triangular, round, or ovate tops, the legs canted outward. Many forms, 1700–1820.

TRIPTYCH: A tablet of booklike form consisting of three leaves; any threefold picture, usually religious in character.

TRIVET: Three-legged stand; any flat stand on legs to hold a dish. Iron stand used in fireplace.

TROMP MARINE: One-stringed instrument for plucking to make music; a cone-shaped box on long neck, played in an upright or vertical position.

TROWBRIDGE CANDLES: Made by Trowbridge at Catskill, New York, established 1818.

TROXEL POTTERY: Made by Samuel Troxel in the manner of early Staffordshire potters. Slip-decorated and sgraffito-decorated red ware with lead glaze. Often inscribed. Pennsylvania, c. 1825–40.

TROY CANDLES: Made at Troy by the Converse family. Fine candles.

TRUE PEWTER, RIGHT PEWTER: Seventy-five to ninety parts block tin; ten to twenty-five parts copper. No lead, no antimony, or bismuth added. True pewter is really a *white bronze*, and the ratio of tin to copper is exactly the reverse of the brown-red bronze. No matter what information so-called experts may put forth, this is the old recipe for right, or true, pewter.

TRUHE: A dower chest.

TRUMPET TURNED: A turning simulating a trumpet; William and Mary style.

TRUNDLE BED: A low bed on rollers which was trundled under the high beds in daytime and pulled out at night.

TUCKAHOE: Any edible fungus; any mushroom.

TUCKER PORCELAIN: Tucker and Hemphill porcelain made at Philadelphia, 1820–40, under various managements. Deserving of greater interest on part of collectors. Classic in design and reflecting the French taste in décor.

TUDOR: Of the English royal house, 1485–1603. Elizabeth was the last of the line. Architectural style reflecting the last phase of the perpendicular.

TULIP CHESTS: Chests with carved or painted tulips made in New England (1650–1750), in New Sweden (1650–80), and the revival of tulip painting by (or for) German immigrants in Pennsylvania, after 1780. Finnish and Swedish chests have been found in New Jersey, with tulip decoration. TULIP WARE: Originating in Staffordshire about 1680, in imitation of tulip-painted wood trenchers of Tudor days, occurring also in The Netherlands, Flanders, France, Austria, and Russia. To call these German, or German in origin, is ridiculous. The Germans copied them from others. Most Pennsylvania German tulip ware was copied direct from tulip ware then common, but most surviving early English pieces were purchased by scouts (1880–1900) and shipped back to England, where there was a ready and high-priced market for it, as it was early Staffordshire and Bristol delft.

TUN: 252-gallon container.

GLOSSARY AND INDEX

TURKEY SOFA: Low sofa, standing only a foot above floor. Introduced by Sheraton, from the Turkish ottoman.

TURKEY WORK: Imitation oriental weaving accomplished by gros point, crewel, cross-stitch, and other devices of the needle. Drawn through coarse linen and used for chair covers, rugs, et cetera. Same technique used later to make hooked rugs. Seventeenth century.

TURK'S HEAD: Metal or pottery baking dish with deeply molded swirls. Sponge-cake molds were so swirled in nineteenth century. Baked piece came out looking like a finely twisted turban. Hence Turk's head. 1820–90.

TURNED FOOT: The terminal of a turned leg, usually a ball or bun.

TURNER: The trade of wood turning.

TURTLE STOPS: Doorstops of glass (also known in iron) made by New England Glass Works and also at Lancaster, New York, 1855–68.

TUTENAG: White copper; white brass; German silver. Chinese in origin.

TWEYFOLD: Double up; fold over. Empty. A saddlebag.

TWIBIL: An ax.

TWIG BASKETS: Actual baskets of twigs, or imitations in pottery and china; bread baskets. The real twig type made as early as the thirteenth century.

TWILIGHT (TOILET): A covering cloth for chests and tables, 1690–1720. Later a light scarf for the person.

TWIST LEG: Leg carved in spiral form.

TWO-BACK SETTEE: Literally a double chair, with two backs, joined. Actually wide enough for three people. 1700–1850.

TWO-FACED DOLLS: Doll heads mounted on pivots and having two faces, either of which could be brought to front of a headdress. Usually a smiling and a crying face. Dolls with as many as five faces are known. Doll collectors seek these as unusual examples. Students are referred to *The Fascinating Story of Dolls* by Janet Pagter Johl.

TWOFOLD TABLE: Early name for what we call gate-leg or thousand-leg tables.

TWO-PART MIRRORS: William and Mary and Queen Anne mirrors, usually made up of two pieces of glass, the lower filling two thirds of frame. Two reasons for this are given: (1) the high cost of large pieces of glass, and (2) evasion of the tax on large mirrors by making them in two pieces. Take your choice—the mirrors are lovely.

TYG: Wide and capacious earthenware pot, straight-sided and with two to three handles. A seventeenth-century loving cup or family mug. It was passed from hand to mouth, as the saying goes. Red ware, tulip-decorated. Staffordshire.

UMBLE PIE: Pastry made from the umbles of deer; *not* humble pie, as is the almost universal error of usage and spelling.

UNDERDISH: Plate usually made to accompany a bowl, especially of glass. Most so-called baptismal bowls (really syllabubs) were sold with an underdish.

UNFOLDING CHAIR: Ancient fold-up chair, made from sections of wood joined at one spot, through the entire assembly. Such chairs folded quite flat. Seats were of tapestry or turkey work. Rare.

URN STAND: High stand to hold urns. Usually four-legged. From Queen Anne period through to Federal. Some have cabinet tops, the precise use of which is now obscure.

URN TABLE: High table of pedestal type, with plain, dished, or galleried top, to hold urns, statuary, and flowers. Also used as lamp stand. Eighteenth and nineteenth centuries.

VARGUENO: Spanish cabinet on legs with doors or falling front. Known in all Spanish settlements that are now states in the Union. Sixteenth century to 1790.

VASE AND COLLAR: A form of turning which embodies two vase forms springing from a collar.

VASE SEWING STANDS: Actually wooden stands of fine cabinetwork but made in skeleton vase forms with the rare exception of a conical type that is apparently solid, and rising from feet to a round top. There are drawers and doors in these; they are made hollow throughout. Mostly Federal style.

VAUXHALL MIRRORS: Glass made at the Vauxhall Works founded by Duke of Buckingham in seventeenth century. The first mirror works in England. Plate glass, with slight bevel.

VEILLEUSE: Pottery stand in form of miniature stove, with apertures to insert candle and for circulation of air. On the stand is a small teapot. A bedside piece; heat of candle kept contents hot throughout the night. Eighteenth and nineteenth centuries. Known in some very decorative forms.

VENEERING: Thin slicing of fine burl and rare woods, began about last, or perhaps third, quarter of the seventeenth century. Used on William and Mary furniture in form of burl ash and burl walnut. When the cutting was reduced to a fine art the slices of wood became almost as thin as paper. The early veneer was hand-cut and is considerably thicker than late veneers.

VENETIAN BLIND: Actually the jalousie of France made into an interior shutter. Used in America before use in England. Advertised and made here from 1800. Almost every town in America had a venetian-blind manufactory by 1845.

VENETIAN GLASS: Glassmaking began at Venice (and Murano) about the thirteenth century. Most European glass techniques spring from these early works.

VERNIS MARTIN: Martin's varnish, made by the Martin brothers of Paris, c. 1740. Their "secret" was an approximation of Chinese lacquer. They made all sorts of articles to which they applied their varnish.

VERSO: Left-hand pages; left side.

VERTICAL PIERCED SLAT: Vertical slots cut through chair backs in a pattern. Chippendale and Hepplewhite styles show this vagary. Vertical is hardly the appropriate term as some of the piercing is fan-shaped.

VERTUGADIN: See Crinoline.

VITRIC PANEL: A pane or sheet of glass.

VITRINE: A glass-enclosed cabinet; a glass cover for anything; any glazed compartment.

VITRINE ÉTAGÈRE: Open bookshelves over a glassed-in cabinet.

VITRINE SCREEN: Wood frame fitted with sliding glass panels.

VOIDER: Woodenware, wickerwork, or metal basket or box to hold used trenchers, table scrapings, et cetera.

VOLCANO CHIMNEYS: Trade name for lamp chimneys of extra globular shape, 1870–1900.

VOYDER: Same as Voider; cachepots for crumbs, scrapings, and soiled trenchers. Used as early as 1633 in America.

WAFERS: Letter sealers of dry paste in round wafer form. When moistened they held letter sheets together. Also large ceremonial and sacramental wafers, baked in WAFER IRONS: pairs of heavy iron molds mounted on a large scissors-like pair of arms. Many designs, mostly of continental European origin, but some known (rare) with shield of United States. It is believed the latter were used in pressing wafers of wax to tapes on official documents.

WAGON-SPRING CLOCK: A fine type of American-made clock (Connecticut) using the considerable pressure of a wagon spring to take the place of a weight. Such clocks ran thirty days at one winding. The mechanism was rather complex in that it had to translate the great power of the spring into a slowly exerted pressure. Also called CART-SPRING CLOCK.

WAG-ON-WALL: A weight-driven clock with movement only cased, the weights and especially the pendulum exposed. This was the "wag," and wag it did as the clock ran.

WAINSCOT CHAIR: Seventeenth-century solid-back, plain or carved chair, the back section having the character of wainscoting.

WAINSCOTT, WAGENSCHOTT: Literally, oak of the best quality, riven from the bole of the oak tree. Choicest oak. From the Danish *Wagenschott*.

WALKING HORSE: A device like a baby creeper but made for helping invalid adults to get about.

WALLIS FURNITURE: Made at Salem, Massachusetts, by Joseph Wallis. He also made the palm-leaf mattress, c. 1835–50.

WALLPAPER: First made, it is said, by François, at Rouen, about 1620. Patent granted to Jerome Lanyer, England, 1634. He invented fflock paper. Bahre, England, patented a method of coating paper with glue, oil, and sugar to produce a brilliant finish and surface for color printing. Wallpaper first made in America (1737) is tradition; it was offered but probably not made here. Records show early makers in Philadelphia and Boston, 1763 and 1787. *Historic Wall Papers*, by Nancy McClelland, is the book we recommend for further study by students interested in wallpapers. *Wall Paper, Its History, Design and Use*, by Phyllis Ackerman, is another book worthy of note on this subject.

WALL VITRINE: Hanging cupboard framed in glass.

WARDIAN CASES: A herbarium under glass; a sweat box for growing plants indoors.

WARMING PAN: Flat metal pan with pierced lid, fitted with long turned handle. Filled with live coals, it was passed between the sheets to warm a bed.

WASHINGTON MEMORIAL HANGING: Wallpaper memorializing Washington made 1800 by Clough of Boston, a paper stainer.

WASHSTANDS, NIGHT TABLES: Stands of cabinetwork to hold bowl and pitcher of water, and other necessities of the bedroom. Drawers for linen, and spaces for toiletries. Eighteenth and nineteenth centuries.

WATCH CLOCKS: Many seventeenth-century timekeepers designated as watch clocks were really alarm clocks or "alarums." The watch as we know it today was once called a pocket clock.

WATCH COCKS: A recent wave of interest in these in the United States is simply a reflection of a collecting vogue of some years' standing in England and the Continent. Watch parts, especially the housing of the balance wheel, were, in the seventeenth and eighteenth centuries, finely shaped, engraved, and damaskeened. These are now torn from early watches and made into jewelry or arranged in collectors' cabinets. The vogue may have its devotees ready to defend it, but it is comparable to collecting Queen Anne furniture legs only, or Chippendale drawers, or only the brasses and hinges from antique furniture. Innumerable fine early watches have been scrapped just to supply the watch-cock craze.

WATCH PAPERS: Early watches were cased first in a case for the movement and then in a two-, four-, or six-leaved case of silver or gold. To prevent shifting in the space between movement case and carrying case, watch papers were used as padding. These originally were issued by watchmakers, but a vogue for handmade ones, with love tokens, memorials, et cetera, developed. Fancy cut paper ones, painted ones, pen work ones, all these are known and collected. They date 1700–1860.

WATER CLOCK (CLEYPSYDRA): Water thief; a clock which ran by stealing water drop by drop from a reservoir.

WATERFORD GLASS: Made at Waterford, Ireland, eighteenth and nineteenth centuries. Factory owned by the Stourbridge works, England. Finest kind of cut and blown glass.

WATER-GILDED: Gold leaf applied to a surface coated with a size of Armenian bole, boiled parchment, and wax. Applied with soft brush to surface, the gold leaf was floated on the size. Such gilding always was done on a surface previously prepared with whiting. Even though named water gilding, it will be ruined if washed with water.

WAX PORTRAITS: Three-dimensional portraits, modeled in wax, mounted and framed. Originals are modeled; fakes are castings. *American Wax Portraits*, by Bolton, tells the story.

WAXY PLASTER: Common plaster-of-Paris work, kiln-dried and waxed by plunging in warm linseed oil for half a day, dried and rubbed.

WAY-WISER: Early name for mileage meters, cyclometers, et cetera.

WEAVER'S CHAIR: High-legged chair for use at side of loom. Known in the form of stools and armchairs. Best types have turned legs, rush seats and arms, looking like adult-sized high chair.

WEDDING MIRROR: Upright box-frame mirror with painted glass border, enlarged to a painted panel on top and having painted folding covers, making a triptych form. Persian in origin. Glorified form of courting mirror.

WELL DESK: Slope-fall secretary desk with a sliding panel to provide for access to first drawer, which is always hard to get at when the falling front is down. 1690–1760.

WELSH DRESSER: Properly a sideboard without cupboards. When fitted with latter, piece is a Welsh cupboard.

WESTCHESTER HIGHBOY, CUPBOARD-TOP HIGHBOY, PRESS-TOP HIGHBOY: Full-size highboy with three or four drawers in the lower section, but with cupboard instead of drawers in the upper section.

WHALE-OIL LAMPS: Metal, glass, and china lamps for burning whale oil.

WHEEL BACK: A chair back of ovocircular form, fitted with fancy spokes emanating from oval hub. An Adam-type chair.

WHITE: To cut, or to planish.

WHITESMITH: Same as Whitster (originally), later applied to workers in tin, tin plate, and all white metals. Listed in directories as a trade as late as 1860.

WHITSTER: A planisher; one who hammered iron white.

WICKER: Willow.

WIG STAND (TRUE): The true wig stand does not terminate in a ring but in a skull pan or rounded surface to hold a wig for dressing. Actually like a milliner's bonnet stand. Those with a round ring at top are really basin stands.

WILLARD CLOCKS: Aaron Willard (1780–1823), Ephraim Willard, and Simon Willard, clockmakers, of Roxbury, 1780–1839. Simon Willard invented the banjo clock, 1802.

WILLIAM AND MARY STYLE: See Section 4, page 10.

WILLOW-PATTERN HANDLES: Decorative brasses of Queen Anne, Georgian, and Chippendale periods, deriving from Chinese patterns.

WINDOW HARP: A box as wide as a window and about 4 × 5 inches high and deep. Musical strings stretched inside box so that, when window was raised, incoming air passed over strings and caused harplike sound.

WINDOW SEAT: Any seat or stool designed for placing in a window recess, but specifically a small backless sofa, usually in Greek Revival influence, Federal style.

WINDOW SHADES: The jalousie or venetian blind was more popular in America (1790–1825) than in England. They were first advertised in France 1750. Advertised in America 1791. Transparent shades were advertised early in the nineteenth century. Holland window shades also advertised about 1830. Holland shades were originally on heavy rollers operated by a cord.

WINDSOR CHAIR: See Section 20, page 52.

WINDSOR TRAY: According to Esther Stevens Brazer, oval-shaped tin trays were known as Windsor trays. They date from about 1820.

WINE BIN: Any cabinet tub or jardiniere-like piece, designed to hold bottles of wine.

WINE COOLERS, WINE COOLERS ON STAND: Urn-shaped buckets with or without stand in which bottled wine was cooled in ice or cold water. Fine woodenware, usually zinc-lined and with brass or silver hoops.

WINE TABLE: Small, knee-high table with dish or galleried top, on a pedestal with tripod base. Used in serving wine formally after dinner.

WINE TASTER: Small bowl-shaped vessel of silver, sometimes with a silver coin in bottom, used in tasting wine at the merchant's, for approval of the buyer, or by experts in classifying wine.

WINE WARMER: A stand with a shield or back, usually of metal, to hold the bottle of wine by the hearth, to bring it more quickly to room temperature.

WIRE PATTERN: Any object made of looped and twisted wire. Of gold, silver, brass, et cetera.

WITCH-HAZEL MATTRESS: A bed ticking or bed sack filled with shavings from the twigs of the witch-hazel bush.

WOAD: A blue dye.

WOLVERHAMPTON PAPER WARE: Wolverhampton, England (1770–1825) had several important makers of papier-mâché.

WOODEN CLOCKS: This term applies to clocks with wooden works, a feature of many cheap clocks made up to 1850. They are usually 24-hour clocks, weight-driven, having a brass escapement wheel.

WOODEN INDIANS: Tobacconists' signs used generally in America during the nineteenth century. Almost life-size effigies of Indian braves and Indian squaws. Also "Black Boys," Mr. Punch, and other characters were used. Smaller effigies were used in the eighteenth century. The practice comes from the Dutch, who used effigies of Indians and blackamoors to advertise tobacco after 1600. Also used in England 1610–1750.

WOODENWARE: Name given to any utensil or object carved, turned, or otherwise fashioned from wood, and especially from burls and from ash wood. There were factories for the production of woodenware as early as 1815.

WOOD LATCH: Door fittings fashioned from wood because iron was not available. Seen on early New England and Swedish-type houses in what is now Pennsylvania. Also on many pioneer cottages.

WOOD SKIMMER: Woodenware; an oval-shaped, shallow, spoonlike skimmer with handle carved as a part of the whole. Handle is almost always cut at a 30-degree angle to the bowl. Used as a cream skimmer.

WOOL-ON-WOOL: Designation given a type of handwork coverlet, made in the Connecticut Valley, c. 1750–1850. There is an elaborate design worked somewhat after the manner of rug hooking, in wool yarn on a heavy woolen base fabric.

WORMED GLASSES: Another name for the air-twist or cotton-stem wineglasses.

WORN STRETCHERS: Many slat-back and other chair types having a ball-wheel stretcher between the front legs display stretchers showing much wear, believed due to the resting and scraping of feet on the stretcher by the occupant of the chair. This theory of wear is doubted by many research workers. It is now believed that most of the wear is due to use of stretcher as a shoe scraper, and sitting on one chair and resting the feet on the stretcher of another chair. Unscrupulous dealers sometimes fake wear on a stretcher by rubbing new ones down with a rasp.

WRITING BOX: Silver, pewter and plated boxes, often with a pair of lids opening as wings from the center of the top. Fitted with inkwell, box of wafers, quill cutter, and compartments for writing quills.

WROUGHT CHEST: It is likely this term as used in the seventeenth century meant carved.

WRYTHIN: A term meaning swirled, ribbing and fluting.

WYVERN: A heraldic winged beast.

YONKER, YOUNKEER: A yeoman.

ZOETROPE: A form of motion picture machine of early nineteenth century. A paper barrel, slotted around its upper edge, revolving on a wooden stand. Films of paper about a yard long, and bearing on their surface a series of pictures, each of which had a change of attitude or position, were placed inside the barrel. Spinning the barrel and looking through the slots gave you the first Silly Symphony. Edison used the Zoetrope, put the films on celluloid, and used the magic lantern to project it. That's how the movie was born.

Author's Note

SPACE did not admit of the inclusion of some 3,000 additional terms which might have been included in this Glossary. Any reader desirous of having definitions not in the foregoing listing may address the author on a reply-paid postal card. If the word or term is in our files, you will receive the information in due time. Also, any reader having information as to purely local terms and colloquialisms for objects and customs now antique is invited to send same to the author, giving the locale and approximate date of use. The author may be addressed in care of the publishers.

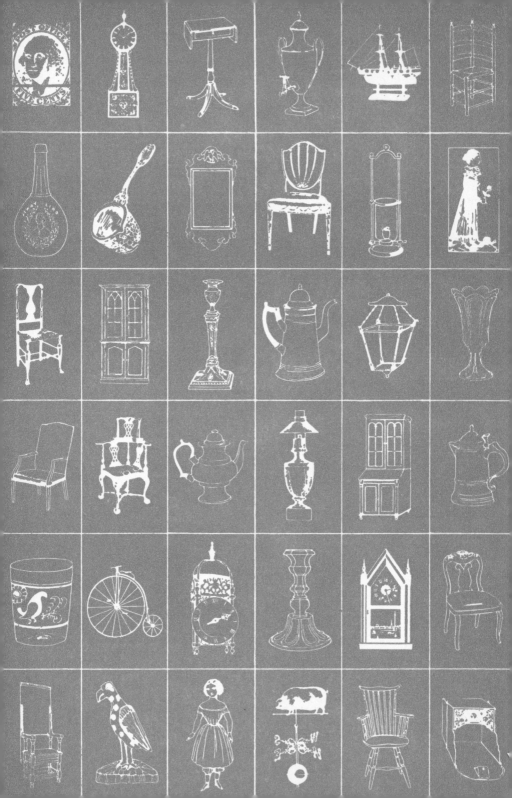